Pico Iyer was born in Oxford in 1957, and educated at Eton, Oxford and Harvard. He is an essayist for *Time* magazine and the author of *Video Night in Kathmandu*, also published by Black Swan. His literary pieces have appeared in *Partisan Review*, *Smithsonian*, the *Village Voice*, *The Times Literary Supplement* and many other publications. Just before he completed *The Lady and the Monk*, his house burned dramatically to the ground, leaving him with nothing but the clothes he was wearing and the manuscript of his book.

'A narrative that, in its richness, its complexity, its elegance and its vast contradictions, accurately reflects the culture that inspired it'
Sunday Telegraph

'As an insight into both ancient and modern Japan this book is every bit as successful as Oliver Statler's *Japanese Pilgrimage* or Alan Booth's *The Roads to Sata*. I'd also add it's the first travel book on Japan I can remember reading that's actually made me want to go there'
Time Out

'Evocative . . . a thoughtful book, full of quiet pleasures'
Observer

'Like Thoreau, Iyer combines an acute sense of place with a mordant irony. The revealing detail is his specialty . . . a *Madame Butterfuly* for the 90s'
Time

'Like a cultural archaeologist, Iyer digs into the dead metaphors of poets and beneath the antiseptic glitz of love

Also by Pico Iyer

VIDEO NIGHT IN KATHMANDU

and published by Black Swan

The Lady and the Monk

Four Seasons in Kyoto

Pico Iyer

BLACK SWAN

THE LADY AND THE MONK
A BLACK SWAN BOOK 0 552 99507 X

Originally published in Great Britain by
The Bodley Head Ltd

PRINTING HISTORY
The Bodley Head edition published 1991
Black Swan edition published 1992

Set in 11/13pt Melior by County Typesetters, Margate, Kent

Black Swan Books are published by Transworld Publishers Ltd,
61–63 Uxbridge Road, Ealing, London W5 5SA, in Australia
by Transworld Publishers (Australia) Pty Ltd, 15–23 Helles Avenue,
Moorebank, NSW 2170, and in New Zealand by Transworld
Publishers (NZ) Ltd, 3 William Pickering Drive, Albany, Auckland.

Made and printed in Great Britain by
Cox & Wyman, Reading, Berks

For Michael Hofmann,
and my friend Hiroko

Permissions Acknowledgments

Grateful acknowledgment is made to the following for
permission to reprint previously published material:

New Directions Publishing Corporation: Excerpt from
poem from *100 Poems from the Japanese*, translated by
Kenneth Rexroth, and excerpt from poem from *Women
Poets of Japan*, translated by Ikuko Atsumi and Kenneth
Rexroth. Reprinted by permission of New Directions
Publishing Corporation.
Charles E. Tuttle Co, Inc: Three poems, #7, #47, #54,
from *Tangled Hair* by Akiko Yosano, translated by
Sanford Goldstein and Seishi Shinoda. Reprinted by
permission of Charles E. Tuttle Co., Inc., Tokyo, Japan.
Warner Chappell Music Limited: Excerpt from
'September Blue' by Chris Rea. Copyright © 1987 by Magnet
Music Limited. Reprinted by permission of Warner
Chappell Music Limited.
Weatherhill, Inc.: Excerpt from poems from *One Robe,
One Bowl* by Ryokan, translated by John Stevens, and
five haikus from *Santoka* by Santoka, translated by
John Stevens. Reprinted by permission of Weatherhill, Inc.

Acknowledgments

Like any foreigner in Japan, I suspect, I encountered more kindness and consideration than I had ever found elsewhere, and certainly much more than I deserved. The two to whom this book is dedicated exemplify that spirit in more ways than I can articulate.

I also, however, owe especial thanks to Mari Gotō, who not only taught me a great deal about her country, but endured my gaucheries – and my Japanese – with angelic patience. Somehow, in the midst of an inordinately busy schedule, she took time out to answer all my endless questions and to conduct tireless researches on my behalf. In the process, she taught me by example about much of the sweetness, attentiveness, and thoughtfulness that are so remarkable in Japan.

While I was in Kyoto two of my kindest guardian angels were Barbara Stein and Naohiko Iwasa, who not only opened their home and hearts to me, but also provided me with tea and warmth and friendly conversation even as I was depriving them of their study and their peace. I consider myself very fortunate, too, to have been introduced to Yūko Yuasa, an exemplar of all that is most elegant in Japan and most civilized in any place. Many of the most beautiful parts of Kyoto, like many of the finer points of Japan, I would never have seen had it not been for her; she opened windows for me as well as doors.

I profited greatly from the conversations I enjoyed in Kyoto with Tyrrell O'Neill and Andrew Hartley, among many others, and hope they do not feel let down by what I have produced; Eric Gower was my smiling *sensei* on all things Japanese, a model of how to live in Japan without losing a sense of humor or proportion. Back home, I was, as ever, buoyed and uplifted beyond measure by Kristin McCloy and Mark Muro, who read what I was scribbling with extraordinary sympathy and care, at once cheering me on and holding me to the very highest standards; Steve Carlson, with his genius for conversation, got me to say things I didn't know I knew; and the late Kilian Coster provided me, and many others, with a model of fairness and calm. I am very grateful too to Charles Elliott at Knopf, and Elizabeth Grossman, for all their help in actually seeing my words into print: in the former, I enjoyed the rare luxury of an editor who not only showed exceptional insight and understanding in training a searchlight on my prose, but was even able to correct my Japanese misspellings.

All the time I was living in Kyoto, nobody could quite understand how I was supporting myself while simply reading old poems, wandering around temples, and doing as I pleased. I would not have understood either had I not known *Time*, whose editors continue to find ways of sustaining me even as I go off in stranger and stranger directions. Without them, and the forgiving cooperation of their Tokyo Bureau, I could not even have gone to Japan.

Finally, all the time I was at home, and away, I was kept upright by my long-suffering mother, who reconciled herself with typical patience to a son who always chose to live in the most inconvenient of places, and without a word of complaint, collected my mail, deposited my checks, and looked after my well-being – showing that grace, no more than kindness, is hardly peculiar to Japan.

*All that a man has to say or do that can
possibly concern mankind is in some shape
or other to tell the story of his love —
and to sing; and if he is fortunate and
keeps alive, he will be forever in love.*

—THOREAU

Autumn

One

The first time I ever set foot in Japan, I was on my way to Southeast Asia. Japan Air Lines was putting me up for the night, not far from Narita Airport, and after stumbling out into a silver late afternoon, I was taken to a high-rise hotel set in the midst of rice paddies. After a brief, disjointed sleep, I woke up early on an October morning, clear, with a faint touch of approaching winter. I still had a few hours to spare before my connecting flight, so I decided to take a bus into the local town. Narita could not be a very distinctive place, I thought, as the Japanese equivalent of Inglewood or Heathrow. Yet I was surprised to find a touch of Alpine charm in the quiet of the autumn morning. A high mountain clarity sharpened the October air, and the streets were brisk with a mountain tidiness.

As I began to walk along the narrow lanes, I felt, in fact, as if I were walking through a gallery of still lifes. Everything looked exactly the way it was supposed to look, polished to a sheen, and motionless. Shoes were lined up along the entrances to tiny houses. Low tables sat, just so, on impeccably brushed tatami mats. Coffee-shop windows gazed out upon vistas of rocks and running water. A clatter of kettles rattled outside a silent teahouse.

Then, turning through some wooden gates, I found myself inside Narita Temple. Everything, here too, was held in a state of windless calm. An old man sat on a wooden bench, alone. A swan flapped noisily, and then set graceful sail. A baby, pouched on her mother's back, cast huge eyes up towards the sky. Black and gold swished past, the rustling robes of two young monks. A gong began to sound, and a column of thin smoke rose high in the clear air.

And then, walking round a corner, I came of a sudden upon a flutter of activity, a cluster of school-children scattered this way and that around the quiet paths, hunched over the ground at strange angles like a flock of odd birds. No more than six years old, perhaps, these curious little creatures were dressed all alike in tidy uniforms: pink and blue hats, white skirts and shorts, sporty white socks. Occasionally, one of them would find what he was looking for – a bean, apparently, or some kind of acorn – and toss it into a cellophane bag, then hurry off in search of more. Otherwise, they all remained so deep in concentration, and so inviolate, that none of them seemed to notice me as they crouched along the tree-shaded path, silent and intent. Around them, in the freshly minted morning, was the coming autumn's faint chill of regret.

And somehow the self-contained quiet of the children, and the elegiac softness in the air – the whole rapt stillness of the scene – took me back, in a flash, to faraway mornings on October days in England, when the Oxford parks were pungent with the smell of burning leaves and crisp with the crackle of leaves underfoot. For the first time in twenty years, I was back in a duffel coat, futureless and blithe, running through a faintly sunny morning to throw bread to the swans in the lake, then hurrying home for tea in the darkening afternoon. Called back through the years to distant childhood, I was back, too, in the blue intensity of knowing nothing but the present moment.

There were many features of Japan that might have

reminded me of England: the small villages set amidst rich green hills, all scaled with a cozy modesty; the self-enclosure of an island apart from the world, not open to sea and light, as tropical islands are, but huddled in upon itself, an attic place of gray and cold; a sense of polite aloofness, a coolness enforced by courtesies and a language built on shadows; even the sense of immovable hierarchy that made both countries seem like giant Old Boys Clubs, where nobody worked in college because the name of the college alone was enough to decide every future. But none of that could explain the urgency of a Wordsworthian moment on a mild October morning, in a place I had never seen before. And the moment stayed inside me like the tolling of a bell.

That first fleeting taste of Japan felt like the answer to some unspoken question. For through whatever curious affinities propel us towards people or places we have never met, I had always been powerfully drawn towards Japan. Ever since boyhood, I had only to glimpse a Hokusai print of peasants huddled under driving rain, or to enter the cold beauty of a Kawabata novel, to feel a shock of penetrating recognition. For years, the mere mention of an 'inn', or 'snow country', or even a 'prefecture', had sent a shiver through me, and a chill. And though I knew almost nothing about Japan and had never had the chance to study it, I felt mysteriously close to the place, and closest of all when I read its poems – the rainy-night lyrics of Japanese women, the clear-water haiku of itinerant Zen monks. From afar, Japan felt like an unacknowledged home.

The next year, I happened to return to Japan, for a slightly longer stay. This time I was there with my mother, on a brief sight-seeing tour, and as soon as we arrived, we found ourselves propelled through the modern nation in all its bullet-trained efficiency. For four days, we glided through uniform hotels, in and out of tour buses, through one fluorescent coffee shop after another. At night, I went out alone into the streets and lost myself in the clangor of their amusement-arcade surfaces, the crash of white signs, bright lights, neon colors – a toyland gone berserk with an intensity that could not have been further from the lyrical land I imagined. Yet even here, in the midst of commotion, images would occasionally bob up and pull me down below the surface of myself: just a picture, perhaps, of a girl alone beside a rain-streaked window; or a monk all in black, alone with his begging bowl, head bowed, in the midst of shopping crowds.

One evening, I wandered through the ancient geisha quarter of Kyoto as night began to fall over the houses, and life to stir within them. The crooked, narrow streets were secret in the dusk, but still I could catch snatches from within: laughter from some inner passage, figures outlined in an upstairs window, the whitened face of an apprentice geisha slipping like a ghost into a waiting taxi.

By the time the street led out on to a busy road, it was dark, and I could just make out, in front of me, the entrance to a park. Inside the giant *torii* gates, I found myself amidst a carnival of lights like nothing I had ever seen, or dreamed, before. Families were gathered by the side of a pond, ringed by lanterns, and lamplit stalls were set along their paths. A surge of people were marching up a path, and as I hurried after them, the way led through the darkness and into another, broader path, framed on both sides by lanterns. The lights, red and white, bobbed ahead of us, up another slope, and then along a further path, until, of a sudden, the path gave way to a kind of plateau. Around me, families ducked under lanterns or darted into shrines to have their fortunes told, inscribed in sweeping calligraphy on wooden blocks. Above me, lights danced across the hill like fireflies.

As I began to climb, the noise fell away, and the crowds started to thin out. Soon I was far above the town, alone in a world of lanterns. For on this, the Night of a Thousand Lanterns, lights had been placed beside every grave, to lead departed spirits back to Buddha. And I, somehow, without knowing it, had found my way alone into an ancient graveyard. For many minutes I stood there, in the company of ghosts and shivering lights.

When finally I made my way back down, and into the festive streets, the spell did not shatter, but only gained texture and animation. Round businessmen in loosened ties went reeling arm in arm amidst the weaving lights, and gaggles of giggling girls shuffled behind, fluent in their best kimono. The teahouses along the Kamo River were strung with lights this summer night, and large parties were gathered on their wooden terrances, set on stilts above the moonlit water. Along the darkened riverbank, lovers sat side by side, spaced out at regular intervals, as self-contained as in some *tableau vivant*. I had passed through a looking glass and into a world of dreams.

That second trip was enough to decide me: it was time to put my visions of Japan to the test. At home, these days, one heard constantly about the zany forms of modern Japan, the double standards of its political system, the strategies of its companies, all the craft of the collective rising sun of economic power that seemed to be the capital of the future tense; but the private Japan, and the emotional Japan – the lunar Japan, in a sense, that I had found in the poems of women and monks – was increasingly hard to glimpse. If this imaginative Japan existed only in my mind, I wanted to know that soon, and so be free of the illusion forever; yet if there were truly moments in Japan that took me back to a home as distantly recalled as the house in which I was born, I wanted to know that too. Residing six thousand miles away, I could only remain as distracted as when one tries and tries to recover the rest of some half-remembered melody.

In Japan, moreover, I wanted to put another daydream to the test: the vision I had always cherished of living simply and alone, in some foreign land, unknown. A life alone was the closest thing to faith I knew, and a life of Thoreauvian quiet seemed most practicable abroad. Japan, besides, seemed the ideal site for such an exercise in solitude, not only because its polished courtesies kept the foreigner out as surely as its closed doors, but also because its social forms were as unfathomable to me, and as alien, as the woods round Walden Pond.

In the fall of 1987, therefore, as a kind of dare to myself, I bought a ticket for Japan. I took nothing more than a little money that I had saved: no plans, no contacts, no places to live. In my suitcase I had a few essentials, and copies of Emerson, Wilde, and Thoreau; in my head, the name of a temple, a few phrases I had learned from a Buddhist priest in Santa Barbara, and a schedule of the festivals by which the Japanese measure their seasons. On 22 September – the first official day of autumn, a new-moon night with an eclipse of the sun, and, as it happened, the day on which the aging Emperor underwent an internal bypass operation that threatened the central symbol of the land – I took off for Japan.

Two

So it was that one day later, I found myself standing in Kyoto, two cases in my hand, outside a tiny temple in the rain. A shaven-headed monk, an albino as it happened, with vague eyes and a face like baby's milk, appeared before me, smiling. 'Do you speak English?' I asked him, in Japanese. *Litteru*, he replied, and so I asked once more. 'One night, three thousand, five hundred,' he said. 'Free breakfast.' Then he pointed to a courtyard behind him, crowded with bicycles, motorbikes, and mopeds. 'My hobby,' he explained.

That, it seemed, was the end of the conversation, of small talk and of big. Eyes bulging, the pale monk motioned to a pair of slippers, then led me through a maze of gleaming corridors, past a tidy rock garden, across an altar room equipped with gong and elegant calligraphy, and into another tiny room. A room was all it was – a bare rectangle of tatami mats bordered by sliding screens. Pulling out a mattress that was standing in the corner, he nodded in my direction, and I collapsed.

Later, many hours later, when I awoke, the world was dark. I looked around, but there was no way of telling whether it was night or day. On every side of me was a sliding door: one that gave on to another tiny, empty space; another that led into the darkened shrine, spectral now in the gloom; a third that proved to be nothing but a wall; and a fourth that, when I slid it open, afforded me a glimpse of the garden behind and,

19

rising high above it, the silhouette of a five-story pagoda, the moon a torn fingernail in the sky.

Fumbling my way through the dark, I stumbled through the shrine and out into the entrance hall, and then into the narrow street. Everything, here too, was hushed. Temple roofs and spires haunted the brownish sky. Banners fluttered from the wooden eaves of teahouses. The darkness was pricked by nothing save white lanterns and the blue-and-white badges of American Express.

I walked along the empty lane in a dream of strange displacement. No other pedestrians walked these midnight streets; no cars purred through the ghosted dark. Only occasionally could I catch the distant murmurs of some secret entertainment. Then, as the first speckles of rain began prickling my arms, I hurried back into the temple. All night long, the rain pattered down on wooden roofs, and I, now sleeping, now awake, sat alone in the darkened shrine, not really knowing where I was.

The next morning, when I got up and made my way uncertainly out to the altar room, the monk bustled up to greet me. The first item on the agenda was a guided tour. And the first stop on the tour was what appeared to be the only piece of decoration in the place: a framed photograph of himself, seated atop a tricycle, looking astonished, a bobble hat on his shaven head and a Mickey Mouse shirt under his alabaster face. 'This me,' he explained. 'I am Buddhist monk.' Then, in the same provisional tone, he proceeded to recite the American sites he had seen – 'San Francisco, Los Angeles, Monument Valley, Grand Canyon, San Antonio, El Paso, New Orleans, Washington, Philadelphia, New York, Buffalo.' Then he led me to a low table, overlooking the temple garden, and vanished.

A few minutes later, my bewilderment now almost mirroring his own, he hurried in again and laid down before me a black lacquer tray filled with elegant little bowls of vegetables, fruit, pickles, and rice; later, a toaster, some bread, and a thermos of hot water for my tea. Then he disappeared again.

I was just beginning to enjoy the feast, looking out upon the green and silver stillness, when suddenly his astonished-looking face appeared again, speeding through the garden atop a motorized contraption. He rode up to the room where I was sitting, looked astonished some more, waved like a queen, and then roared away again in a minicloud of smoke. The next thing I knew, he was at my door, on foot this time, peering in with a hesitant smile. 'Tricycle,' he said, pointing at the offending instrument, Mickey and Minnie grinning on its license plate. With that, he disappeared.

My second day, as I sat in the alcove looking out on to the other garden – a stream, a wooden bridge, a stone lantern, and, beyond, Yasaka Pagoda rising through the trees – the second, and only other, monk of the temple, an older man, with the breathless, fright-ened voice of a perennially bullied schoolboy issuing from a spherical wrestler's body, padded over to me. He spoke even less English than his colleague, but that did not seem to matter, since his was not a verbal medium. Huffing and puffing, but without a word, he sat down beside me and pulled out six sheaves of snapshots: himself (wide-eyed) in front of the Taj Mahal; himself (bemused) on a bridge above the Thames; himself (bewildered) on l'Île de la Cité; himself (perplexed) on the steps of the Piazza di Spagna; and himself with a variety of other scenic wonders. Then, show complete, he trudged away again.

A eunuch and an albino: the monks with whom I was living were the strangest-looking pair that ever I had seen, and a cynic, no doubt, would have had no trouble explaining why they had turned their backs on the world before the world could turn its back on them. Yet they were an eminently kindly pair, and peaceable, and I began in time to think of them as good companions. Every morning, as I took my seat in front of the rock garden, they laid before me a four-course breakfast, and every morning – with a thoughtfulness and precision I could imagine only in Japan – they gave me something different. Every evening, when I went out, I found them squashed together on the floor, at a tiny table in a tiny room, drinking beer before some TV ball game. 'Catch you later,' the albino monk would call out after me, waving his bottle merrily in my direction, chalky white legs protruding from tomato-red shorts.

The area where I had settled down was, by happy chance, one of the last remaining pilgrims' districts in Japan, an ancient neighborhood of geisha houses and incense stores built in the shadow of the city's most famous temple, Kiyomizu, the Temple of Pure Water. Wooden boards still marked the places Bashō had admired, and monks still bathed in the ice-cold Sound of Feathers waterfall above. My own street, as it happened, was still a center of the *mizu-shōbai*, or 'water trade' (of women), and also the place where the widow of the city's fiercest shogun, Toyotomi Hideyoshi, had retired, on her husband's death, and built a villa and a temple. In the temple, I had read, *yama-nekko*, or 'mountain lion', geisha had entertained at parties for the monks, and even now the elegant characters on the lanterns denoted the names of the women who worked within.

Thus the whole area was preserved as carefully as a museum treasure. My local café was a rock-garden teahouse, sliding blond-wood screens opening out on to a clean geometry of wood and water; the neighborhood stores were polished galleries selling sea-blue Kiyomizu pots, silken fans, and woodblock prints, all silvered with the sound of water music; and my next-door neighbor was a forty-foot statue of the goddess Kannon, majestic against the mapled hills.

Few places in Japan were as self-consciously Japanese as Kyoto, the romantic, templed city that had been the capital for a thousand years and even now was faithfully preserved as a kind of shrine, an antique, the country's Greatest Living National Treasure. Almost a hundred thousand tourists (mostly Japanese) came here every day to pay their respects to the 'City of Peace and Harmonious Safety', and the city, accustomed to their worship, handed itself over to them like a collection of gift-wrapped slides – even the place mats at the local McDonald's (which had once set a world record for serving two million burgers in a single day) were maps of the city's lyrical conceits, locating the temple whose floorboards sang like nightingales and the rock garden that traced the pattern of infinity.

Yet even the efficiency of its charm could hardly diminish the city's beauty. My first Sunday morning in Kyoto, I hurried out of the temple at first light and climbed the steep cobbled paths that lead up to Kiyomizu. Taking the wrong path without knowing it, and passing through a side temple, I slipped out into a rock garden. A woman, mistaking me for a VIP, came out with a gold-and-indigo tray bearing a cup of green tea. The maples before us climbed towards the blue. Everywhere was a silence calm as prayer.

Minutes later, I was walking through the teeming basement of a department store, overflowing with more fruit, more pickles, more high-tech gadgets than I could easily take in; sorbet houses and wineshops, noodle joints and macaroni parlors, melon outlets and chocolate-makers. I bought an ice cream from a girl, and she wrapped it in a bag with a smart gold twizzle around the neck, put that bag in a larger, foam bag, complete with two blocks of ice to keep the whole from melting, and wrapped it all in the stylish black-and-gold bag of her company; I went to temples and was handed entrance tickets that looked like water-color prints; I walked into a park again, in the cloudless exaltation of a perfect Sunday morning, and could scarcely believe that I had stumbled upon such a flaw-less world. To partake of the gleaming splendors of the *depāto* and to sip green-tea floats in teahouses; to find moonlit prints in convenience stores and damascene earrings in coffee shops: it shook me out of words.

It sometimes seemed, in fact, in those early days, as if all Japan were at once charging into the future with record-breaking speed, and moving as slowly as a glacier; both sedative and stimulant, a riddle of surface and depth.

And so, in time, the days in the temple began to find a rhythm of their own, and I to set my watch by the pat-tern of their calm. Every morning at 6 a.m., the sound of the tolling gong and the husky rumble of chanted sutras, broken by the silver tinkle of a bell. Then the patter of receding footsteps. Sweet incense seeping under the screen, making the space all holy. Then breakfast in first light, beside the garden, and random walks through lemon-scented mornings, rainbow ban-ners fluttering above the wooden shops. At noon, the elder monk would take his dog, Kodo, for a walk and then, regal in black robes, clap his hands above the pond, summoning the carp to lunch. A little later, the temple was silent again, and the tidy pairs of slippers outside one room, and the squeak of a TV hostess, told me that the monks were eating.

At night, when the city was asleep, I took to slipping out of the place to make phone calls to my employers in Rockefeller Center (New York offices were open from midnight to 8 a.m. Kyoto time). And only then, as I stood in a squat green phone booth, plastered all over with trim stickers advertising topless girls – a novel kind of convenience shopping – did I see the other, shadow side of Japan begin to emerge: the derelicts with wild hair, the crazy-eyed vagrants and disheveled beggars, venturing out into the pedestrian arcades or huddled together under department store eaves, tidy in their way and self-contained, as if, in some part of themselves still good Japanese, they were determined not to intrude upon the world around them. Watching these denizens of the underworld – all but invisible except in the city center and late at night – I recalled that such a one, six centuries before, had gone on to found Daitokuji, the Temple of Great Virtue.

By day, though, the temple was mostly deserted: just me, the two monks, and their dog. Sometimes, on the wall above the toilet, another visitor appeared, a vile, pale-green lizard, with eyes like raisins on the top of his head. And one bright morning, after I had finished breakfast, I met the only other member of the household, a laborer who came each day to make the gardens perfect. As soon as I returned the gardener's smile, he came on over and shook my hand in the glassy autumn sunshine. 'Are you wealthy?' he began. A little taken aback, I did what I had been told to do in every meeting with a Japanese male: handed him my business card. This he scrutinized as if it were Linear B.

'My hobby is making money,' he went on, and then, before I could get him wrong, interjected, 'Is joke!' I see, I thought, a joke. Then the conversation took a literary turn.

'Have you read Milton? And Shakespeare? How about Nietzsche, Kant?'

'Sometimes,' I said. 'Have you practiced English with many foreigners?'

'Oh no.' He waved his hands at me. 'I very embarrassed. I cannot. Especially girls. I very, very shy.'

This, I thought, was familiar enough terrain. 'So you like American girls?'

'At first.' He paused. 'But gradually, no.'

'They are not *shizukana*,' I tried.

He nodded happily. 'Not modest.'

'You must be working hard today.'

'Not so hard. One hour I talking monks. Now Grand Sumō tournament. Monks love Sumō very much; every day they watch. Three hour.' Yet another surprising arrow to their quiver!

The other unexpected feature of the temple was that it was ringed, in large part, by the gaudy purple blocks and curtained parking lots of love hotels. This was, of course, in a way, quite apt: monks and women had always been close in Japanese literature – had, in fact, been the main purveyors of classical Japanese literature – and Gion itself, the name of the 'flower district' here, was also the name of a famous temple. Professional women had long been known as 'Daruma' (after Bodhidharma, the first patriarch of Zen) because, like legless Daruma dolls, they tumbled as soon as they were touched, and then bounced back. And 'dark willows, bright flowers' – a Zen metaphor for the Buddha nature – had long been a euphemism for the pleasure quarters, or so I had learned from a scroll

I had seen in Santa Barbara, by the eighteenth-century Zen monk Gakkō, suggesting that Daruma could as easily be found in a brothel as in a temple. Even one of the most famous episodes in Bashō had found the wandering monk and a disciple in an inn, spending the night next to two concubines and their elderly consort. The next morning, the girls, on a pilgrimage to Ise, had expressed their wish to travel with the monks, and Bashō, regretfully, had demurred:

> At the same inn
> Play women too were sleeping,
> Bush clover and the moon.

Nonetheless, it came as something of a shock to me, on the night of the harvest moon, to return to the temple to find two pairs of delicate white pumps resting neatly in the yard of motorbikes. I wondered whether the monks were entertaining, but I could hear no whispers in the dark, no rustling behind doors. Next morning, I stumbled off my mattress at the sound of dawn prayers, as usual, and wandered into the breakfast room, to find two young Japanese girls – perfectly composed, of course, and tidily dressed, even at this extremely godly hour – standing in the garden, while the elder monk fussed all about them. Then, with a gallantry I had not expected of him, he effected an introduction of sorts, led us to the low table, and presented us all with a full, five-course Japanese breakfast. A little awkwardly, we sat around the table, the two girls exchanging giggles and dainty jokes, then shy smiles and painful pleasantries. They asked me a question, and then giggled. I returned the favor, and there was more giggling. Their giggles came close to hysteria when they looked across the table to see the foreigner flapping around wildly with his chopsticks, and losing, by a technical knockout, to a piece of sushi.

Then, just as fun was at its maddest, up roared the albino, astride his motorized tricycle and giving us all his Empress wave. With that, he zipped away. We were only just beginning to catch our breath after this unexpected command performance when suddenly he materialized again, pale legs pumping furiously as he pedaled through the delicate garden on a baby-blue tricycle, Donald Duck chuckling on its mudguard. The girls clapped their hands in delight and giggled some more, and the monk, flushed with his success, gave another majestic wave and pedaled off again.

The idea of living in a temple while stealing out after midnight to make contact with New York appealed to my sense of incongruity, and I felt open and uncluttered in my empty room. But I could tell that it would be an encumbrance to continue staying there, not least because my after-midnight telephone calls disturbed the monks' early nights as surely as their dawn prayers disturbed my early mornings. Besides, the main purpose of monasticism, I thought, was to help one build a shrine within, so strong that time and place were immaterial. I decided, therefore, to find myself a basic, functional room and to keep the temple as my secret hideaway.

When I told the monks that I was leaving, there was a great commotion. The albino asked me, again and again, if I could not stay but a single night more, and the gardener, with whom I had grown accustomed to having daily chats, announced that I was the first foreigner he had ever met who was 'reserved, polite, and modest' (an encomium that his own politeness doubtless prompted him to deliver to every foreigner he met). The elderly monk invited me into his chamber for a final cup of tea, and only the lizard seemed unmoved.

28

Three

On one of my first days in Kyoto, a poet from Boulder, whom I met by chance in the Speakeasy 'American-Style Coffee Shop', urged me to go, that very evening, to a once-a-month happening called the Kyoto Connection. On my way there, in the bus, a frizzy-haired potter from Santa Cruz sat down next to me and told me that she was going there too. Five minutes later, we found ourselves in a quiet Londonish square, in front of a murky little dive with blackened windows on which was inscribed: 'Studio Varié: Le Chat qui Fume'.

Inside was a small stage in front of a bar, and lots of smoky little tables at which were seated a ragtag group of Bohos: foreigners with shaven heads, foreigners in dreadlocks, shiny-faced Japanese men with ponytails, and bright-eyed Japanese girls. Two girls came in and joined us at our table – friends of Siobhan's, I gathered – dressed in scarves, with kohl around their eyes and hennaed hair and bangles. One, with a ring in her nose, was just back from Tibet; the other, wearing a yin-yang necklace and maroon Nepali trousers, was settled now in Angola. The first talked about 'the full moon on the terraces of Lhasa', the other about 'the powerful kind of energies in Luanda'. An emcee got on the stage, an Aussie with a thick black beard – a former Rajneeshee, I was told, from Tasmania – and announced that this was to be the 'Peter Tosh Memorial Evening'. A Japanese 'salaryman' in his middle years strolled in and sat down at our table, whispering to me urgently, 'Please help me. I want to meet foreign girls.' And then the show began.

The first group was a quartet singing 'Blowin' in the Wind' in Japanese, and soon they were followed by another Japanese group, a trio of young students with soft high voices and angel harmonies, singing, 'It never rains in southern California', and then 'I'm proud to be an Okie from Muskogee', and then, in words I could scarcely recognize, 'Good morning, America, how are you? Say, don't you know me, I'm your native son . . .'. Next up was a local bluegrass sextet delivering 'Tennessee Homesick Blues', and I began to wonder whether people here sang songs only if they had American place names in their titles.

Then the foreign acts began: satirical stanzas, shouted out in confrontational Beat fashion, that began, 'I am a clump of cottage cheese'; poems about Mao, poems with allusions to Godard, and – inevitably – love poems about persimmons wet with summer dew ('Well, she liked it,' huffed the bearded American poet when the audience began to jeer). A Japanese girl got up, holding a white rose, and sang a plaintive ancient melody, '*Hamabeno Uta*', by Narita Tamezo.

> *In the morning on the beach I walk around, remembering.*
> *The sound of wind, the shape of clouds, the surf, the color of the shell;*
> *In the evening, my lover wanders on the beach,*
> *Remembering the waves come up, go down;*
> *Moonlight, starlight.*

As I was taking all this in, my eye happened to catch that of the quiet foreigner beside me. He was a shy-looking fellow in plaid shirt and scuffed gray corduroys, sitting by himself and doodling in a sketchbook.

Seeing me watching him, he explained that he was an artist, and came from San Francisco, and had lived here on and off for fifteen years, learning to paint in the traditional Zen *sumi-e* tradition. Before that, Mark went on, he had been a student in Santa Barbara, and when I told him my name, he told me that he had taken a course in Spinoza from a Mrs Iyer – my mother – and we were off, busily exchanging names in common while, around us, a potbellied character in glasses, so overcome with emotion – or something like it – by the Philip Glass variations being played by a Japanese waiter on a Chinese harp, got up and began swaying to the music, rolling his hands around like a Balinese nymph, and various others started humming 'Om' or sat back rocking on their chairs, eyes closed.

Four hours later, sometime after midnight, the show was over, and a mix of strange spirits spilled out into the half-lit lanes: a ponytailed imp from New York, whose claim to fame was painting the patriarchs of Zen with Marty Feldman faces; a girl from Minnesota who was married to a Japanese flamenco dancer; a slightly unsteady Japanese woman, whose American husband had been the translator of some of Japan's most famous love poems; a vivacious Japanese girl seemingly on the lookout for foreigners ('I live in Gion' – pretty giggle – 'you know, the entertainment area?'); and two hearty beer-swilling German students, one bespectacled, besweatered, and apparently keen to hear more about Gion, the other long-haired and leather-jacketed, with a blasé look that suggested that he, with his rock-star looks, had already found a local girlfriend.

Meanwhile, the diligent salaryman kept sidling up to one foreign girl after another, whispering something in each one's ear and then standing erect and nodding solemnly as he got the bad news, receiving each rejection like a gift.

A few nights later, as I shuffled through the business cards I had collected at the gathering, I noticed, to my surprise, that the street on which Mark was living had the same name as my own. Japanese streets are notoriously as straight as their sentiments and as easy to follow as their sentences. But still, I thought, this was a lead worth following. Going to the nearest phone booth, I gave him a call.

Two minutes later, I was seated in Mark's creaky old Japanese-style house – the very Santa Cruz vision of what a Zen painter's house should be, its central paper lantern reflected in the window twice over, twin moons, as we sat cross-legged on cushions at a low, worm-eaten table.

The old room was rigorously spare and clean: just a few cassettes in a wooden cigar box, a collection of brushes in a tin, and, on the wall, some paintings of Zen themes and a nude. From next door came the steady, monotonous chanting of a Buddhist woman; from the rafters, the scuttling of rats. Putting on some tea, Mark told me a little of how he had come here.

He had grown up, he said, in San Francisco, surrounded by artifacts from Japan, brought over by his aunt and uncle, and fascinated by the stories they had told him of the land where they once lived. Yet he had never really had any contact with the island until his senior year in college, in Santa Barbara. 'And then this man called Shibayama came over from Kyoto. Only for a week. But somehow – it was one of those things – everywhere I went that week, I kept running into him.' He shook his head at the memory. 'He was this really amazing guy, the head abbot of Nanzenji: gentle, but very direct. I'd never met anyone like him before.'

This was '69, and having survived the student riots,

Mark had taken off with a blackjack dealer from Nepal, across the Overland Trail – through Turkey, Iran, and Afghanistan – and ended up living with a Tibetan family in Kathmandu. But as he'd settled down there and begun to take the measure of his trip, and to read deeper in the book of Shibayama's that he'd been carrying around with him, he began to feel 'that there must be some reason for my meeting him. So that really confirmed my sense that I ought to come over to Kyoto to study with him.'

By then, however, he was beginning to run out of money, so he went back to the West Coast, started saving up again, and finally, three years after that first meeting, made it to Kyoto. 'My first day here, I went over to see the *rōshi*, and his first question was what I wanted to do over here. Jeez, I had no idea! But I'd done some sculpting in Santa Barbara, and Shibayama's interpreter and assistant – this really amazing woman called Miss Kudo, whom I'd met in California – had suggested that I mention my interest in painting as well. So I did, and he instantly said, 'Oh, I have this friend who's a painter. Let me introduce you.' And so, the very next day, I was introduced to Jikihara-sensei, who's one of the top *sumi-e* painters in the country. He didn't speak any English and I didn't have any Japanese, but we got on without any problems. And when I told Shibayama that I was also interested in Zen, he sent me to a temple – Antaiji – and as soon as I arrived there, I ran into an American monk, who found me a place to live with another student of Zen.

'So anyway, my first few days here, everything pretty much fell into place, and I met all these people who were going to have a big influence on my life – Shibayama-roshi, and my teacher, who's still my teacher now and probably the main force determining the course of my life, and these two Zen students who are still in many ways my closest friends. Fairly soon there were also these two friends I knew from Santa Barbara, who came over to become monks.' A quiet smile. 'Just kind of karma, I guess.

'Two years later, after I'd settled into an artists' village in the mountains – and into the rhythms of my new discipline – the *rōshi* died. On the day of his funeral, there was a thin drizzle, really thin. A line of pilgrims stretched all the way from the main hall to the next subtemple. And all of them were carrying bells. I still remember the sound of their bells ringing in the drizzle. A little later, Miss Kudo died too.'

Handing me a gift before I left – a friend's homemade map to the city's secret places – Mark invited me to come with him next day on a walk through some of the nearby temples. By the time I arrived, early on another blazing morning, the sun was flooding through his wood-framed windows. Pulling the screen door closed behind him – he never locked his door, he said – he led me down a maze of alleyways and towards the eastern hills. As we walked, I asked him a little more about the practice of Zen.

He had never been a monk himself, Mark explained, but he had stayed in a temple sometimes and had attended monthly sessions of *sesshin* – five days of almost uninterrupted meditation, even in the unheated monasteries in the depths of December. Many of his closest friends were monks, and though his teacher too was not a formal Zen master, he had a temple of his own on an island near Osaka. And though Mark took care not to say it, I could quickly tell that Zen had given him a discipline and a focus: in the cycle of vagrancy and stillness by which he led his life – now spending two years in Kyoto, now taking off for Grenada or Mexico or California for a while, then returning again to Kyoto; in his devotion to his teacher, with whom he had lived for two years as a personal attendant; and, most important, in his training in an art that was, of course, a training in a life.

Though many of Mark's friends had left their temples by now, that was mostly, he implied, because they had reached a stage at which the temples would not leave them. Many of them, he said, had wearied of the worldly aspects of the monastic life – the politicking, the emphasis on sheer willpower, the need for subservience, the stress on hierarchy: all the qualities, in short, that could make temples seem just like any other affluent, rule-bound Japanese company. Yet the temples had given them a certain intensity, a sense of discipline, that stayed with them even now.

We walked past a temple graveyard – newly cut flowers at the base of many headstones, and candies still fresh in their eighty-yen wrappers – and Mark pointed out how such rites were the source of many of the temple's riches: a single headstone here cost twenty thousand dollars. Recently, in fact, the temples had made headlines by refusing to pay taxes to the city and threatening to close their gates to visitors – thus paralyzing the city's most lucrative tourist attractions – unless they were granted an exemption. This much, I knew, was in keeping with Kyoto's history: spiritual and temporal powers had always clashed as often as they had conspired here. If the purity of religion had occasionally touched and elevated the *daimyō*, the chicanery of realpolitik had more often lowered and implicated the monks, who had famously become warriors and libertines and even moneylenders. Poems regularly punned on the closeness between *sen* (a kind of money) and Zen.

'You'll also notice,' he went on, as we mounted a steep hill, framed by orange *torii* gates, 'how the

35

Buddhist temples here are always dark and somber; black. People associate them with death. And usually they come to them only for funerals – or as tourist sites. The Shinto shrines, by comparison, are always red and orange – these really bright and happy colors – and that's where people come for marriages and New Year's Day and other festivals.'

Nowadays, of course, he continued, Zen had much more appeal for foreigners than for Japanese (who generally entered monasteries only if they had to take over a family temple): this despite – or maybe because of – the fact that outsiders had a great deal to give up before they could even enter the front portals of Zen, and the surrendering of self and cerebration clearly came less easily to us than to many Japanese. 'I remember this one Zen teacher told me, soon after I arrived, that the appeal of Zen to many foreigners was like a mountain wrapped in mist. Much of what the Westerners saw was just the beautiful mist; but as soon as they began really doing Zen, they found that its essence was the mountain: hard rock.'

And so we wandered on, past quiet mothers wheeling prams, and age-spotted men pulling yapping dogs; past schoolgirls shuffling their slow way home along canals, and coffee shops where women sat alone, the autumn moon above them in the blue.

Finally, our path meandered into the Tetsugaku-no-michi, or Philosopher's Path, a narrow, tree-shaded walkway along the base of the eastern hills, beside a slow canal. Above us, a thick camouflage of trees carpeted the slopes, broken, now and then, by the severe spire of some temple; on the other side, pink coffee shops and teddy-bear boutiques rested placid above the bustle of the city. I noticed the Bobby Soxer pizza and spaghetti house, and the Atelier café, run, so I'd heard, by a former mistress of the novelist Tanizaki;

36

I noticed too, amidst the trees, the small temple of Anrakuji, where once – in one of the most famous of all Kyoto's scandals – two of an Emperor's favorite concubines had stopped to hear two priests, and been so bewitched by them (or by their message) that they had chosen to forsake the court and join the temple as nuns. Upon hearing of this defection, the enraged Emperor had sentenced both Anraku and the other monk to death.

We stopped in a café, owned by a *samurai* actor, and as we walked on, were given salted plum tea by two chirpy salesgirls. Farther on, inside a shrine almost Chinese in its solemnity, with stone lions perched on either side of its imposing orange entrance, Mark pointed out a small statue covered with a scarlet bib and surrounded by knickknacks – stuffed animals, frilly shirts, flowers, and piles of stones. Jizō, he explained, was the patron saint of children and of travelers (very apt, I thought, since every child is a born adventurer and every traveler a born-again child). These offerings, in fact, were remembrances of *mizugo*, or 'water children' – children who had died young or been stillborn or, in most cases, aborted. 'Is that a sign of real sorrow or just a kind of ritual?' I asked, assuming, as always, that the Japanese were not like other people (the same assumption that so enrages us when the Japanese apply it to us). 'Well,' said Mark quietly, 'I've known a number of women here who've had abortions, and they're always really affected by them.' Having lived here for fifteen years, Mark was clearly well accustomed to dealing with wide-eyed romantics from abroad.

Finally, we arrived at the sprawling compound of Nanzenji – Shibayama's temple – and stopped in a small room to drink green tea, the dark, red-carpet chamber lit up by a rush of silver down the rocks it faced. In the rooms that followed, we saw stylized paintings of white cranes and prowling tigers on gold-lacquer screens, and then the famous rock garden designed by Kobori Enshu ('Approach a great painting,' he had written, 'as you would a great prince'). I noticed how the pines and maples on the hill behind, faintly red and orange and green, blended seamlessly into the pattern of raked gravel, Nature consenting to become a part of art. 'This was the first painting I ever did,' Mark explained. 'The "Leaping Tiger Garden". The first time I visited my teacher, he just gave me three sheets of paper and said, "Come back in a week with three paintings." I did. And when I showed them to him, he just redid them himself – right on top of my drawings!' His quiet voice caught fire. 'And I was breathless. The vitality he gave to the scene! The stones had real power, tension. He caught the sound of the water, the softness of the hills behind. He made the whole place come alive!'

Then, as we wandered back into the streets, watching two models set up for a TV ad, Mark asked me with a quiet smile if I thought I might find a Japanese girlfriend.

'Oh no,' I replied easily enough. 'I've come here mostly to live alone; and besides, I don't think any Japanese girls are likely to have much time for me.'

'Well,' he said with a penetrating glance, 'it would have to be an exceptional girl. But that's the only kind that you would want.'

That night, Mark introduced me to two of his closest friends, Shelley, a funny, warmhearted lawyer from Brooklyn, and her husband, Kazuo, trim in his jeans, with close-cropped hair and glasses, a teacher of animal sciences at Kyoto University, the most high-powered site of higher learning in the country. Over mounds of curry, a 'Positive Thinking' tape reproducing the lap and hiss of the ocean behind us, Mark and Shelley reminisced a little about the folklore of the foreigners (or *gaijin*) here: of *gaijin* who had been directed to the vet when sick, of *gaijin* who, after three years in a firm, were still listed in the company directory as 'Mr Foreigner', of *gaijin* who had been made to sign confessions if ever they were late in renewing their Alien Registration forms.

Kazuo, meanwhile, sat silent in his chair.

'How was your summer?' Mark asked him.

'I was in the temple,' he said tersely. For three whole months, he went on, he had been up Mount Hiei, the famous sacred mountain in the north-east of the city, training to be a Tendai Buddhist monk. For the first month, he had had to get up at five every morning, take a cold shower, and then climb the mountain to collect pure water from a well. In their second month, the apprentice monks had had to get up at two and do the same, while praying three or four times every day. The food was sparse, and the days were cold and hard. But that was only the first stage. Those who were serious would have to complete another course, lasting three full years – sweeping leaves for six hours a day – and then another, for five years, and then, if they were ready, they could try the famous thousand-day circuit, the 'Great Marathon' around the mandala mountain and in and out of the city, in which they would have to run, in handmade straw sandals, fifty miles a day for one hundred days at a stretch, year after year, until they had done the equivalent of running around the world. Part of their training involved going nine days without food or water or rest, watched around the clock by two monitor monks. Many of them lost weight, fell ill. Some even died. Any who failed to complete a single part of the course felt obliged to slash their own throats. But those who survived, anointed as 'Living Buddhas', took on the unearthly glow of souls that had almost passed through death; during their nine-day fasts, they grew so sensitive that they could hear ash falling from an incense stick, smell food being prepared many miles away.

For years, I recalled, women had not even been allowed on the three-thousand-temple mountain. Now, though, Kazuo told me, a woman was actually trying the thousand-day course – a woman, in fact, from Santa Barbara.

I asked him why he was putting himself through all this. He looked very gloomy. 'My mother's father and uncle have a temple,' he explained. 'I am the only male who can carry on the succession. So I must become a monk.'

Four

When I abandoned the temple, I moved across town
into a tiny four-and-a-half-tatami room in an undis-
tinguished modern guesthouse near the base of the
eastern hills. The name of the house was I.S.E. (though
not, alas, in honor of the great sacred shrine of Japan),
and the district into which it was tucked, as tidy as a
paperback in one of the area's crowded bookstore
shelves, was called Nishifukunokawa-chō, or Western
Happy River Neighborhood. It was a quiet area, of
sleepy dogs tethered to their red-roofed villas, and
elderly ladies in kimono, with thinning hair and backs
so stooped they walked almost parallel to the ground.
Outside my room, in a lane too narrow even for cars, I
could hear the sounds of a drowsy world: the cries of
playing children, the occasional scuffling of a cat, the
patient, insistent tinkle of some conscientious student
trying and trying to get a piano melody correct.

My new home was a simple enough space, appointed
only with a desk, a heater, a cold-water tap, a hot
plate, and a futon; in the corridors were two toilets, a
phone, and two showers to be shared among the
house's fifteen residents. Outside, the props were no
less simple. Every morning, at eight-twenty exactly,
there came a high, tinkling cry of *'Okā-san!'* (Mother!)
from the tiny lane, and soon thereafter, a procession of
quiet, tidy children on their way to school, faces well
scrubbed and hair shining, animal-faced satchels on
their backs. At noon, an autumn silence along the

streets: old women leading their grandchildren by the hand, in shuffling steps, to local grocery stores and flower shops. In midafternoon, young mothers carried their tiny, silent, wide-eyed charges home from school on the backs of shiny bicycles; and then, after dark, on the other side of town, there came the counter-procession of the night – the hostesses of the 'floating world' slipping out of taxis at five minutes to eight, shoving change into the drivers' white-gloved hands, and wiggling, in black leather skirts and high heels, down the neon-blazing alleyways.

It was, indeed, almost entirely a world of women and children that I found myself inhabiting in Kyoto. Not being part of the working world, I had no contact with the gray-suited office worker, the bowing interpreter, the straphanging commuter, that form so much of our image of corporate Japan. Japanese men, who were generally captive to the office from eight until eight each day, and then sequestered in their closed-door bars until they went home to sleep, were almost entirely absent from the world I saw. So whenever I was in temples or coffee shops or movies, I found myself, apart from monks, most often amidst groups of young girls, all frightened gravity and giggles, or tidy matrons. And whenever I was downtown, I moved among troops of postcard-perfect young women, the picture of impassive chic in their expensive Dior dresses, lustrous hair waterfalling down their downturned heads as they marched in well-pressed battalions from one shop to the next. In public at least, in their official demeanor, Japanese girls seemed to conform not only to a model but to a peculiarly uninflected model: with their ritual giggles and the mechanical bird song of their voices, they looked to me like public-address systems on two legs.

The sweetest of all the Kyoto scenes, though, took place right outside my window. For every morning, round about nine, the small area in front of my guest-house filled up with two or three young mothers, prettily lipsticked, and trendy in their denim jackets, together with their tiny charges. And every day until five, six days a week, I would find them there, the neatly dressed mothers looking on with infinite patience while their quiet toddlers bumped around on tricycles or waddled about the courtyard with an air of grave purpose. I never saw any of the children shout, or squawk, or throw a tantrum, and I never saw any of the mothers lose her smiling equanimity: both parties formed a tableau of contentment. In New York, the near-absence of children had struck me as a denatur-ing almost, and in California, the sense of endless possibility that was the state's greatest hope seemed all but a curse in the hands of its young. But here, wher-ever I looked, I found images of madonna-and-child, in a world that seemed so settled that it almost cast no shadow. Even Pierre Loti – I read in my first few days in Kyoto – while writing off nearly all Japan as a giant playpen, had grumpily admitted, 'It was the only thing that I really liked about this country: the babies and the manner in which they are understood.'

Five minutes to the east of me in my new home was a temple, where I began to go on hazy mornings when the grayness seeped inside me and my mind would not engage. Sitting in its spacious silences, the tree-thick hills rising beside me towards the blue, a tolling gong behind me, I was brought into focus by the details: an old monk brush, brush, brushing a pathway clean; a young girl seated on the temple platform, as clear as the pond before her; another stone Jizō littered with the offerings of disappointed mothers; a sitting Buddha imparting a peace so strong it felt like wisdom. The temples in Kyoto, around the eastern hills, took one literally out of the world, leading one up through narrow flights of stairs between the pines, away from the rush and clamor of the everyday. Yet one could never forget the world entirely. Floating up from below came the sound, plangent and forlorn, of a garbage collector's truck playing its melancholy song.

Five minutes to the west of me was a blast of pachinko parlors, convenience stores, and shopping malls more modern than anything I had ever seen at home. Walking the shopping streets in Japan, I felt as if I were wandering through some children's wonderworld of indulgences, soothed by jingling Muzak and singsong reassurances. My local video store, whenever I entered, greeted me with a robot's voice that cried, 'Welcome!' and, later, 'Thank you very much!'; my local supermarket, after piping in chirpy messages all day, serenaded its customers when it closed each night with an unbearably mournful rendition of 'Auld Lang Syne'. And the dizzying *depātos* – compact boxes within the great gift-wrapped box that was the modern country – not only glittered with accessories and video screens, hallways of food in the basements, and twenty or more restaurants on the top floor, but even provided whole rooftop amusement worlds, not playgrounds but entire Playlands, sprawling cities in the sky offering views of the hills and the temples on one side and, on the other, a dazzling array of robots, panda trains, goldfish tanks, mechanical raccoons, and Ferris wheels.

Sometimes, in fact, it seemed as if all Japan were a kind of tinkling dollhouse, with props from around the world reconstituted in shops that were peddling foreign dreams. In my neighborhood alone, I found the Ergo Bibamus restaurant, Notre Quotidien Pain (just a

44

couple of blocks from Our Daily Bread), and La Casa Felice – nearly all of them filled with Kyoto Valley Girls who wore warm-up jackets with legends such as *'Style vivant: nous nous aimons et nous vivons'* and who tended, I gathered, to do *arubaito* (part-time work) in order to pay for their *vacances*. Not far away were the Café-Bar Selfish, the Café Post-Coitus, and the Ringo coffee shop, which had Beatles posters plastering the walls, nonstop videos of the mop-tops jamming, menus designed like copies of *The White Album*, and even an ad soliciting members for the Ringo Stars American football team. Yet every time I went into one of these imported theme spaces, be it the Shalom restaurant (all its signs in Hebrew and English), or the Moghul (advertised by a bowing subcontinental cutout in a turban), or the Mozart coffee shop (which specialized in Sacher torte), I was met by exactly the same scene: a team of flawlessly polite Japanese women on both sides of the counter, playing their parts impeccably amidst the exotic stage sets.

Along the cosmopolitan streets, moreover, it often felt as if every need was somehow taken care of and every person treated as a VIP (in the formula phrases of the PA system, customers were given the honorific suffix generally reserved for gods and rulers). On one of my first extended trips downtown, I found exquisite French pastries, orange *givrés*, Lata Mangeshkar tapes almost impossible to find outside India, the entire inventory of New and Lingwood, haberdasher of my youth. Whole liveried ranks of servants came literally running out to serve me, gold buttons gleaming, each time I slouched, in torn jeans, into a large hotel to use the rest room. And where even the affluent in New York could sometimes feel like prisoners, with cockroaches in their sinks and garbage outside their doors, even the poor here, I sometimes thought, could feel like dignitaries, each purchase wrapped for them like priceless treasure.

That Japan was colonizing the future with its ingenious conveniences was already, of course, a universal given; yet still I was startled to find waitresses taking their orders with computers; washbasins at the exits of Kentucky Fried Chicken parlors; special machines in my tiny local laundromat for dry-cleaning sweaters or washing old sneakers. And it was not just that the Japanese had designed telephone cards to get around the inconvenience of stuffing coins into a slot, but that they had made their inventions artful, decorating the cards with images of rock gardens or Hokusai mountains, of cartoon characters or the Golden Gate Bridge, of sumo stars and teen idols, and even – I later learned – of oneself or one's loved ones. And one could buy these conveniences in the streets, from machines, or in stores, laid out in little bags to keep them magnetized. The perfect world, gift-wrapped.

Nor was a single speck of time or space to be wasted. Banks provided magazines so that one's waiting time would be well spent, coffee shops were as well equipped with video games and diversions as amusement parks, and Sony was in the process of perfecting a portable VCR that executives could use while waiting for traffic lights to change. Even the tiny, unvisited alleyways around my house were pressed into service for the larger good, crowded with ranks of vending machines: vending machines for noodles, soup, and every kind of fruit juice; vending machines for cans of tea and coffee and cocoa, with every permutation of milk and sugar, so hot one could hardly hold them; vending machines for tickets to movies or temples or zoos, with additional machines for giving change. There were vending machines for batteries and beer,

huge bottles of sake and cartons of milk, and even –
should one suddenly get the urge after midnight, without a twenty-four-hour convenience store in sight – for
hard-core pornography, their little windows crammed
with thirty-one skin mags, six X-rated videotapes, and
eight inscrutable sex aids.

To find such appurtenances in a quiet family neighborhood – row after row of dimpled teenagers posed in
positions of compliant ease under (English-language)
titles such as *Dick, Deep Special* and *Mad Sex* –
dramatized most graphically this society's difference
from our own. Yet whether these shots of innocence in
transit – cherry blossoms in the flesh, in a sense – were
an incitement to perversity or a defusing of it, I could
not begin to tell. Certainly, in a city where I never saw
couples even holding hands, and where the streets felt
cleansed of every sexual threat, I suspected that public
impulses were as separated from social ones as the
'floating world' was from the family home. So perhaps
these magazines, with their secular cult of the virgin,
served only to encourage sex in the head, catering to
that famously sentimental Japanese Romanticism that
prefers the idea of a thing, its memory or promise, to
the thing itself. And if sometimes I felt I was living
inside a gallery of antique canvases, sometimes I felt I
was living in a world of vending machines, shining
sentinels humming through all the quiet lanes in the
dark.

My first social engagement in Japan came one windy
evening when Mark invited me to a meeting of
Amnesty International – less for the meeting itself, he
suggested, than in order to meet a friend of his, an
uncommonly cultured and philanthropic woman who
had lived for many years in England and was head
now of the local group. Ready to try anything, I

strapped on a helmet, and on a chill night full of stars, through a whipping wind, we rode his Honda through a maze of twisting little lanes up to an elegant old house. Inside, the walls were lined with musty, arcane volumes that had an attic air to them, and after making voluntary donations at the entrance, we were ushered up to a comfortable room where various Japanese, mostly young, were seated on the floor.

'*Dōzo, dōzo,*' cried a man as soon as he saw us, jumping up to usher us to a couple of chairs placed near its front.

Typical, I thought: foreigners were given the best seats in the house (a sign of Japanese graciousness) and, in the same act, were segregated from all locals (a sign of Japanese prudence). My suspicions were only confirmed when, a couple of minutes later, two other foreigners – a tweedy, very distinguished-looking couple from Massachusetts – were ushered to the front. '*Gaijin* ghetto,' muttered the old gentleman as he took his place, looking every bit the retired foreign service officer in his gray slacks, Ivy League jacket, neat red tie, and faultlessly aristocratic bearing.

Good Lord, I thought, what on earth could have brought these New England patricians to this shaggy little gathering of student radicals? Were they CIA? Or worse? And then, in a flash, all my impudent questions were dispelled, as Mark's friend Etsuko swept in, greeting the man as she passed with a dainty 'Good evening, Reverend Farnsworth.'

Behind her came the guests of honor, a family of three Argentines eager to describe their torture at the hands of the military government. The father was a gaunt, long-faced man in his late thirties, who looked the part of a workers' hero, a Latin Walesa in his denim jacket and jeans; his wife was a plump madonna type, dressed all in black, with thick raven hair that fell to her waist; and their perky little son, twinkling impishly at every Japanese girl he passed, was now an eleven-year-old sixth-grader.

Etsuko delivered a brief introduction to the audience, in Japanese, and then, looking over in my direction, asked sweetly, in her bell-like English, 'Shall we begin?'

Nobody else said anything, so I replied, 'Oh, yes.' Maybe this was her way of acknowledging me?

And then the man began speaking, delivering a sentence or two of introduction, in the rough Argentine Spanish that turns *yo* into *zho* and *vas* into *vasch*. There was silence. The man looked at me. Etsuko looked at me. Thirty pairs of Japanese eyes looked at me. I looked at everyone else. And then, with a sinking heart, as the silence deepened, I realized what was going on: mine was not, it seemed, just a foreigner's place of honor – it was the translator's chair. Apparently, my Spanish-sounding name and vaguely Hispanic looks had been enough to have procured for me, unbeknownst to me, the job of interpreting from Spanish, a language I had never learned, to Japanese, a language Francis Xavier himself had considered the work of the devil. My only qualification for the task, I thought bitterly, was that I was probably the only person in the room who spoke neither Spanish nor Japanese.

Glumly, I leaned forward, thirty pairs of Japanese eyes following me as I did so.

The tortured man looked back at me. 'Do you speak Spanish?' he asked under his breath, in almost unintelligible Spanish.

'Not really. I'm not Spanish, you see; I'm Indian.'

'I see,' he said, looking gloomier than ever. 'OK.'

'But if you speak very slowly and simply, I can probably follow.'

'OK,' he said, looking very much as if he had come seven thousand miles in vain.

And so I began. 'It was like a movie,' I found myself saying. 'He put a gun at my head, and said, "Juan Carlos, you are a dead man." Then they put handcuffs on me and threw me under a blanket in the car.' Etsuko duly relayed this information to the goggle-eyed audience, and the narrative went on. 'I will not go into the methods of torture they employed, but they laughed and joked at me, and I remembered that there was a school of torture in Argentina, a school for the members of the death squads.' On and on the torture ran, and all I could do was try desperately to tell the difference between *cabeza*, which means 'head', and *cerveza*, which means 'beer', between *esposas* meaning 'handcuffs' and *esposas* meaning 'wives'. Only a couple of weeks earlier, in the temple, I had read Scott Spencer's *Walking the Dead*, about a family of Chilean refugees led around by radical groups to meetings such as this one. Now, as I tried not to say, 'They tied me up in wives and wrapped a blindfold around my beer,' I felt as I myself were waking the dead.

'When I was released from prison, I was of two minds,' I went on, morosely. 'I was happy at the prospect of seeing my wife and son, my only child. But I was very sad at the thought of all the dear friends I was leaving behind. The Mothers of the Plaza de Mayo have embarked on something very dangerous and difficult, spontaneously forming their group. Some of them have themselves disappeared.'

As the terrible litany ran on, I found more and more that the Japanese words that always deserted me when I needed them were now the only words I could remember. When I had arrived in Japan, fresh from Cuba, I had often found myself saying *Sí* or *Permiso* to frightened-looking Japanese who looked more alarmed with every syllable. Now, however, I found myself saying, *'Hai, hai'* to the anguished Argentinians and *'Ah sō, desu ka?'* to their heartfelt explanations of the 'Dirty War'. *Tabun* in Japanese means *tal vez* in Spanish, I kept telling myself, *casa* means 'house' in Spanish and 'umbrella' in Japanese. Meanwhile, Reverend Farnsworth was squirming in his seat and muttering imprecations each time I uttered the words 'liberation theology', and the Japanese on the floor were looking increasingly unhappy and perplexed. Finally, the narrative ended.

Before I could catch my breath, however, the audience, eager to hear more about these alien horrors, started firing questions at the long-suffering Argentinians. 'Were there any Japanese among the detainees?' 'Do you know of any Japanese who have disappeared?' 'Are there Japanese among the prisoners still in jail?' all of which I deftly turned into Spanish sentences about wives and umbrellas.

Then, out of nowhere, a Japanese man in the audience, unable to wait for the interminable process of translating Japanese into English and then into Spanish and back again, suddenly spoke directly to the family, in Spanish. 'Do you know this friend of mine,' he began, 'who disappeared? I lived in Argentina for many years, and I know all that you are describing.' Madre de Dios, I thought, my mind on anything but the *desaparecidos*: here was a man who was perfectly equipped to translate from Spanish directly into Japanese, and vice versa. I was off the hook!

Which only shows how little I understood Japan. *'¡No, no, me olvidado de todo!'* the man cried out, with enviable fluency, when it was suggested he serve as translator. *'¡No me acuerdo de nada!'* And try as I might, I saw that there was no way at all of persuading him to speak a tongue in which he might possibly, just possibly, in the space of several paragraphs, make a single tiny error. And so I went back to my horrible task, stumbling through more accounts of torments made scarcely more pleasant by the dawning realization, as the Argentine speaker interrupted my translations and the whole family fell into animated debate about which parts I was distorting most, that the main speaker knew more English than I did Spanish; that his wife, who had sat through it all with a look of great pain, spoke both languages well; and that their son, who was enrolled in a Manhattan junior high school, was fluently bilingual. 'And so I say to you, my friends,' Juan Carlos said through me, my unhappy look a fair translation of his own, 'that your efficiency and discipline and unity have turned this country into the third-strongest power in the world. Just think what you could do if you worked on behalf of human rights!'

Later that night, Mark and I went to a *yakitori* house nearby for dinner. Just as I happened to look around, in the midst of our conversation, the young Japanese man next to me caught my eye. 'Excuse me,' he began. 'May I talk English with you?'

'Of course,' I said, more than grateful to be back in my own tongue.

'What country do you come from? How long are you in Japan? How do you find Japan?' Trying to find answers compatible with these phrasebook questions, I felt as if I were being worked on by a student doctor eager to practice his still-unformed skills.

'I saw the American movie *2010*,' he went on, though whether in a spirit of bonhomie or bewilderment I could not tell. 'I could understand the computer – Hal. No problem. But I could not understand the human beings.'

'Really?' I said, not sure how to take this.

'But she' – he pointed to his glumly chic young consort – 'she is student of English literature.'

Ah, I thought, my years of study were not in vain.

'What courses are you taking?' I began.

'One course,' she said haltingly, and with some apparent pain. 'It is in Henry James.' I registered surprise that they would be given the most byzantine of English stylists to begin with. 'And,' she went on with a bulldozer determination, 'in other course, we study nineteenth literature.'

'Nineteenth century?'

She nodded unhappily, her eyes never once leaving her bowl.

'Dickens, for example?'

'Not Dickens,' she said with some authority. 'Dickens is twentieth. We do Swift.'

Ah, I thought: the inscrutable Orient.

'Don't worry,' said Mark consolingly as we made our way home. 'You'll soon find ways of getting out of that. Everyone does, sooner or later.'

Back in his house, while making some tea, Mark put on an old tape of Ry Cooder: lazy, sunlit songs about the border.

'Nice album,' I remarked.

'Yeah. It's funny! This was the very same tape that Ray had with him while he was living in the monastery. Did I tell you about Ray? No? Well, anyway, Ray was this huge, king-size guy from Dallas, who came over to join the Peace Corps in the Philippines and somehow ended up as a Zen monk over in Daitokuji. And somehow, he had this deal worked out whereby he kept a motorbike outside the monastery walls, together with his cowboy boots and leather jacket. And every few weeks, he would steal out to visit his girlfriend. Or occasionally he'd come over to my house. And every time he came, whatever time it was, it was always party time, because this was the only chance he was going to get. Jeez, he was something! He just had this incredible energy, which living in the monastery only intensified. And the monks couldn't come down on him so long as he made it back before morning prayers at four a.m.

'Well, he had the stamina to keep this up – slipping in just before four a.m. every time he left – for months. But one day, on New Year's Day, he left when he shouldn't have, and the head monk, who had never much liked him in the first place, seized the opportunity to get back at him, and told him that he would have to go back to the beginning of the course – become a training monk again! After seven years in the place! So he put all his things in a wheelbarrow and rolled them out of the monastery gates. And he went off to his girlfriend's house and spent a month with her. And of course, after seven years in the temple, he was totally defenseless – totally unprepared to live in a regular domestic situation – and she just sliced through him, completely ate him up.'

He paused. 'It's funny; many of the so-called Zen masters in America have the same problems – with money or sex or alcohol. Anyway, Ray decided to go off to Berkeley to write. He'd been corresponding with Anaïs Nin from the temple, and she'd given him some really good contacts in the Bay Area. So he had a book of poems published – by a press in Santa Barbara, in fact – and he was going really strong until an old girlfriend from high school came over and dragged him back to Texas. So suddenly he ended up in this clean suburban town where everyone thought he talked funny and nobody could begin to understand what he'd been through. He got a few odd jobs and tried to write a novel. But pretty soon, his relationship fell apart, and he did too. The trouble was, poor guy, he just wasn't ready for the world. The monastery had prepared him for everything *except* the world. Last thing I heard, he was a bouncer in a reggae bar.'

Five

As autumn began to draw on in Kyoto – and the first touches of color to grace the eastern hills – Mark invited me one day to attend a special private initiation ceremony. A longtime friend of his, now a head priest at Tōfukuji, one of the Five Great Temples of Kyoto, was about to ascend to a new rank, the youngest Zen master in Japan to attain such a position. It was a closed ceremony, of course, but Mark had been invited, as a friend, and he thought that I might be interested too. Certainly, it sounded like a rare opportunity to see a little behind the enigmatic transparencies of Zen, if only to the next layer of its public face. So when the day arrived, I dusted off my best jacket and tie, put on a black motorcycle helmet, and, thoroughly incongruous, popped on to the back of Mark's Honda. Whizzing through the crowded streets, we veered along a maze of narrow lanes and ended up at last outside the temple compound, all abustle in the brilliant morning.

By the time we arrived, sober parishioners in their best suits were already heading under purple banners into the temple, along with monks who looked like giant bats, black robes billowing out around them. 'That's Soto-san,' Mark whispered as one such figure hurried past. 'I knew him in California.' In the glorious sunshine, the thickly forested hills that rose above a plunging gorge were glowing almost, and the maples, through which the sunlight streamed, were just beginning to turn. In the shadeless gravel courtyards of the temple, monks were scattering this way and that, some of them in special orange-and-black raiment, some waving tidy scarlet flags. Inside one of the temple's Buddhas, I once read, the beautiful poetess Ono no Komachi had secretly stashed her love letters.

Slipping off our shoes at the entrance to the monastery, we followed a shaven-headed monk (from California) into an antechamber and there were offered tea. This, I gathered, was the *gaijin*'s corner: it included a middle-aged American student of Zen with his teenage Filipina bride; another eager-eyed American; and a New York woman with granny glasses who handled words as if they were thorny roses. Beside her, and next to me, sat a seamlessly elegant Japanese lady in a flowing dress, who apparently found it incumbent on her to make conversation with me. Where did I come from? she began hesitantly. How long had I been here? What was I doing in Japan?

At that moment, bells began tolling, and we were led off again, in our little group, around a rock garden and over the famous hanging causeway and along a wide stone pathway to the great *zendō*, a celebrated National Treasure usually closed to the public. There, under a dragon-writhing roof, the ceremony commenced. Drums sounded sonorously as the monks walked in, one by one, in purple and orange robes, with orange sashes and pointed Chinese shoes. A screeching came from within, and the *rōshi* himself appeared, followed by a long, muttered wailing that sounded like a coyote's howl. A monk waved a bamboo whisk above us all, extending a skinny, but commanding, hand in each of the main directions. The solemnity was broken, in our corner, as the Filipina, giggling brightly, asked if we knew where the rest room was. Four men blew on bamboo flutes, piercing, mellifluous, and sad.

Outside once again in the radiant morning, men in dark suits, women in kimono, stood on the Tsuten Bridge, bowing with the ceremonious elegance of characters from *The Makioka Sisters*. One woman glittered like a brooch in a blue-and-golden sari and metallic blue fingernails, her temple dancer's features sharp under kohl-ringed eyes. Old men in grave suits sat on Coca-Cola benches, reclining in the autumn sun like ageless school friends of the Emperor.

When we returned to our places in the monastery, we found beside every seat an elegant purple carrier bag with golden lettering, loaded high with gifts; in front of each setting, two wooden boxes on a tray, stuffed with every kind of delicacy; and – since there was no way that anyone could begin to eat all this – another elegant bag, and a stylish lavender cloth, or *furoshiki*, in which to pack the boxes and take them home.

Again I found myself next to the decorous Japanese woman. Again the obligatory questions began. Who was my favorite musician? What was my age? How did I like Kyoto? Apparently, my answers were the right ones – she, too, was thirty and liked Bruce Springsteen and felt that Kyoto was 'little magic town' – and so, as we munched our inexplicable food, she ventured a little further. 'Sunday, my daughter little have birthday party. Please come here my house.' Sure, I replied, game for anything, and she wrote down meticulously the name of a train station and then her telephone number. 'Please you come. Maybe two o'clock, begin.' 'Thank you very much,' I said, and then, with a mother's brisk efficiency, she whipped out my *furoshiki*, packed my food away into my boxes, wrapped the boxes in the lavender cloth, and handed it all back to me as if it were her gift.

Later, back home, I peeled back layer after layer of

the elegant cloth. Simply opening the temple's treasure was an almost sensual experience. Caskets of Japanese cake sat inside, and bottles of expensive sake; a poem in flowing calligraphic script, written by the *rōshi* himself, and a screen on which to mount it; and, of course, the purple cloth, touched now with the lady's perfume.

Five days later, I was spending all morning writing on Ruth Prawer Jhabvala, my mind on the follies of credulity, when suddenly I remembered the woman's birthday party. It had been a fairly casual invitation, I thought, with no meaning attached to it, but I felt that courtesy alone suggested I attend. 'You never know what to expect with these things,' Mark had advised me, but I felt pretty sure that children's birthday parties must be something of a universal: fifteen or twenty kids careening around, amidst a mess of many-colored balloons and party hats, alternately laughing and screaming, while mothers stood by the kitchen, enforcing order and swapping gossip. So I packed the bear that I had bought as a ceremonial offering, and timed my arrival to be a safe forty-five minutes late. That way, I thought, I could slip into the background and easily make my escape.

When I arrived at the station written down by the mother, I walked out into the street and found myself inside a honeycomb of unmarked alleyways. Streets forked this way and that on every side of the diverging railway tracks. Narrow lanes led off into the distance. Signs were nonexistent. I looked for the nearest phone.

'*Moshi-moshi,*' came an excited voice at the other end, up to its neck, I assumed, in children and chaos.

'*Moshi-moshi.* This is Pico Iyer.' There was a silence. 'The man you met in Tōfukuji Temple?'

'Ah, hallo. How are you? What place you now?'

'I'm not sure. I'm just outside the station.'

'What name street?'

'I don't know. I came down the stairs, and I'm standing outside a coffee shop called U.C.C.'

'U.C.C.?' she repeated, incredulous.

'Oh, I'm sorry. That's the name of the coffee they're advertising. Anyway, I'm near the stairs.'

'Stairs?' She giggled nervously. There was a long silence. 'You come here my house?'

'Oh, I'm sorry. I thought it was your daughter's birthday party.'

'I think maybe you no come. Now three o'clock.'

'Oh, I'm very sorry.'

'Please you wait station. I come.'

Two minutes later, a small and pretty figure bounced up to me, long hair tumbling over her shoulders, a bright turquoise scarf over her black shirt, and leg warmers covering her acid-washed jeans. I was not quite sure who this was, but I assumed it must be the funky teenage sister of the woman I had met at the temple, maybe ten years younger than that elegant matron with the severely swept-back hair and the long brown dress. As she flashed me a dazzling smile, though, I recognized the look, and the soft, melodious voice – and realized that this was the same woman, remade now in a different role. She led me down the station stairs and, breathless, filled me in on the plans.

'Other person little telephone my house. They little late. Maybe five o'clock.'

'Oh fine. Well, if it's easier, I can come back then?'

She looked at me, confused. 'You no want come my house?'

'Either's fine really. Whatever's easiest.'

'You not want come *ima* now my house?'

'Sure – if it's no trouble.'

60

'Maybe other person come five o'clock. Maybe six. Are you OK?'

'Oh yes. No problem.'

She led me through a sliding door, and I found myself inside a compact modern flat. The main room was utterly silent. It had the look and feel of a teenage girl's bedroom. On the walls were two posters of the teen-idol pop group a-ha (a latter-day Osmond family from Norway, so far as I could tell) and one of Sting, in all his open-shirted glory. Album covers of Sting hung from the doors, and more beefcake posters of a sultry-eyed a-ha. From the ceiling, an upside-down sea otter chuckled down at me, and all along the gleaming bank of high-tech stereo and video equipment that were the room's main decoration were stickers from Tokyo Disneyland. The teenage artifacts sang out strangely in the quiet of the room on this sleepy afternoon.

'Please you sit,' offered Sachiko-san, motioning me towards her small paisley sofa. 'You like Sting?'

I felt I could hardly admit that I found him one of the more disagreeable creatures on the planet. 'Oh yes.' With that, she gave me a pretty smile of delight, pressed a few buttons on the stack of gleaming black consoles, and disappeared. I sat alone in the silent, empty room and listened to the maestro sing dirges about Quentin Crisp and Pinochet.

A few minutes later, Sachiko-san reappeared, bearing two cups of Twining's tea on a tray (I recalled that I had mentioned, *en passant*, at the temple that I preferred English tea to Japanese). She sat down beside me and smiled shyly.

'You seem to like the West,' I began.

She nodded gravely. 'My brother go Kansas City study. Three year. My mother very sad, many time say, "Don't go!" But then he send picture from your country, always biggg smile! America, he say, little animal

61

country. He think he living movie world – little Disneyland cartoon. But he much much want return.'

'So he's here now?'

'Now Switzerland. Jung Institute. You know this place?'

'Oh yes. Have you visited him there?'

'I like.' She paused. 'But now I am mother part. Japanese system, man visit other country, very easy. But woman must always stay Japan.' A long pause. 'Very sad.'

A difficult silence fell. Then she brightened up. 'But, my son now little learning English. He want go Switzerland. He much love Matterhorn. T.G.V.'

'Really?'

At that moment, the record finished, so she popped up and stepped over to the tower of video monitors, laser videos, and speaker systems. 'You like Chris Lay?'

'I'm sorry, I don't know him.'

Her brow creased up in confusion. 'You not know Chris Lay?'

'No.'

'Please you try.'

At this, she put on another record, a very, very slow love song, delivered by a husky, infinitely gentle male voice, about a lovers' parting. We listened in silence to the slow, heartfelt ballad, with its drawn-out, wrenching climax: 'I'll always love you . . . September Blue'.

There was silence.

'Very nice song,' I said brightly, hoping to lighten things up.

'You like? Please one more time.' She bounced up again, pressed a button, and again, in silence, in the empty room, we sat side by side on her couch, listening to the husky, heartrending strains of the teary love song.

When it was finished, Sachiko-san jumped up again. 'I write word,' she announced proudly, and then pulled down from the wall a computer printout on which was typed, ' "September Blue" by Chris Rea', and all the words in English.

> *I'll be all right, though I may cry,*
> *The tears that flow, they always dry,*
> *It's just that I would rather be,*
> *With you now . . .*
>
> *And every time I see that star,*
> *I will say a prayer for you,*
> *Now and forever,*
> *September Blue.*

'You have a computer too?'

'My husband buy.'

'Is he here?' I looked around. Now it was my turn to be confused.

'Not here. He cannot holiday. Every day, much much work.'

'Sunday too?'

'Sunday too. Every day, he come home twelve o'clock.'

A long silence.

'Your country same?'

'No, not really.'

At this point, two small heads suddenly peered around the screen door: one belonging to a boy of about seven and the other to a five-year-old moppet. 'Ah, please,' said Sachiko-san, smiling happily. 'Please you see. This my son, Hiroshi. This Yuki.'

They stood in silent shyness at the door.

'And today's her birthday?'

'No. Today no birthday. Two day before.'

'I see,' I said, though of course I didn't.

Both children stared at me in neat decorum, at once intrigued and, I assumed, faintly unsettled by this funny-looking foreigner. Then their mother invited them to sit down, and the four of us sat in silence in the small room, presided over by rock stars, and listened again to the slow and emotional ballad, with its air of tender intimacy. 'I'll always love you . . . September Blue'.

The song was just starting up again when Sachiko-san vanished into the kitchen. I looked at the children. The children looked at me. Chris Rea murmured his love. Then Sachiko-san emerged again, bearing a beautiful cake, with fresh strawberries and melon slices – the ultimate Japanese luxury – pieced around the message *O-tanjōbi Omedetō* (Happy Birthday). Lighting the five candles, she went over to the system, turned off 'September Blue', and turned off all the lights. Then, flashing a smile of encouragement at me, by the light of five flickering candles, she began singing, in quavering, high-pitched English, 'Happy birthday to you . . .' I joined in, and her son did too, three wobbly voices in a plaintive refrain in a room lit by candles. When we finished, the birthday girl blew out all the candles, and we were left again in the dark. I felt Sachiko-san stirring beside me, and then the lights came on again, and she brought us all orange juice to enjoy with our cake, and Chris Rea began to sing of love once more.

I liked Sachiko-san very much – she seemed unusually warm and openhearted, as well as demure and chic in the approved Japanese fashion – and her sleek-haired, almond-eyed, utterly quiet children were entirely irresistible. My sense that mothers and children were the two great blessings of Japan was only getting confirmation. But still, I thought, this was a rather sad and awkward way to celebrate a fifth birthday, and I could not help shuffling a little in embarrassment as we sat there in a silence broken only by the song and my occasional mutterings of 'Yuki-chan, O-tanjōbi omedetō!'

Then, suddenly, I remembered the bear that I had brought for Yuki and withdrew it from my bag. And Yuki, in delight, bundled off and brought back a rabbit, a koala, a fluffy bear called Pooh, and even an orange raccoon. Delighted in turn, I inquired after their particulars and then, pointing to the Tokyo Disneyland stickers on the front of the stereo system, mentioned how much I enjoyed the place, and the children scurried off to show me their photos of their visit. Paging through the album, I pointed to the photos of Yuki and asked if she was Mickey, pointed to Mickey and asked if that was Goofy, pointed to her mother and asked if it was her father, and the next thing I knew, the little girl's sides were shaking with laughter, and she was beginning to tickle me, and I was retaliating with the aid of a bear, and Hiroshi was making a counterattack with a rabbit, and all of us were making mayhem.

A few moments later, the children were pulling me out, one by each arm, into the street to play ball, and we were bouncing a tennis ball back and forth while Sachiko-san kept throwing her long hair back and saying, 'Oh, I'm sorry. Children very happy. I'm so sorry. Are you OK?' And then Hiroshi decided that I must see his school, and all of us marched off to the shrine of the Meiji Emperor nearby, and then to the shrine of General Nogi, to play hide-and-seek, and soon the children were racing off to bring me sprigs of flowers, and Hiroshi was feeling bold enough to tell me the name of his best friend, which I ritually mispronounced, and his mother was smiling anxiously, and clicking away with her camera, and saying, 'You tired?

I'm very sorry. I'm so sorry,' and Yuki was clinging to my hand, and we were all running races up and down the darkening lanes.

By the time night had fallen, all four of us were back home, and Yuki was clambering all over me, giggling helplessly as I pointed to pictures in her new Richard Scarry book, of hippos in aprons and rabbits playing golf. *'Tanuki wa doko deshō ka?'* (Where is the raccoon?), I kept asking. *'Kono dōbusto wa tanuki deshō ka?'* (This animal here, is it a racoon?) As one whose Japanese was strongest when it came to animal words, I realized that this was a conversational opportunity not to be missed. And Hiroshi was driving his trains all over my stomach, and Yuki was bouncing her flattened orange raccoon up and down on my chest, and Sachiko-san, as if in proof of Ruth Benedict's claims about the blurring of apology and gratitude in Japan, was saying, 'Thank you. Sorry. Thank you. I'm so sorry.'

And then I threw still more oil on the fire by teaching all three of them the English word 'raccoon' and telling them how much I had always been taken by the *tanuki*, the mischievous masked figure, half badger and half raccoon, who stood outside most sake bars, advertising in his potbelly the Dionysian pleasures of the open road. All the while, Sachiko-san kept asking me, doubtfully, 'You like raccoon? Really? True you like raccoon?' and I kept saying, *'Hai, hai!'* until she told me that the Japanese, as a rule, were not very fond of him: the raccoon was the rival to the fox, the other malefic trickster said to disguise itself as a beautiful woman to bring down innocent priests. Undeterred, I recounted how the Germans called them *Waschbär* and explained how they were famous in California for making raids on carp ponds.

And that night, when I got home, I was so caught up

in the spirit of the day that I sat down on my futon, imagining Yuki by my side, and wrote out a story for the children about a princess trapped in a castle by a jealous father, and the two raccoons, gallant, resourceful, and speaking in couplets, who spirit her away to a new life of freedom.

Six

As I began to settle down in my new home, I began, very slowly, to make my way, in translation, through some of the great works of Japanese literature. And as I did so, I was struck again and again by how much Japanese writing was touched with a decidedly feminine lilt and fragrance, a kind of delicacy and a lyricism that I associated, however unfairly, with the female principle. This softness was apparent not just in the watercolor wistfulness of Japanese poems, but also in the very themes and moods that enveloped them – loneliness, abandonment, romance. This was, perhaps, as much a reflection of my own tastes as of anything, and in men like Mishima, or the modern-minded Abe and Ōe, there were, of course, some towering exceptions. Yet still it seemed to me that much of Japanese writing, right down to such near contemporaries as Tanizaki and Kawabata, was devoted to the private world, a Jane Austen stage of domestic passions. The world of state, the striving of the office and the marketplace, the realm of public affairs – all these were scarcely glimpsed amidst the quiet, unworldly dramas of the soul. Even gangsters, at their deaths, wrote poems to the seasons.

Historically, of course, there were good reasons for this. For one thing, the Japanese syllabary, though invented by a Buddhist priest, had originally been used almost exclusively by women – to such an extent that it had become known as 'woman's hand'; and

68

while men had been confined to the public, official script of Chinese, women had all but invented Japanese poetry. As a result, perhaps, early Japanese poetry was all love poetry (where its model in China dealt more often with friendship). And by the tenth and eleventh centuries, and the great cultural flowering of the Heian period, the Japanese alphabet was so much a woman's domain that men actually pretended to be women if they wanted to use the native script, and even fit themselves into the conventions and emotions of women.

> By and by I'll come
> he said and so I waited
> patiently but I
> saw only the moon of the longest month
> in the dawn sky.

That plaintive love poem was written by a Buddhist priest.

Many of these verses, clearly, were as ritualized as thank-you notes, especially in a culture where writing poems was as *de rigueur* as dancing might be in other courts; clearly, too, in a society whose public life was close to formal pageant, it was only in private, behind closed doors, that people began to seem interesting to themselves. Yet whatever the reasons – or the qualifications – poetry and femininity seemed almost interchangeable in Japan, as they would never be in the literature of Chaucer, Milton, and Johnson, say; and every modern scholar seemed to agree with Kenneth Rexroth in saying that the Heian period was 'certainly the greatest period of women's writing in the history of any literature'.

Certainly, too, as I began reading *The Pillow Book* of Sei Shōnagon, one of the two great testaments of the Heian court, I felt that much of its charm, as with Lady

Murasaki's *Genji*, lay in its girlishness, its womanly refinement, its sensitivity to nature, and to the lights and shades of relationships. Here was the poetry of the paper screen – of delicate walls and sliding panels, of shadows and suspicions, of secrecy and stealth.

Yet all this was also of a piece with Sei's extreme fastidiousness about the observation of ritual courtesies, a kind of hypersensitivity that amounted, in the end, to snobbery. Obsessed with impressions and reputations, with what was and was not 'cricket', Sei revealed herself as something of a stickler for protocol, even when it came to matters of the heart. Everything to do with the common folk she found contemptible; everything to do with the Emperor or Empress – even their bad moods – she found a source of great delight. And in her habit of anatomizing emotions and cataloguing poetic sights as if even the motions of the heart were finite, she betrayed something of the stylized reflexiveness of a society in which not only gestures but feelings themselves were prescribed; one of the 'Rare Things' she exalted was 'a person who was in no way eccentric or imperfect', and one of the 'Embarrassing Things' was 'to hear one's servants making merry'. One could almost hear the lady-in-waiting at Buckingham Palace saying, 'But really, my dear. It's simply not done.'

Thus Sei's delicacy in responding to Nature turned into a kind of pedantry when she dealt with human nature; she read people as if they were gardens and as if both should be raked into the same kind of impersonal perfection. And in her fussiness regarding the proper associations of blossoms, the emotional effects of the moon, and the etiquette of the morning-after letter, one could see how love of beauty in such a world might often mean no more than the beautiful gowns worn by aristocrats in Florence or Versailles.

The elegance we ascribed to Japanese souls belonged sometimes only to their tastes; Sei, in a sense, had designer views.

I was more taken aback, though, to find this same preoccupation with niceties, and with the right way of doing things, in the other great classic of the *zuihitsu*, or 'follow the brush', form of collected sayings, the *Essays of Idleness* of the fourteenth-century monk Kenkō. The title, with its distinctly Thoreauvian air, promised typically serene meditations on silence, solitude, and impermanence, and all these it did indeed provide; the monk did much to enunciate the aesthetic of Japanese Romanticism, explaining why it was better to dream of the moon than actually to see it, and how longing was better than love. Yet in between were reflections on women ('devious but stupid'), interviews with backgammon champions ('You should never play to win, but so as not to lose'), lists of 'Things Which Seem in Poor Taste' ('A man should avoid displaying deep familiarity with any subject'), and descriptions of 'seven kinds of persons [who] make bad friends'. The monk wrote about his frissons of pleasure when passing an unknown woman on a night of moon viewing, and the protocol of making love; how 'lamplight makes a beautiful face seem even more beautiful', and 'beautiful hair, of all things in a woman, is most likely to catch a man's eye'. Most unexpected of all, at least to me, were the priest's anxious obsessiveness with appearances ('A man should be trained in such a way that no woman will ever laugh at him'), and his strongly worded snipes about lower-class men and other 'insufferable' or 'disagreeable' types ('It is unattractive when people get in a society which is not their habitual one'). If the lady-in-waiting occasionally wrote with the exalted purity of a monk, the monk often wrote with the sharp-tongued worldliness of a lady-in-waiting.

At times, in fact, it became hard to tell the two of them apart. Sei wrote that one of the 'Unutterable Things' was 'snow on the houses of the common people. This is especially regrettable when the moonlight shines down on it.' Kenkō echoed her almost to a fault. 'Even moonlight when it shines into the quiet domicile of a person of taste is more affecting than elsewhere.' Sei flaunted her irreverence by mischievously declaring, 'A preacher should be good-looking . . . an ugly preacher may well be the source of sin'; the monk returned the favor by writing, 'A man may excel at everything else, but if he has no taste for lovemaking, one feels something terribly inadequate about him.' Both of them, weighing fashion against tradition, seemed – even more than their counterparts elsewhere – to be writing almost impersonally. And yet the effect was ravishing. That, in fact, was the confounding paradox of this land of pragmatic romantics: If you find something beautiful, it seemed to say, why not simply reproduce it and reproduce it *ad infinitum* (even if it was a woman or a poem or a gesture)? If you've found something pleasing, why ever deviate from the norm? And what answer could one provide when the finished product shone with such an enameled perfection?

It did not take me long, in the autumn afternoons, to find that whenever I tried to find any particular place in Kyoto – to locate, that is, a specific site on a map – I ended up wandering around in circles, through riddles of dead-end lanes, thoroughly defeated by the maze of Japanese planning. There was, I thought, a metaphor in this: one could not plan epiphanies any more than one could plan surprise visits from one's friends. Expectations would only defeat themselves. So as the days went on, I tried to keep as open as I could, waiting to see what kind of things found me.

One day, I was just walking home down the narrow lane, when suddenly I was hailed by a strapping, red-faced fellow with a mat of straw-blond hair. 'Excuse me, mate, d'you live near here?' He pointed to an ad for my guesthouse. 'Yes, I do.' 'Would you mind if I tagged along and took a bit of a look at it?' 'Not at all.' Bob, I quickly discovered, was a former professional Aussie-rules football player and sometime engineer who had recently moved here from Surfers Paradise. I would not have believed that such a place existed, with so immodest a name, except that the previous day I had met a man in my very own house who also came from 'Surfers' (the Santa Barbara of Australia, so it would seem). Bob was something of a larrikin – he still walked eight hours a day, he said, to keep himself in shape – and as he eagerly accepted my offer of a cup of tea, I began to see that he was more in need of company than a room. But still he struck me as a friendly fellow, in the Aussie way, and he seemed to have a genuine wish to do well. 'Thing with the Japanese is,' he declared, 'they're a clever group of bastards. Found out how to be hard the nice way. I've been living in the youth hostel over in Osaka' – he made it sound like an Irish pub – 'two months now. Way I see it, you get here for a year, learn a bit of the culture, give yourself a chance to crack the language. Jesus, I'm learning more English than my students – grammar, y'know, and all that bullshit! Way I see it, you've got to know something if you know nothing.' (The Zen of Surfers Paradise, so it would seem.) 'Not like a chapter from a book, but in a real sense. Mind's a tough bastard to control.

'I'm also interested in Asian girls,' he went on disarmingly, 'as a possible partner for life. Went over to the Philippines a couple of times, for a month or so, looked it over. Nice girls, if you know what I mean. But psychologically – naw! I mean, you want to have a chat now and then, if you know what I mean. A lot of my friends over in Queensland, they have these Filipina brides. But they're just simpleminded guys; as long as they've got someone to take care of them and have sex with a lot, they're as happy as pigs in shit, if you'll pardon my French.

'See, the way I look at it' – Bob apparently did a lot of looking – 'you've got up here' (he put his hand parallel to his head) 'all these incredibly obnoxious, dominating, demanding American and Australian women – you might think this is sour grapes, but it's not; it's just a statement of fact – and you've got down here' (he put his hand at heart – or was it breast? – level), 'down here, you've got all these really feminine Asian girls, and sexual too; I mean sex not just for sex but for other things too. Way I figure it, it's easier to bring these girls up than the other ones down, the ones who are busy saying, "You guys have had it good for a thousand years, now it's our turn to take over." So you raise the girl, and you're raised yourself.'

I wasn't entirely persuaded by his logic, but I kept my ideas to myself, and Bob brought his Sunday sermon to a rousing climax. 'Nice to talk to you, mate,' he said, extending his hand, and headed off for more of his eight hours walking.

The East, of course, had always been filled with Bobs, with Western men seeking Asian wives, as well as Asian wisdom, and not always troubling to distinguish between the two. Romance and religion had long constituted the double lure of the Orient, and in recent years, the confusion of the two had grown even more intense as the presence of U.S. troops on the continent – in Japan, then Korea, then Vietnam and the Philippines – had turned every war zone into a kind of erogenous

74

zone, leaving more and more Westerners smitten with Buddhism, and with the other graceful attractions of the East.

In Kyoto, however, the division was especially vexed. Here, after all, was a city built on an imperial grid, yet curlicued with scented gardens and pretty floral canals. Here was a city still inscribed with the bloody feuds conducted in its hooded temples and dark castles, yet a city that was now a repository of all the country's female arts. Kyoto today was the center of kimono and flower arrangement and geisha; of lacquer-work, paper umbrellas, and fans. Even the Kyoto dialect was famously a girls' tongue, best suited to a high, melodious delivery, in which *arigatō* became *okini*, and *wakaranai, wakarahen*. 'Every city has its sex,' Kazantzakis had pronounced unequivocally. 'This one [Kyoto] is all female.'

Thus the 'City of Purple Hills and Crystal Streams' had always been defined, for the foreign world at least, by the monks who lived in the hills and the women who dwelt along the streams. The two great mountains surrounding the city were known as the 'Mount of Wisdom' and the 'Mountain of the Cave of Love'. The mountains themselves were supposed to carry the male energy of yang; the rivers, yin. Yet the division had never been as clear as its designers would have liked. For temples had famously been used as tryst-ing places, and Buddhist storytellers had sometimes doubled as prostitutes. Paintings had shown Daruma dressed in courtesan's clothes, and vice versa. Even today the classic postcards of the city showed fledgling geisha standing, coquettish, outside temples. And for foreigners, who came to Japan in search of 'a good life' and 'the good life' and were not always able – especially in a country whose language has no articles – to tell one from the other, the dialectic was especially bewildering. I was probably typical, having long been drawn to the aesthetic and the religious elements in Japan, and wishfully hoping that the two were one and the same (the Japanese made a religion of pure beauty). Even the latest of the Western poets to settle in Kyoto, Brad Leithauser, had taken as the epigraph for his novel about the city Shakespeare's sonnet 144, the classic statement of the conflict between two loves, one heavenly and the other of the earth.

I was just musing on all this when Mark, as he had promised, gave me the book of poems by his friend Ray Coffin, a book whose very title, *Poetry for Crazy Cowboys and Zen Monks*, announced the same dialectic (one poem was even entitled 'Ode to Narcissus and Goldman'). He had gone East, the American monk had written, in search of 'some simple, sound horizons' and had found them in Japan – in his memories of Texas. As for Zen's immersion in the moment, its sense of immediacy and intensity, he had found that mostly with his girlfriend, in their unsanctioned kind of moving meditation. His love nights, he wrote, were 'rich, gusty and full of the ever-fleeting NOW'.

The stay in the temple, in fact, seemed to have made him only more Texan – because more himself – and his poems read like old Dylan songs set to an irregular Zen beat. They hymned faraway girls, Mexican bars, 'the sweet easy drone of a steel guitar on a summer night' – all the pleasures, I assumed, that had grown more piquant for him as they grew more distant. And so the dialogue gained force and fire, the cowboy on his bike, in handmade Nocona boots, chafing at the monk, head bowed in meditation. Sometimes the monk disciplined the cowboy, sometimes the cowboy liberated the monk. And finally the unlikely duet concluded with 'Cowboy sun Monk moon friendship – A total eclipse'.

*   *   *

The very next day, I was reading Zen poems in my room when a call came for me on the guesthouse telephone. A call? I thought. Whom did I know in Japan? I answered it and heard a high, breathless female voice. 'Hallo. My name is Sachiko Morishita.' I could almost hear the phrasebook flapping in the background. 'Thank you very much coming here my house. I'm sorry. Children very happy. Very fun. I'm sorry. Thank you very much.' Amidst a confusion of girlish giggles and long pauses, I slowly dug out her meaning: in return for my playing with her children, Sachiko-san was offering now to show me around Nanzenji. Like every Japanese citizen, she apparently had a schedule as precisely organized as that of any head of state, what with going to her part-time job, taking her children to school, collecting her children from school, taking her children to swimming lessons, ballet lessons, piano lessons, and English classes, doing her aerobics, paying duty visits to her parents and her in-laws, and preparing her husband's food, bed, and bath each night. Still, she said, she could be free for a couple of hours on Wednesday morning. Sensing both her loneliness and her openness, I did not have the heart to tell her that Nanzenji was one temple I had seen already.

A couple of days later, when I arrived at the Heian Shrine, I found her waiting for me eagerly, a tiny figure of casual chic in a thick U.S. Army jacket with a Sting sticker on one pocket, hands shyly crossed behind her back, and bouncing on the soles of her feet. Exchanging greetings in languages neither of us could really understand, we began wandering together through the sleepy backstreets of Kyoto. Ambling into a garden, we found an arrangement of rocks and water, and Sachiko-san backed away when she saw the gliding carp below. In the street, a dog strained at its leash, and again she started, moving quickly to the other side. But her sheltered smallness was most apparent in her enthusiasms. 'Last night,' she said, 'I go Chris Lay concert. Osaka Festival Hall. Very beautiful concert. "September Blue" encore. I very, very excited. All day I cannot eat. Stomach big problem. Heart cannot control. Very beautiful day.' The epiphanies of her world seemed almost sadder than her trials.

As she fell into a pregnant, thoughtful silence, I tried to lighten the mood by telling her that I'd been so invigorated by her daughter's party that I'd written a story for her children, about two heroic raccoons.

Having learned this new word just the previous week, she tried it out with glee. 'Raccoon story?'

'Yes,' I answered with some pride.

'You write raccoon story?'

'Yes.'

She frowned. 'You job, raccoon story writer?'

Some things, it seemed, got hopelessly lost in translation.

And so we wandered on, down drowsy lanes, past noodle shops and china *tanuki*, to Nanzenji, and there, on the platform overlooking the Leaping Tiger Garden, we sat side by side, looking out upon the maples, as I had done with Mark two weeks before. There was, as Mark had noted at the temple ceremony, a curious kind of intimacy that Sachiko-san established – she seemed to draw a net around one as if to shut out the rest of the world. And as she explained the symbols of Zen to me in the giddy autumn sunshine, I caught snatches of her perfume, saw silver bracelets jangling on her tiny wrists, realized that her eyes – finely folded and alight – were the first Japanese eyes I had ever really seen. Sometimes, in the sun, I saw the red lights in her hair, hair she fastened on one side with a mother-of-pearl comb and let fall free across her shoulder on the other.

Sachiko-san's influence was soft and subtle as a mild spring breeze, yet still I could feel the warmth in that breeze, and as we walked back into town, I could sense her straying closeness. This strange, unlooked-for intimacy was only formalized when, as we walked along the Kamo River, I suddenly saw a familiar figure on his bicycle. The last time I had seen Billy, a former U.S. Army man, he had been hanging out with two other foreigners, eyeing Japanese girls over their beers. I tried as hard as I could not to see him, but Billy was quick to see me – or at least my companion.

'Hey,' he said, turning round, getting off his bike, and walking back towards us. 'I can see you're settling down quite nicely.' He looked her up and down. 'You seem to be doing really well.'

'In a way.'

'Great. Looks like you're doing real good.' He gave me a conspirator's grin.

'How are things going with you?' I said, eager to change the subject.

'Aw, pretty good. All my students tell me I look like Randy Bass – you know, the slugger for the Tigers?' He flashed Sachiko-san an engaging grin. I refrained from telling him that this was more a reflection on his students than on him, since the Japanese apparently thought that every bearded foreigner looked like Randy Bass. I had heard one portly white journalist likened to Michael Jackson.

'So anyway,' he said, 'bring her along to a Halloween party we're having.' Then, after a final inspection, he got back on his bike. 'Costume required!' he called back as he began cycling away.

'Can I come as an Indian?' I shouted after him.

'Sure,' he called back. 'I'm going as a *gaijin*!'

'Very nice man,' Sachiko-san giggled sweetly as we went on our way. 'I like your friend. Very kind, very warm.'

'Oh, sure,' I muttered sullenly.

At the Montessori kindergarten, Yuki proudly showed me her agility on the swings. Then, through shifting sunlight, all three of us made our slow way to a sushi restaurant. 'I wonder if it'll rain,' I said, looking up at the sky.

'Old Japanese people say, *"Onna-no kokoro, aki-no sora,"*' said Sachiko-san, shooting me a sidelong glance (The autumn sky is like a woman's heart). 'Your country same?'

Ten minutes later, little Yuki was seated in front of a mountain of eight empty sushi bowls, while I, incriminatingly, had nothing to show but one. Sensing my unease (I had yet to make my peace with sushi), Sachiko-san suggested that it was time for them to leave. Outside, in the street, the clouds were turning to sun again. 'Like woman's heart,' she said, and looked at me again.

Seven

One reason I had always been interested in Zen was my sense that for people like myself, trained in abstraction, Zen could serve as the ideal tonic. For Zen, as I understood it, was about slicing with a clean sword through all the Gordian knots invented by the mind, plunging through all specious dualities – east and west, here and there, coming and going – to get to some core so urgent that its truth could not be doubted. The best lesson that Zen could teach – though it was, of course, something of a paradox to say or even think it – was to go beyond a kind of thinking that was nothing more than agonizing, and simply act. In that sense, Zen reminded me of Johnson's famous refutation of Berkeley by kicking a stone. It was unanswerable as pain.

This training had particular appeal for me, perhaps, because I had often thought that the mind was, quite literally, a devil's advocate, an agent of diabolical sophistry that could argue any point and its opposite with equal conviction; an imp that delighted in self-contradiction and yet, though full of sound and fury, ultimately signified nothing. None of the truest things in life – like love or faith – was arrived at by thinking; indeed, one could almost define the things that mattered as the ones that came as suddenly as thunder. Too often, I thought, the rational faculty tended only to rationalize, and the intellect served only to put one in two minds, torn apart by second thoughts. In that sense, God could be said to be nothing but the act of faith itself. Religion lay in the leap and not the destination. And Zen was as much as anything a refutation of doubt itself; a transcendence of the whole either/or sensibility that makes up all our temporizing. Instead of temporizing, as Thoreau might have said, why do we not eternize?

In all these ways, Zen seemed the natural product of a culture that has little time for philosophical speculation but stresses instead the merits of ritual, rigor, and repetition. The directness of Zen appeared to reflect the utilitarian concreteness of modern Japan, where people seemed rarely to dwell on suffering or to give themselves to close self-study. Zen, after all, was about whole-heartedness – or, at least, whole-mindedness. Strictly speaking, I knew, both Shintoism and Jodo Buddhism, the other great faiths of Japan, were equally free of doctrine and scripture, and, moreover, Zen had been invented by an Indian monk in China. The first Zen temples were active in Korea before the teaching had ever come across the Tsushima Strait to Japan. Yet still the finest achievements of the discipline today were associated with Japan, not least because the qualities sought out by Zen – spareness, self-discipline, precision – seemed closest to those of Japan. Did Zen help to create the features of Japan, or did Japan help to form the distinctive qualities of Zen – it was a question as old in its way, and unending, as the famous Zen conundrum 'What was your face before you were born?' Whatever the answer, I thought, if Zen had not existed, the Japanese would have had to invent it.

Talking to Mark, though, and to Kazuo, had already brought me a little closer to earth. Besides, I knew that coming to Japan hoping to find a world guided by the stern and gentle precepts of Buddhism was as misguided as going to America hoping to find a society graced at every turn by Christianity (but America was shaped and strengthened by Christian writers, one could almost hear a visitor saying – Jonathan Edwards, Emily Dickinson, T. S. Eliot: how could modern America be so forgetful of its inheritance?). I realized, too, that the very qualities that made Zen so attractive to me were also the ones that made it so alien. Most of all, I suspected that if the Japanese really did have a religion, it was very likely one that outsiders like myself would not be able to recognize if we saw it, since it would probably have more to do with rituals than with texts. That religion could have a shifting relation to morality; that religious affiliations could be taken off or put on again as easily as costumes; that the Japanese could partake of what Rexroth had called 'a secular mysticism, which sees experience as its own transcendence' – that religion, in short, could be capricious and practical as love, that other celebrated act of nondenominational faith, was something we Santa Barbarians found hard to understand.

I got a glimpse of this one day when Mark and I came across a Zen student from New York, who was all marshmallowy softness. ('And what are *you* doing in Japan?' she cooed. 'A journalist? Oh, how *wonderful!*') As we walked away, Mark, usually so gentle, could hardly contain his impatience. 'Jeez,' he began, shaking his head, 'that's the kind of stuff the Zen guys can't stand! Because they know what it's really like – how tough and rigid and down-to-earth it is: waking up at three a.m. in the winter and sweeping leaves in the rain and going begging in the snow. Yet these Zen students are always coming over from America and putting on this weird, goody-goody kind of sweetness. And the Zen guys know that has nothing to do with it.'

As he talked, I could see how right he was, yet also, perhaps, how protective of the Zen he knew. The hardest part of this discipline, like any other, must be to free oneself from a notion of what it was to protect.

Because I was interested in this aspect of Japan, Mark invited me one day to come and meet his best friend, an American who had lived in a temple for a while but now devoted most of his energy to his wife and children, while teaching English, translating Japanese, and spending long hours reading or playing the piano.

The next thing I knew, we were seated inside Joe's house and some frenzied Dennis Hopper madness was exploding on every side of us. *Ghostbusters* was blasting out of the video set, and some throaty jazz was thrumming out of the stereo system. Joe's four-year-old son was somersaulting across a tiny room jammed with 'Hello Koala' bags and a tank of fish, while his three-year-old daughter was scampering around on all fours like a dog. The master of the household was blowing up balloons as fast as Mark could draw feet on them, and his nine-month-old baby was scattering toys and juice on the floor and feeding at the breast of a mother who was muttering something in Japanese. 'She wants to know if Ringo Starr is homosexual,' said her husband, setting up a chessboard for the two of us, and then the phone began to trill. He picked it up. 'A hundred fifty thousand? Listen – what's your problem, man? If I say it, you can believe it. Yeah, all right, one forty-five thousand. Jesus fuck, I don't believe this, man. One forty thousand,' and then he slammed down the phone and picked it up again. 'Listen, Umeda-san, we really had a great time last night,' and then, 'Oh shit, man. I just dialed the number of the same guy I was talking to. Wrote down his number, man, and then dialed it again. He must have thought I was crazy or somethin', callin' about a piano and then me thankin' him for dinner . . .'

Joe looked over at us, his unshaven face cracking, and began laughing. His laugh got started like an aging Plymouth on a winter's day, until he was chortling and chuckling infectiously. His unorthodox directness was hitting me like a slap in the face. But I could see that it was the most Zen-like quality about him and, if nothing else, he was very much his own man. Cackling, uncombed, talking with the crazy intensity of someone forever under some foreign influence, he put on another tape, and as *The Neverending Story* went on neverendingly, he began telling me about Japan. 'Like my students, man. One time, I had to teach them the meaning of the words "necessary", "useless", and "useful". So I asked them to rate all their subjects in one of these categories. And you know the one all of them – one hundred percent of them – listed as "necessary"? Sports, man! Fuckin' sports! And the one that every single one of them listed as "useless"? Religious education! Except for one guy, who put it as "useful". But everyone else laughed at him and said it was because he was a Christian. Weird, man, fuckin' weird. But I thought about it, and it makes sense. Not just because sports makes them healthy. But it instills in them this sense of the team. And it makes them competitive. And in most ways, this is a very competitive society. The place is like a pyramid, man; the whole place is a fuckin' pyramid. And the one subject you *never* mention to them is politics. *Never*, man. Makes them go dead. It's like in the U.S., if you had a class on Byzantine Church doctrine or somethin' – they don't care about it. They don't know anything about it. It's not their concern. It just makes them dead. Not a single fuckin' political science department in the entire country. No-one here gives a damn about politics.

'There are two myths that the Japanese have about

themselves. One is that they're a small country. They ain't small, man. France and Spain are the only countries in Europe that are bigger. And look at the fuckin' population, man. Sometimes I get out an atlas and say to them, "How many people in Denmark, man? Five fuckin' million." And they say, *"Ah sō?"* This country ain't small, man. Look at a map. And they think that this is an old country. It ain't old. Ask any Japanese high school graduate to read somethin' before 1868. He can't to it, man. They have no connection with their literature. In the old days, before Meiji, they didn't have this Emperor-worship thing. One old Emperor was just this nothin' guy who had to sell his own calligraphy to keep goin'. But then in Meiji they built a new nation and trained people to think a certain way. Education didn't mean broadening horizons. It just meant learning to be a part of society. And hey, man, if they decide to bring back Emperor-worship, you better have short hair, man.' Joe's eyes were wild now. 'And you better get new clothes. And you better not talk in the street. No fooling around with those guys, man. You watch what you're doin'.'

Joe was certainly giving me a crash course in one-pointedness – and in the frustrations of a longtime resident. The next thing I knew, he was flinging down before me a box that featured a floppy-eared rabbit above the legend 'I Am Somebunny Special'. Inside was a novel, flawlessly typed, called *Tree-Planting in America*, by someone from Little Lake, Michigan, who was, Joe said, just some penniless guy living in a cabin without a toilet, electricity, or running water. 'I knew this guy way back – in Massachusetts. We were buildin' a *zendō* together. But he never talked about Zen. Never. Or writing. Then, last summer, he gave me this manuscript. I read it by kerosene lamp in his cabin, man, and I was gettin' more and more excited.

86

This is a true book, man. At fifteen, this guy tried to be a painter. Then at eighteen, he decided to be a writer. By twenty-two, he had all the skills, he says – more than he's got now – but he hadn't anything to say. So he put it aside for twenty years. Now, he says, he's got somethin' to say, so he writes this, supporting himself by slayin' deer. That's integrity, man. He didn't want to make money out of his writing; he just wanted to make art. He's starving to do it, doesn't have any friends. He's kind of like Kundera, I think – it's funny, but it makes you think.'

Integrity at any cost, I thought; a rigor of dissent. 'D'you like Jim Harrison?' I asked, casting around in my mind for any other Zen-minded writer who came from Michigan.

'Sure. I read *Warlock* and some other book by him. Better than Saul Blow or John Updick. Man, I can't stand those guys. Best place I ever found for buying books was Taiwan, man – I'd go into this store, buy five books, read 'em, and sell 'em back to the guy the next week. I remember two books I got there. One was *The Big Sleep*. The other was by this guy called Ben Garcia, and I'm ashamed now that I gave it back. Ben Garcia, I'll always remember the name.' He shook his head at the memory. 'You could tell his wasn't a learned style or anything, but this guy had truth! It was a true book, man, a true book. About this Mexican who lived with the Indians. I remember its beginning: "I've got a ranch, wife, and kids, but for seventy years I feel like I'm living in a coffin. Ranching, making money – none of it means a thing." That's how it starts, man. Only book he ever wrote. True book, man, fuckin' true book.

'Taiwanese, though, they only like food. When I asked my students what they wanted for their birthday, they'd just say, "Food", man. That's why you'll

87

find a Chinese restaurant anywhere you go. Anywhere in the world, man, you go and you'll find a Chinese restaurant – even Grenada, or Huehuetenango.'

Noticing his four-year-old son careening like a dervish around the room, Joe suddenly told him to stop. Abruptly, the boy sat down where he was, cupped his hands, and folded his legs in a perfect lotus posture. Eyes closed, he fell into a silent meditation.

'Man, I was reading Charlie Chaplin's autobiography the other day,' Joe started up again. 'Chaplin, man, the only guy I know who started out life with no ideals – just tryin' to survive – and then he got famous and started havin' ideals. Great, man. Fuckin' great!' And then there was more, about R. K. Narayan and *Travels with My Aunt*, about the infighting of monasteries and piano techniques, about bilingualism and the chess game that lay finished in one corner. And finally, it began to rain, pittering and pattering on all the flimsy roofs and walls.

'*Shito-shito*,' said Joe softly. 'And *goro-goro* for thunder. *Zā-zā* for heavy rain. *Pica-pica* for starlight. You don't have words for these things. Just sounds, man, perfect sounds.'

And I thought how well you could always hear rain here, on wooden walls and roofs, in every Japanese poem and home.

Eight

As the October days eased on, Autumn stole like a thief
into Kyoto, in one fluent succession of days so calm
they took my breath away. Wandering through the
buoyant days, I felt I had never known autumn before,
not even in New England. For the mild and milky
afternoons were graced with a distinctly Japanese
touch, unintrusive in its effects, and hesitant, and still.
The reticence gave dimension to the beauty.

Sometimes it rained, but when it did, it truly poured;
other times, everything was a radiance of blue. The
weather here was rarely indifferent, rarely caught in
the bleary in-betweens of England; whatever the
inflection, it usually seemed unqualified, and the days
often passed with a kind of metronomic regularity, of
sun and rain and sun and rain and shine. Sometimes
the rain came down steadily, relentlessly, with an
unlifting persistence that blurred the world for days;
other times, mornings dawned crisper and clearer than
any I could remember outside the Himalayas in winter.
Occasionally, the two extremes would alternate on a
single day, but still, even then, the pattern never
wavered: either rapturous or foul.

Besides, Kyoto was lovely in the mist – the air rising
clear above the hills, the dogs barking in the hillside
temples. The singing cries of children rang out in the
ringing air, and everything was green and cleansed.
Kyoto back streets were lovely too, on shiny afternoons after days of heavy rain: the tangerine trees in

bloom, and monks on slow-moving bicycles, and ladies bent over rain-washed alleyways, rearranging flowers. The Heian Shrine was all patterns of sunlight and reflections in the water: girls crouched meditative over ponds; orange gates solemn under blazing autumn skies.

Autumn, moreover, was beginning to be observed in every corner of Kyoto, as a religion might be, but in a place where religions were often both secular and consumerist. Coffee shops now were advertising 'Autumn ice cream sundaes', and vending machines, like towel-bearing waiters, were changing their offerings from cold to hot. One trendy boutique had chalked a new slogan on the window: 'Autumn is the season to do pretty things for you'. And at Koshien Stadium, where the local baseball team, the Hanshin Tigers, was playing its last game of the season, the air was thick with elegy. Before the game began, the great star of the Tigers, the huge and gentle Oklahoma farmboy Randy Bass, got up on the rostrum, bowed all round, and stepped down again. Then he got up on the rostrum, bowed all round, and came down. Then he got up . . . eleven times in all, while Bass flags fluttered everywhere and a little boy next to me, in a flowing white happi coat with 'R. Bass' on its back, looked on in wonder. After the game ended, every member of the team came out on to the field and bowed in unison to the fans. For fifteen minutes, not a supporter left the stadium. All of them – all of us – stood to attention, singing every last verse of the sober, martial Tiger fight song, in one massed, mournful choir. Here, I thought, was a team in last place, thirty-six games out of first place, which had lost two games out of every three for more than six months – yet still its faithful were rising to give it this heartfelt show of support. *Sayōnaras* were hosannas here.

*   *   *

A few days later, on another brilliant morning, the trees beginning to turn under skies that were blue and puffy white, I went to see one of the three great occasions of the Kyoto year, the Jidai Matsuri, or Festival of the Ages, in the Imperial Palace.

When I arrived, an hour or so before the procession was to begin, the performers were relaxing backstage, on the lawns of the spacious compound. Little girls whose ghost-white faces and twisted hairdos reproduced the high elegance of Sei Shōnagon and Murasaki sat erect in priceless kimono under trees. Old wooden carriages stood at rest on gravel walkways, forgotten props from some period movie. Wrinkled men in fierce warriors' dress glared for cameras in the shadeless courtyards. Incarnations of great figures from the city's past, the performers were as shiny as the apple-polished day around them.

And as the parade began, one stately procession of spirits walking and breathing through the high-rise town – *daimyō* and *samurai*, courtiers and geisha, caparisoned and costumed, and fighters all in armor, watched in respectful silence by the crowds – I could not help but think of the last such celebration I had seen, just two months before I arrived in Japan: Carnival in Havana. It was an absurd comparison, I knew, yet the difference was as striking as between real life and art. For Cuba, however circumscribed by government edict and reduced by poverty, was still one pulsing, writhing explosion of lust and liquor, of bikinied girls and wriggling dragons and foot-high paper cups of beer foaming over beside the seaside Malecón. Here, by contrast, all was grave formality. Boys in black walked two by two, in synchronized steps, playing pipes; ancients regal on slow-stepping horses passed in noiseless dignity across the gravel;

girls as stately as Heian courtiers glided with phantom steps through coffee-shop streets. The audience was as silent as a congregation. Everything, timed to the moment, was as rigid as a catechism.

All festivals, of course, are acts of collective myth-making, chances for a nation to advertise its idealized image of itself. In Cuba, for all the privations, that meant abandon, gaiety, and bacchanal; here, it meant mellifluous order, solemnity, and grace. In Cuba, one could feel the effusions of a passionate, rhetorical people able and eager to give themselves over to the sentiments they voiced so recklessly; here, the effect was one of strange, almost awestruck, disengagement. It seemed as if the Japanese were almost paying homage to the fact of ritual itself – and to the religion of Japan – so that the ceremony became pageant, and the festival a kind of memorial service.

Before the day was out, however, this, like most of my generalities about Japan, found its refutation in the country's other side, the side that came out after dark – in this case, in the mysterious Fire Festival held that very night in the village of Kurama, in the hills to the north. I had heard for days how terrible the crowds would be, so I took pains to leave home early, arriving at the train station just as the late-afternoon sun was turning faces to gold and catching the firelights in hair. This was the magic hour of the Kyoto autumn, the last hour of light in the waning days: the hills silhouetted with a shocking clarity, the sky a burnished strip of gold and silver.

The minute the train drew into the station, the whole huge crowd piled in until we were packed as tightly as nuts in a bag of Japanese sweets. I bumped against rows of silky hair, was shoved into pockets of expensive perfume, buried myself in a new Springsteen tape.

Through all the crush, the Japanese remained unfailingly calm, some of them even sleeping where they stood.

As soon as we arrived at the village, the crowds piled out again and into a steep, narrow main street, so thick with bodies that one could scarcely move. A smell of bonfires redolent of Guy Fawkes Night, on a blazing, chill November evening in England, the details of the world smoothed down now in the dark. Lanterns all about, and the shadows of hills, and ashes spitting into the night like fireflies in some Peter Brook production. Along the tiny, toylike streets, the crowds expectant, a loud speaker conferring on everything an air of panic and authority.

Finding no room amidst the crowds even now, four hours before the festival was due to begin, I started to climb up the hill, away from the town, up towards Kurama Temple, towering solemn above the crowds. There I sat, and walked about, hands stuffed into pockets, and waited. I waited some more. The night grew chilly, with a winter snap to it. Still there was nothing to see but crowds. I watched a pair of German boys attach themselves to three smiling 'office ladies' and smiled to myself as the Germans, new to the country, took the shy giggles and polite questions for encouragement and began sliding hands behind backs, as the girls, smiling sweetly, edged away. I listened for a while to the Springsteen tape, rented today, the very day of its release, from a neighborhood store. I watched a teahouse high above the street, where VIPs were sedately taking dinner in a perfect Tokugawa tableau of high elegance. I nibbled on corn chips, stamped up and down in the cold, began to wish I'd never come.

And then, of a sudden, there came a quickened intensity, and then a roar, and a flash of fire, and a rush

93

of boys, naked save for loincloths, arms lifted in the dark, streaking furiously through the winter streets, bearing torches, shouting, 'Sareyā, sareyō,' eyes blazing. It was like nothing I had ever seen in Japan: wild, pagan, full of danger. The torches played crazy games on the faces they passed, and the shouters raced to the shrine like intoxicants, faces lit up by their torches. Pointing their torches to the middle, they started building a huge fire. Flames licked the air, torches began to waver, the crowd let out a gasp. Sparks were flying this way and that, policemen were roaring through megaphones, the whole crowd, pressed as closely as in some rock concert, was shaking and wobbling as one. Shouting 'Sareyā, sareyō,' the men in loincloths, bodies glistening in the night, poured more heat on to the fire, the flames racing up in the sky above them, their eyes alight. I could feel the danger in the air, sense the pull of some ancient force. I could feel an electrical crackle in the air.

All night the fires raged, subsiding shortly before dawn.

A couple of days later, I found myself walking along a broad avenue in the sunshine with Siobhan, the potter I had met from Santa Cruz. 'For a long time, you know, I used to repress this thing about being a witch,' she began, as we walked past groups of horn-rimmed students, remarkable only in their normalcy. 'When I was young, you know, I was always afraid of all that stuff about devils; I believed that knowing anything about them was a form of possession. And then one day, Pam, who I knew from Connecticut – but she's in Santa Cruz now – came up to me and said, "You're a witch, you know."

'And at first I just said, "No, no, I'm not." But she could tell. And she had her own coven. And then one night I saw my dead mother in a dream, and I could just tell she was in a very different place, but a good place. And that's when I accepted being a witch.'

Siobhan smiled, and the day smiled with her.

'Anyway, now I'm in this really comfortable place in the countryside, and everything's cool. Except that my Japanese roommate – she's really into Stendhal and is going to France next year – has fallen in love with this young German boy who lives with us. Fell in love with him just for the way he washes the dishes. Plus, of course,' she said, eyes flashing, 'there's the whole Christmas cake thing. Keiko's twenty-six.'

'Christmas cake?'

'You know. For girls.' I must have looked perplexed. 'You don't know about it? Maybe it's something they only tell girls. Anyway, it's this system they have over here; they even use the word, in Japanese, *Kurisumasu kēki*. You know how on the twenty-third of December a Christmas cake is supposed to be fresh and worth investing in, but by the twenty-fourth it's getting kind of old? And after the twenty-fifth, it's starting to get stale and no-one wants it. Well, that's how they think of women over here. Twenty-three is a good age to get one. Twenty-four is a little close to the deadline. And after twenty-five, forget it!'

'Which is why girls over the age of twenty-five often make a beeline for foreigners – that's their only chance of getting married?'

'Exactly!'

As soon as I heard this, many things began to fall into place. For my initial sense that every foreign male here found some demure but passionate Japanese companion to dance attention on him had only been strengthened by some of the characters I had met in Kyoto. Everywhere I turned, I seemed to run into men who were in a kind of spell here, having not only met girls but dream girls who were the embodiment of everything they wanted in a woman. Lifelong bachelors began talking about marriage; newlywed husbands could not stop extolling the goddesses they had married; hardened Lotharios found themselves disarmed by girls whose innocence was touched by a hint of guiltless sensuality.

And though most Japanese women, I assumed, would still unquestioningly follow their prescribed course towards a Japanese husband, there was, by all accounts, a minority – and an increasingly large minority – who would do anything possible to find a foreign boyfriend, if only for a while, in order to get a taste, firsthand, of the glamorous foreign world they had seen on their TV screens. In the discos of Tokyo and Osaka, foreign men were currently as fashionable as Chanel shirts or Louis Vuitton bags, trendy accessories to be shown off to one's friends. But even in less cosmopolitan Kyoto, foreigners were still agents of escape – like the crickets kept by Kawabata's Kyoto girl Chieko, inhabiting 'a separate realm, an enchanted land . . . filled with fine wine and delicious food from both land and sea'. The Japanese looked on foreigners, I sometimes thought, with the same awestruck condescension that we might bring to heavy-metal rock stars, secretly convinced that they are, at heart, somewhat vulgar and barbarous, yet undeniably seduced by the fact that they belong to a flashy, semimythic world of money, fame, and glamour. We look down our noses at Jon Bon Jovi, but invited to meet him, we jump at the chance.

In Kyoto, however, the attraction of opposites was especially strong, not least because this most conservative of cities, in one of the most traditional of all societies, attracted – indeed, because of its traditionalism attracted – some of the freest and most radical of visitors from abroad, the hiders and seekers, the rebels and dropouts who did not fit in, or did not want to fit in, at home. And Japanese girls had long been the subject of romantic fantasies of our own in the West. Pierre Loti had hired his Mademoiselle Chrysanthème as soon as he laid anchor in Japan; the Santa Barbaran Rexroth had found his Muse in a mysterious Japanese woman poet who lived in the shadow of a Kyoto temple. Even Lafcadio Hearn, who had done so much to bring Japanese Buddhism to the West, had declared that 'the most wonderful aesthetic products of Japan are not its ivories, nor its bronzes, nor its porcelains, nor its swords, nor any of its marvels in metal and lacquer – but its women'. And even today, the *Japan Handbook*, the standard guidebook used by most young foreigners in Japan, devoted an entire section to 'Sex', informing its readers, with guidebook authority, that Japanese women were 'orgasmic', longed to be swept off their feet, and '[expected] you to be an aggressor and in the old-fashioned sense to make [them]' – an alarming suggestion, I thought, in the hands of men looking for 'a possible partner for life'.

Besides, the pairing of Western men and Eastern women was as natural as the partnership of sun and moon. Everyone falls in love with what he cannot begin to understand. And the other man's heart is always greener.

Nine

One sunny morning, I was huddled over some proofs in my room when suddenly a call came for me. It was Sachiko-san again – now, she said, on her way to the zoo, together with her children and Sandy, the American woman with granny glasses I had met at the temple ceremony, and her children too. Would I like to join them? This, I thought, was too good an opportunity to be missed (to show off eleven of the twelve words I knew in Japanese), so I readily accepted, and an hour later, when I approached the giant *torii* gate that bestraddles one of Kyoto's central streets – making it fit for ceremonial processions – I found all six of them in picnic mood. Inside the zoo, we duly inspected the raccoons, the tiger, and the California seals, and I felt more than ever like the only adult male of the human species inside this shop-window collection of stylish young mothers and glossy-haired silent children. I half expected a sign to be hung around my neck identifying the rare, and undomesticated, *Homo subcontinentus*.

When it came time for Sandy and her children to go home, I half expected that Sachiko-san would go with them. But no, she said, her children had asked whether they might possibly come and see my room – their first chance, I assumed, to visit that close cousin of the zoo, the *gaijin* guesthouse. So together we ambled through the sunstruck streets, the children teetering on walls and scuffling after acorns, while Sachiko-san's apologies tumbled out unstoppably.

When finally we arrived at my house, the children apparently found all the excitement they had anticipated. *'Okā-san, okā-san, mitte!'* cried Hiroshi, pointing in horrified astonishment at the American-sized shoes lined up at the foot of the stairs. 'Mother, mother, look at the shoes!' The footsteps of the yeti would, I thought, have been no more remarkable to him. His mother, for her part, showed just how much of a mother she was – and how Japanese – by bending down to tidy up the shoes that the foreigners had left so higgledy-piggledy, arranging them all in a neat, color-coordinated row. Upstairs, when I opened the door to my room, the children's eyes grew even wider as they took in the pile of proofs scattered messily across my desk (convincing Sachiko-san, no doubt, that my job was not that of a raccoon story writer but a proof-reader).

'You like story?' she asked me, taming her children with one hand as she spoke.

'Oh yes,' I said, 'very much.'

And so, as her children careened around the room, she began telling me an elaborate old Japanese folktale – the oldest surviving story in the land – about a princess, Kaguya-hime, who had come to live with an old bamboo-cutter and his wife but then at last had been obliged to leave them and return to her home, in the Palace of the Moon. When Sachiko-san finished the story, I was startled to see, her eyes were bright with tears.

There was a long and awkward pause.

'Maybe we little go home?' she said. Taking the hint, I offered to walk them back to the station, and as the four of us wandered through the crowded streets in the dusk, I suddenly remembered to remind the children of the new word I had taught them just a week before. At that, the day broke open like a smashed window, and the children, thrilled with their new discovery, began reeling through the crooked lanes, crying, 'Raccoon car! Raccoon bus! Raccoon ship!' while I, spurring them on shamelessly, shouted, 'Raccoon coffee shop! Raccoon cinema! Raccoon plane!' and all the while Sachiko-san serenely continued recounting ancient Japanese folktales that left her again and again in tears.

The Japanese were famous, I knew, for their delight in *lacrimae rerum* and for finding beauty mostly in sadness; indeed, it was often noted that their word for 'love' and their word for 'grief' are homonyms – and almost synonyms too – in a culture that seems to love grief, of the wistful kind, and to grieve for love. So I was hardly surprised to learn that most of their stories were sad and that all of them ended in parting. Parting was the definition of sweet sorrow here. Yet still I was taken aback by this curious flash of intimacy: Sachiko-san sinking deep into her sadness, while her children pranced gaily through the gathering dark, shouting out their new mantra with the zeal of proselytes. 'Raccoon train! Raccoon street! Raccoon temple!'

Making plans with Sachiko-san was always, I had found, an uncertain business, not least because whenever she called me, both of us would engage in a polite, but ruthless, tug-of-war as to which should be the medium of confusion. Both of us were determined to speak the language we didn't know (she to practice her English and I to try out my Japanese), and so, very often, we ended up communicating in a kind of jangled bilingual hybrid in which nothing was lost except meaning.

Whenever we tried to fix meetings, therefore – she confusing 'Tuesday' and 'Thursday', I mixing up *kayōbi* (Tuesday) with *kinyō-bi* (Friday), she routinely transposing 'yesterday' and 'tomorrow' – the result was madness. 'Where would you like to meet?' I would ask her, in Japanese, and she would reply, in English, 'You want to come here my house?' in a tone that suggested more apprehension than delight. She would say she was free at two, and I would arrive, for a brief encounter, only to learn that she was free for two hours. I would say that I was leaving for three days, and she would assume I was leaving on the third. That first day, when she had casually invited me to drop in on her daughter's birthday party at around two and I had casually dropped in at two forty-five, only to find that there was no party at all and I was forty-five minutes late, increasingly seemed an augury of all that was to come.

Once we met, of course, the craziness would only accelerate. For one thing, Sachiko-san was as unabashed and unruly in her embrace of English as most of her compatriots were reticent and shy. Where they would typically refuse to utter a single sentence unless they could deliver it perfectly, she was happy to plunge ahead without a second thought for grammar, scattering meanings and ambiguities as she went. Plurals were made singular, articles were dropped, verbs were rarely inflected, and word order was exploded – often, in fact, she seemed effectively to be making Japanese sentences with a few English words thrown in. Often, moreover, to vex the misunderstandings further, she spoke both languages at once, as if reading simultaneously from both columns of a phrasebook: '*Demo* but where are you *ima* now?' she sometimes asked, hardly stopping to bother about the fact that *demo* means 'but' and *ima*, 'now'. Other times, she suddenly came up with an affirmative 'Sí!' suggesting that somehow or other she had got hold of a French or Spanish phrasebook instead of an English one. Often, too, I could see in her sentences the scorch marks of an all-too-hasty trip through the dictionary: 'Is America very high?' she asked me (since *takai* in Japanese means both 'expensive' and 'high'), or, to more alarming effect, 'The bullet train is always very early' (since *hayai* in Japanese means 'early' as well as 'fast'). Sometimes, when she said something like 'I have this happy feeling touch,' I could tell that she had whizzed through a list of synonyms fatally unseparated (in her mind at least) by a comma.

I, of course, was hardly better, turning Japanese nouns into adjectives, using feminine forms for myself, and sometimes just deploying English words, with random vowels hopefully stuck in at the end, foolishly confident in the belief that Japan had incorporated an enormous number of English terms (*Hamu to tōsto, kudasai!*). Having picked up most of my Japanese from a businessman's handbook and bilingual editions of poetry – a fitting combination, I had thought at the time – I was able to deliver nothing but sentences like 'Please give your secretary the autumn moon.'

To complicate matters even further, Sachiko-san, in the classic Japanese manner, contrived to make everything as ambiguous, as circumspect, as consensual as possible – even in English. If ever she wanted to use the English word for *itsumo*, which I had been taught meant 'always', she always said, 'usually', so as to soften the assertion and allow for the exception that might one day prove the rule (leading to such statements as 'Usually, the first day of the year is January one'). And where we would say yes, she always said *tabun*, or 'maybe'. When once she told me that Yuki was sick, I replied, with empty assurance, 'I'm sure she'll be better soon.' '*Tabun*,' she replied. 'Maybe.' 'No, really,' I insisted, 'I'm sure there's no problem.' 'Maybe,' she replied, all caution. The effect was one of instant melancholy, though really she must have been as sure as I that all would be OK. And of course, every adjective that was less than entirely positive – and much else besides – was qualified with a *chotto*, meaning 'little', so that Frankenstein became 'a little strange', and traveling to the moon 'a little difficult'.

Much of this, clearly, was as much an act of courtesy as of caution, and not so different, really, from the reflexive softenings in which I too had once been trained in England. Always prefer a rhetorical question to a bald assertion ('Might it not be easier perhaps to try this road?'). Never disagree outright ('I'm not absolutely sure that's true'), and sometimes soften the dissent further, with – what else? – a rhetorical question ('It's so hard to know for certain, don't you find?'). If absolutely forced to say no, say anything other than 'no', diluting every term in the sentence ('I'm very sorry, but I'm afraid it might be just a little difficult'). None of these were lies, as such, only stratagems for easing the social machinery.

Thus the intricacies of Japanese protocol were compounded by those of my own English training, and both were made nonsensical by the relentless exchange of gibberish. Whenever I said anything that made her happy, she assumed I was being polite, and whenever she replied, I assumed this was mere Japanese indirectness. So I would say, 'Do you want to have some coffee?' and she would answer, 'OK. Do you want some coffee?' and I would have to say, *Iie, kekkō desu* ('No, thank you, I'm fine as I am'), and both of us would end up exactly where we had started.

'Should we meet on Tuesday?' I asked her. Sachiko-san gave me a smile. 'No problem! Yesterday, Thursday, OK!'

Nonetheless, we did occasionally manage to meet, at

almost the same time and place, and one day I found myself sitting with her in a shrine, on a bare wooden step, the light coming through the ginkgo trees as we waited for Yuki's English lesson to conclude. Carried away with excitement for my latest enthusiasm, I asked her if she preferred Mishima or Tanizaki.

'All Japanese writer, I like,' she replied. 'But my favorite is little foreigner man. His name Hess-e.'

'Hermann Hesse?'

She nodded solemnly. 'I much like this man. *Siddoharuta. Narushisu and Gōrudoman.* And *Petā Kamejindo.* When I little high school size, I all reading.'

'But that's incredible,' I said, pulling out of my bag the book I was reading at the moment, in this city of artists and anchorites, *Narziss and Goldmund.*

She, too, looked taken aback. 'You read this book?'

'Yes! It was my favorite when I was a boy.'

'Maybe you your country reading, I, too, same time!'

'Yes. And did you know that Hesse was a close friend of Jung, whom your brother is studying? And that he lived in Switzerland, where your brother lives? When I was in high school, this book was the only common link between my boarding school in England and California, where I went home in the holidays!'

She shook her head in amazement. 'Also, I like Emily Brontë. You know *Storm on Hill*?'

'*Wuthering Heights*?'

'Maybe.'

'That's one of my favorites too.'

Minutes later, we were seated on a bench in the flowering gardens of the Imperial Palace, while three hundred schoolchildren sat in rows on the gravel before us, patiently listening to a pep talk from their teachers. Sending her daughter off to play amidst the trees, where she set about making a pretty brocade of leaves (Japanese children had a remarkable gift, I noticed, for playing with flowers; their training in Nature awareness started early), Sachiko-san started telling me the story of the 'North Wind's Daughter', an endearing children's story about a bear and his sorrow, made all the more engaging by her ideogrammatic delivery.

'Bear live in house. Mother, father, grandma, all die. All brother, sister, die – hunting! Bear very sad in his heart. But he has much pride; he never not cry. He think music very happy sound, then he little make sign, "Please. I need Music Teacher. I have money."

'Then much banging on door, very big noise. Man in blue there. He have trumpet. Then he play music. Sun shine, and set. Bear very happy. Then very sad in his heart. He try trumpet – but sound very bad sound. Then he blow much much, break tooth. He say man, "Please you teach me." Man say, "You cannot play. You tooth break. Please you give me blueberry pie." Bear give him pie, but in his heart very sad.

'Then blue woman come here his house, North Wind. She has violin. She play violin, very beautiful sound, little silver staircase sound. Sun shine, and set. Bear in his heart very happy. He try violin. But very bad music. He very sad. Very cold. Woman say, "Please look your icebox. Please give me pineapple pie." He give.

'Then much banging his door. Very pretty child there, North Wind daughter. She blue! Bear sad. He has no food in freezer. But girl say, "Please you close eye. Please you count." Bear try, then open eye: hot cakes and chair! Bear very happy. Then girl say, "Please you close eye. Please you count." Bear try, then open eye. Then bear very sad. She not there. She gone. But he still have music, and many beautiful memory.'

'Happy ending?'

'Yes,' she laughed sweetly, her voice like running water, and with that, she took her daughter home.

One delicate autumn day a few days later – the sky now gray, now blue, always like a woman's uncertain heart, a light drizzle falling, and then subsiding, and falling once more – I met Sachiko outside an Indonesian store, for a trip to Kurama. She was, as ever, girlishly dressed, her hair falling thickly over one side of her face, held back on the other by a black comb with a red-stone heart in its middle; the tongues of her black sneakers hanging out from under lime-green leg-warmers.

As we traveled towards the hillside village, she set down her backpack beside her on the train and began telling me excitedly about her friend Sandy, and how it was Sandy who had first introduced her to Zen, Sandy who had first taken her to a temple, Sandy who had first encouraged her to try *zazen* meditation. 'I Japanese,' she said softly. 'But I not know my country before. Sandy my teacher.' More than that, she said, it was Sandy who had shown her another way of life and given her the confidence to try new things. Sandy, supporting two children alone in a foreign country and at the same time embarked on a full-length course of Zen studies, had shown her that it was possible, even for a woman, to have a strong heart.

Now, she went on, Sandy was planning to send her children back to America for high school. 'I dream, maybe Hiroshi go your country, Sandy's son together. You see this movie *Stand by Me*?' I nodded. 'Very beautiful movie. I want give my son this life. I dream, he little *Stand by Me* world feeling.' And what about her husband's view on all this? An embarrassed giggle. 'I don't know. Little difficult. But I much dream children go other country.' She paused, deep in thought. 'But I also want children have Zen spirit inside, Japanese feeling.' I asked her to explain. 'Example – you and Sandy, *zazen* very difficult. Japanese people, *zazen* very easy. I want my children have this spirit.'

'But if your children go away, they may grow distant. Maybe never talk to you. Maybe forget all Japanese things. Wouldn't that make you sad?'

'*Tabun.* Maybe.'

'It's very difficult, I think.'

And so we get off the train, and climb from shrine to shrine, scattered across the steep hills of Kurama, and the rain now drizzles down, now stops again, and the two of us huddle under her umbrella, sweaters brushing, her hair almost falling on my arm. '*Ai to ai gasa,*' I say, thinking of the phrase I had read in a Yosano Akiko poem, describing two people sharing a single umbrella. 'Maybe,' she says, with a lilting laugh, and we climb some more, the hills before us resplendent now, and then still higher, in the gentle rain, till we are sitting on a log.

In front of us, the trees are blazing. 'I like color now,' she says, pensive. 'Later, I not so like. More sad. Leaves die. Many thing change.' And then, carried away by the view, perhaps, she recalls the only other time she has come to this hill. Kurama is only a few miles north of Kyoto, a thirty-minute train ride. But Sachiko has not been here for fifteen years, and all that time, she says, she has longed to return. 'I so happy,' she whispers, as if in the presence of the sacred. 'I so excited. Thank you. Thank you very much. I very happy. Very fun. Before I coming here, little teenage size, together three best friend. We climbing mountain, I very afraid, because I thinking snake. Much laughing, many joke. Very fun. My friends' names, Junko, Sumiko, and Michiko. But Osaka now. Very busy, marry ladies.'

We walk down again, through the drizzle and the mist, then up slippery paths, between the trees. 'I much love Kurama,' she says quietly, as if in thought. 'Sometimes I ask husband come here; he say, "You always want play. I very busy. I cannot." And come here together children, very difficult. Soon tired. Thank you very much, come here this place with me.'

This is all rather sad. She tells me of her adventures, and the smallness of it all makes me sad again: how, when she was a little girl, she went with her cousin and brother and aunt to a cinema, and her aunt allowed her to go and see *The Sound of Music* alone. 'I very scared. All dark. Many person there. But then, film begin, I soon forget. I much love. I dream I Julie Andrews.' She also describes reading about Genghis Khan. 'I dream I trip together Genghis Khan. I many trip in my heart, many adventure. But only in my heart.' She tells me how once, last year, for the first time ever, she went alone to Osaka, forty minutes away, to see the Norwegian teenybopper group a-ha in concert, and then, exhilarated by this event, went again that same week to another of their concerts, in Kobe, with her son and her cousin, all three of them sharing a room in a luxury hotel. The night she spent in the hotel, the trip to the coffee shop after the concert, the way she had chanced to see the lead singer's parents in the coffee shop and then to meet the star himself in an elevator – all live on in her as what seems almost the brightest moment in her life. 'I very lucky. I very excited. I dream, maybe next summer, I go this hotel again. See other a-ha concert.'

And when she says, more than once, 'I live in Kyoto all life; you come here only one month, but you know more place, very well,' I feel again, with a pang, a sense of the tightly drawn limits of a Japanese woman's life, like the autumn paths vanishing in mist around us. For I could see that she was saying something more than the usual 'Tourists know more of towns than their residents ever do,' and I could catch a glimpse of the astonishing circumscription of her life. Even while her brother had been to Kansas City to study for three years and was now in his third year of pursuing Jung in Switzerland, she had never really been outside Kyoto. She now worked two mornings a week in a doctor's office, but it was the same place where she had worked during junior high school and high school, in vacations, just around the corner from her parents' house. Her cousin, a kind of surrogate sister, sometimes worked in the same place. Her own house was in the next neighborhood down, within walking distance of her parents-in-law's house. And her mother still called her every night, to see how she was doing.

Every year, she said, her husband got three or four days of holiday, and the trips the family took together on these breaks – to the sea once, and once to Tokyo Disneyland – still lived within them as peak experiences. Even a trip such as the one today, for a few hours to a suburb, seemed a rare and unforgettable adventure.

'Please tell me your adventure,' she begins to say. 'Please tell me other country. I want imagine all place,' but I don't know where to begin, or how to convey them to someone who has never been in a plane, and what cloak-and-dagger episodes in Cuba, or nights in the Thai jungle, will mean to one who has scarcely left Kyoto.

'I dream you life-style,' she goes on, as if sensing my unease. 'You are bird, you go everywhere in world, very easy. I all life living only Kyoto. So I dream I go together you. I have many, many dream in my heart. But I not have strong heart. You very different.'

'Maybe. I was lucky that I got used to going to school by plane when I was nine.'

'You very lucky. I afraid other country. Because I thinking, maybe I go away, my mother ill, maybe die. If I come back, maybe no mother here.' Her mother, she explains, developed very serious allergies – because, it seemed, of the new atmospheric conditions in Japan. (All this I found increasingly hard to follow, in part because Sachiko used 'allergy' to mean 'age' – she regularly referred to the 'Heian allergy', and when she was talking about 'war allergy', I honestly didn't know if it was a medical or a historical point she was making. I, of course, was no better, confusing *sabishii* with *subarashii*, and so, in trying to say, 'Your husband must be lonely,' invariably coming out with, 'Your husband is wonderful. Just fantastic,' which left her frowning in confusion more than ever.)

'When I little children size, my mother many times in hospital. And Grandma too. And when my brother in Kansas City, my grandma die. He never say goodbye. She see my husband, she think he my brother. Very sad time. So I always dream in heart, because many sad thing happen. But dream stay in heart.' This seemed a sorrowful way to approach the universe, though eminently pragmatic. Yet she held to it staunchly. 'Maybe tomorrow I have accident. I die. So I always keep dream.' That was lovely, elegant, Sachiko: Sachiko, in her teenager's high-tops, keeping a picture of Sting in her wallet and sometimes losing sleep over him – a thirty-year-old girl with daydreams.

All this gets us on to what is fast becoming a recurrent theme in our talks, the competing merits of the Japanese and the American family systems. I, of course, argue heartily for the Japanese.

'It makes me so happy to see mothers and children playing together here, or going to temples together, and movies, and coffee shops. In America, mothers and daughters are often strangers. People do not know their parents, let alone their grandparents. Sometimes, in California, parents just fly around, with very young girlfriends or boyfriends, and leave their children with lots of money but no love.' (My sense of America, in Japan, was getting as simplistic and stereotyped as my sense of Japan had been in America.) 'So fifteen-year-old girls have babies and drive cars, and have money, many boyfriends, and lots of drugs.'

'Maybe. But in your country, I think, children have strong heart. Do anything, very easy. Here in Japan, no strong heart. Even grown-up person, very weak!' I think she means that they lack adventure, recklessness, and freedom, and in all that I suppose she is right, and not only because twelve Japanese CEOs have literally collapsed this year under the pressures of a strong yen. And she, of course, as a foreigner, sees only the pro ledger in America, while I, over here, stress only the con – though when I am in America, I find myself bringing back to American friends an outsider's sense of their country's evergreen hopefulness.

And as we continue walking, a few other people trudge past us up the hill, elders most of them, with sticks, the men in berets and raincoats, the women in print dresses, occasionally looking back through the curtain of fine drizzle at the strange sight of a pretty young Japanese girl with a shifty Indian male. Sachiko, however, seems lost in another world.

'What is your blood type?' she suddenly asks, eyes flashing into mine.

'I don't know.'

'True?'

'True.'

'Whyyy?' she squeals, in the tone of a high school girl seeking a rock star's autograph.

'I don't know. In my country, people aren't concerned about blood types.'

'But maybe you have accident. Go hospital.'

'I don't know.'

'Really? True??'

'Really. Foreigners think it's strange that the Japanese are so interested in blood types.'

'Really? *Hontō ni?*'

'Yes.' I am beginning to feel I am letting her down in some way, so I quickly ask if she is interested in the Chinese calendar, or astrology. All this, though, is frightful to try to translate, and when Sachiko says that she is the sign of the 'ship' and I say, 'Ah yes, you mean the waves,' she looks very agitated. 'No, no waves! Ship!' Now it's my turn to look startled. What is going on here? 'The Water Bearer?' 'No.' 'The Fish?' 'No. Ship!' She is sounding adamant. Then, suddenly, I recall that Aries is the ram. (Thank God, I think, for all those years in California!) 'Oh – sheep! You are the sheep sign.' 'Yes, Ship.'

And then, of a sudden, she plops down on a bench, and draws out from her backpack a Japanese edition of Hesse, and shows me the stories she likes, and repeats how he had struck a chord in her when young. 'When I little high school size, I much much like. But Goldmund, not so like. When I twenty, it not so touch my heart, not same feeling. Now thirty, maybe different feeling. Which you like?'

'I don't know. That's why I'm reading it again now. When I was young, I liked Goldmund. Then, later, I understood Narziss a little better. For a long time, I spent one month living like Goldmund, traveling around the world, and one month like Narziss, leading a monk's life at home. Now I'm trying both at the same time, to see which one is better.'

Somehow the world has misted over as we talk,

and time and space are gone: the world, I think, begins and ends on this small bench. And as we sit there, sometimes with her dainty pink umbrella unfurled, sometimes not, I pointing to the yellow trees, or the blue in the sky, and saying, *'Onna-no kokoro, Kurama-no tenki'* (The weather in Kurama is like a woman's heart), I can see her perfect white teeth when she laughs, the mole above her lips, a wisp of hair across her forehead, another fine strand that slips into her ear. She bends over to look at the magazine in my hands, and her hair falls all about me.

'You tell parent about girlfriend?' she says, looking up.

'Well, for many years, I haven't had – or wanted – a girlfriend.'

'So what am I?' A long silence. 'I man?' She giggles girlishly, and I don't know where that puts us: our discourse is soft and blurred as autumn rain.

'I think you're a very beautiful lady,' I say, looking down at my outstretched legs like a bashful schoolboy. 'Your husband is a very lucky man.'

'I not so think. I bad wife.'

And then, seizing the closeness in the air, she tries to formulate more complex thoughts. 'I very happy. Today, time stop. Thank you very much, coming here this place together me. I only know you short time, but you best friend feeling. I think I know you long time. I no afraid, no weak heart. You foreigner man, but I alone together you, very easy. I think maybe you very busy man. But talking very easy. I very fun, thank you.' All of this is a little heartbreaking, I think, together on a bench on a misty autumn day, and she so excited to see me after only two weeks of acquaintance.

Standing up, we start walking slowly down the hill, through faint drizzle, talking of her closeness to her mother, and the poems of Yosano Akiko. And as we leave the hill of temples behind us, she turns and bows towards the shrine, pressing her palms together and closing her eyes very tight.

That evening, I read Yosano Akiko late into the night and try to recall the short *tanka* Sachiko had recited to me on the hill. But I know only that it begins with *kimi*, the intimate form of 'you', as so many of Akiko's poems do. Falling asleep over the book, I awaken with a start in the dead of night, imagining that I am holding her by the hand and saying, 'Sachiko-san, I'm sorry to disturb you. I know you have a husband, and I'm very sorry, but . . .'

And later in the night, I think of the two of us under her pink umbrella, and flip hurriedly through the book in search of the phrase '*ai to ai gasa*'. When I find it, my heart seems almost to stop: it is, it seems, a classic image of intimacy, and one of the most famous figures in Japan for lovers.

Ten

As I went back and forth between my walks with
Sachiko and my talks with the Zen-minded foreigners,
I was beginning to pick up a little more Japanese by
immersing myself in a bilingual edition of Yosano
Akiko's almost unbearably sensuous poems, *Mida-
regami* (Tangled Hair). Voluptuous and rich as full-
bodied peaches, her *tanka* presented a world quite
different from the one I had found in the haiku of the
monks: hers, indeed, was the world of the temple as
seen from the other side, by a young girl loitering at its
gates, provoking the monks with her come-hither
boldness:

> *You have yet to touch*
> *This soft flesh*
> *This throbbing blood —*
> *Are you not lonely,*
> *Explainer of the Way?*

In the rich nights, I sank deep into Akiko's delectable
tremors; in the bright afternoons, I steadied myself
with the clear-water verses of Ryōkan:

> *If your hermitage is deep in the mountains,*
> *Surely the moon, flowers and maples*
> *Will become your friends.*

Certainly, the more I read of Ryōkan, the more I
found myself thoroughly won over by this gentle
eccentric spirit, wild brother to Thoreau, who lived all

alone in the mountains for most of his life, as good as his poetic word. Yet as much as he savored his loneliness, the friendly old monk seemed never to forget that solitude can only be as strong as the compassion it releases. All his life, according to the folk legends, he drank sake, danced freely in the villages nearby, spent his days playing hide-and-seek with children or stopping for a game of marbles with some geisha.

It was, in fact, his sense of warm mischief that rescued Ryōkan from sanctity and that seemed to make him as much at home with the world as with the universal. ('The great man,' wrote Emerson, 'is he who in the midst of the crowds keeps with perfect sweetness the independence of solitude.') Ryōkan's truth, he confessed, with typical simplicity, was 'not that I do not wish to associate with men. But living alone I have the Better Way' (in almost perfect anticipation of the celebrated Romantic credo of his contemporary Byron: 'I love not man the less, but Nature more'). Yet it seemed only fitting that the light of his last years was the twenty-nine-year-old nun who fell in love with him and tended the sixty-nine-year-old monk in his final four years and then for another four decades after his death. It was she, in fact, who brought out the first collection of his poems – not, she said, as a work of art but rather as a testament to his life. The two terms in any case dissolved in his work.

> *What is the heart of this old monk like?*
> *A gentle wind*
> *Beneath the vast sky.*

One day, legend has it, a famous scholar from Tokyo came to visit the old monk. Ever hospitable, Ryōkan asked his guest to wait for a minute, while he went down to the village to buy sake. Minutes passed, and more minutes passed, the distinguished guest kept

116

waiting, but still there was no sign of Ryōkan. Finally, after more than three hours, the man went out to look for his host – only to find him sitting on the ground just outside, gazing at the moon. 'Isn't it beautiful?' Ryōkan asked his guest. 'Yes. But what about the sake?' 'Oh yes, the sake. I'd quite forgotten about it.'

This was, of course, a classic Zen tale of absent-mindedness, in the highest sense of the word: the mind was absent to the world – but only because it was taken up with something higher. Who, I thought, could resist the figure of this fun-loving monk who took the official name of Great Fool and wrote about his daily life, his walks with the local children, his love?

Yet who, I also thought, could withstand Akiko's sumptuous lyrics, with their almost palpable musk of sensuality, more subtly delicious than any poems I knew, except, perhaps, for the quatrains of Rumi? A kind of overpowering perfume suffused her lines, humid with the pressures of spring rain.

> O this heaviness of spring,
> Surrounding
> Maiden and priest,
> From her shoulders a lock of hair
> Over the sutra.

And her central image of 'tangled hair' suggested all the wildness and abandon that the Japanese generally kept so strictly under wraps (not least, perhaps, because their word for 'hair' was a homonym of their word for 'god'). Hair, for the Japanese, was a way of keeping perfection all about one, and hair, in the Heian period, had been the focus of an attention 'so over-whelming', in Ivan Morris's words, 'as to seem almost obsessive'. Even a millennium ago, Japanese women had prided themselves on their long, straight, glossy hair, making up the deficiencies of nature with their art. Yet Akiko, locked up by her father in her bedroom as a girl, had broken out to write some of the most rebellious verses ever heard in Japan, throwing her hair – and everything around it – into disarray. All her sympathies she had given, subversively, to the women who had traditionally been regarded as mere playthings, and even to such celebrated outlaws as the young shopkeeper's daughter who had been executed for burning down her family house in order to be closer to the priest she loved. Akiko had even committed the heresy of outdoing her poet husband, himself the son of a priest. In her explosive poems, hair was nearly always loose and tangled, as far as possible from the shaven clarity of the monk.

> Pale handsome priest,
> Can you not see
> The girl lost in dreams
> By the tree of pink blossoms
> This spring evening?

And so I read on, across the parallel texts, lady tempting monk, monk renouncing lady.

The first time Sachiko invited me to her house for dinner, I was taken aback, and touched, to come in to find that she was playing a Bruce Springsteen tape (in honor, no doubt, of my stray comment at the temple). Sitting me down at her small round table, she brought out a four-course dinner of all the favorites I had mentioned in passing – a salad lit up by strawberries, a dish of corn, potato croquettes, and Earl Grey tea. On her piano sat a spray of gold and violet flowers. 'Every room need little flower,' she explained, as gracious as a Heian courtier. 'Every day I find new flower. I think person, then I choose flower. This flower you!' The

118

whole room, in short – like Sachiko herself – had been remade for the occasion.

After dinner, she glided through the next act of what seemed as efficient a plan of hospitality as at some geisha house. Inviting me to sit down on her couch, she drew out a guitar and started singing, in a strong, high voice, a series of bluegrass-flavored songs, all of them sounding like 'Red River Valley', yet all, she said, made famous by the Carter Family (yet another all-American institution I had never heard of till I came to Japan). Then she broke into some Japanese folk songs, their melancholy tales of broken love carried by the lilting softness of her voice. As with so many things in Japan, female singing seemed to be done to formula, and yet it was a lovely formula, guaranteed to please. The songs rang out in the quiet room, as fresh as the flowers, and as sweet.

This song, she explained, was about lanterns floating down a river at night, each of them carrying a spirit of the dead, yet seeming, to the children along the bank, nothing more than an exciting play of lights. 'This song little same my father sing in war,' she declared. 'But feeling, little different. This more spring light feeling – *Subaru*,' though here, I gathered, she meant not the car but the constellations for which it had been named.

And as she sang, I was struck again at how the Japanese, shy as they generally are – perhaps, indeed, because they are shy – tend to be professional performers at home, almost as if they feel obliged to shower guests with accomplishments as well as other kinds of gifts. I, by contrast, would rather do anything than perform on cue, though on this occasion, sensing an unspoken request, I glumly sat down at her piano and tried to bang out some half-remembered Beethoven and Bach.

Later, just before I left, I pointed out the yin-yang symbol on the blue scarf she was wearing round her neck. Surprising me yet again, Sachiko put her hands behind her hair, unknotted the scarf, and handed it over to me as a gift. I turned it around in my hands, the cloth smothered in her perfume. It was a dizzying experience, and heady: the scarf in my hands, her fragrance all about.

By now, I felt, I could understand a little more the nature of Sachiko's quiet urgency, her sense of impatience in pushing against the limits of her tightly reined life. At thirty, she had clearly spent her last, perhaps her best, seven years in absolute thrall to her family – or, more precisely, to the dictates of her society. She had, I was sure, played all the roles demanded of her with typical efficiency, and yet by obediently following a schedule imposed on her from without, she had also, I felt, cut herself short somehow, allowing herself to be propelled precipitously through the roles of perfect fiancée, perfect wife, and perfect mother, without ever really having fully worked out other parts of herself. Even now, therefore, something of her youth still lodged inside her, like a slide stuck in a projector, jamming all the images that followed and threatening to blow up the whole system.

This sense of missing the boat was, I suspected, particularly vexing in a society where the boat always, but always, left on time (a feeling I was already coming to know when racing to a bus stop at 10.12 a.m., knowing that there was no chance – absolutely no chance in this relentlessly punctual land – that the 10.10 a.m. bus had not left already). In Japan, stages in life seemed as rigorously demarcated as the hours of the day: just as people changed kimono or bracelets with the seasons, just as restaurants served different

kinds of rice, or tea, according to the time of year –
customs that we, not imprisoned by them, could afford
to find enchanting – so Japanese people had to change
roles and identity on cue, with the seasons of their
lives.

Age, therefore, was always stressed in Japan as
much as it was downplayed in the U.S. (where, in
California at least, a sixteen-year-old girl often looked
so much older than her age, and her forty-year-old
mother so much younger, that mother and daughter
truly did end up looking like sisters, as the soap ads
promised). One reason Japanese generally asked one
another, as soon as they were introduced, 'How old are
you?' was station – a thirty-year-old was expected to
defer to someone thirty-five and to have priority over
someone twenty-five. But it was also, and relatedly, to
give, and enforce, a sense of identity. Just as Sachiko's
life was set up so that she gave her mornings to herself,
her afternoons to her children, her evenings to her
parents, and her nights to her husband, so the stages of
a woman's life seemed all but scheduled in advance:
0–5 for shiny bowl cuts and indulgence; 6–18 for
ponytails and the blue-and-white sailor-suits of school;
19–24 for bangs, high fashion, and a stint in an office;
25–45 for child raising in jeans and pretty sweaters;
and the years that followed for sober matronhood in
perms, a return to the workplace, perhaps, and, at last,
a rounding of the cycle in the licensed second childhood of old age. The *Kurisumasu kēki* phenomenon
was only the most flagrant example of a system that
propelled its people into stages as forcibly as commuters into train compartments.

There was, in fact, a prescribed look, a kind of
uniform, for every stage. So although the old cliché
about all Japanese looking alike was clearly absurd,
there was some truth in saying that all Japanese of a

certain position or age – all nine-year-old schoolgirls, say, or forty-five-year-old executives – were encouraged to look, or at least dress, alike by a society they wanted to conform to an anonymous model, to become generic, in a sense. A sense of interchangeable identity not only helped to enforce unity; it also made one parent's daughter seem almost like another's, and thus enforced a larger sense of duty. So when Sachiko talked of her 'mother part' and 'wife part' and 'daughter part', she caught nicely, if inadvertently, the absoluteness of the way in which people here were both parts and partitions – and parts, in fact, were inflexibly partitioned.

But now, with the years fast slipping away from her, and her children both in school, I could see how avidly Sachiko was grasping after her receding youth, having matured to a point where at last she could appreciate the freedom that she was no longer allowed to have. I could also see how this longing was tied up with all things Western, as if she could not find an authorized Japanese precedent for being a thirty-year-old teenager. This side of her, then, came out through foreign contact mostly – in her giddy excitement at hearing about Phil Collins, or her high school girl's absorption in reading every last detail of Michael J. Fox's life in the Japanese equivalent of *Tiger Beat*. And part of this whole desperate last stand against conformity clearly included the befriending of *gaijin*, not only because the foreign world was associated with the young, the new, the trendy – and, more to the point, the reckless and the self-indulgent – but also because the foreign world was, apart from her posters and her daydreams (and akin to them too, perhaps), her only alternative to reality. Foreigners meant freedom in a land where freedom itself was largely foreign.

So I could see one reason why she was so active in

cultivating me, even if it was a reason, perhaps, that had never consciously occurred to her. One of the first things I was learning in Japan was how easily shrewdness and shelteredness could go hand in hand. When Sachiko lent me a tape, I could see that she was doing so partly in order to ensure that I would have to see her again (to give it back), and when she invited me to dinner, she was binding me up in a debt I would surely feel an obligation to repay. Yet even the subtlest and most elaborate of her emotional gambits were in pursuit of ends that seemed in themselves disarmingly innocent.

Meanwhile, as I fell deeper and deeper into such thoughts, I kept meeting foreigners who could not stop singing of their conquests. One softspoken American told me how he had fallen in love with a girl just by watching the way she sharpened his pencil. Another told me how, upon arrival, he'd been given an option on his best friend's house, his bike, and even his girlfriend. I ran one day into an old friend – from Santa Barbara, of course – a sweet if slightly scatterbrained soul, who had always seemed girlproof, so lost was he in Mahayana meditations and herbal teas. Now, though, he said, after thirty-nine years without ever really having had a girlfriend, he was on the brink of marriage – to a woman he'd met only six weeks before. She was, of course, thirty-eight, and she'd even told him that if he didn't marry her, he could at least, please, give her a baby. I shuddered at the consequences.

Another day, after meeting another shy foreigner, who instantly began telling me about the love letters he had received from his students and how little they meant to him – really, how little – I asked Mark what he thought of these relationships.

'I would imagine,' I said, 'that a Japanese woman would make a very good wife, if only because she has so precise a sense of what it means to be a perfect wife, and a perfect daughter-in-law, and a perfect mother.'

'Sure,' said Mark, with the sharp, smiling glance I knew so well by now, 'and a precise sense of what it means to be a perfect husband.' In his experience, he said, the marriages often worked out well when a Japanese girl was matched with a flighty or irresponsible foreign man, in part because Japanese women were well trained at housebreaking men and, like the heroines in Shakespeare's comedies, were often bright and agile enough to bring their ne'er-do-well partners to heel. But the marriages that brought more sensitive, and passive, kinds of foreign men together with Japanese girls often seemed to founder. Because, of course, the kind of Japanese woman who was interested in a foreign man was, by definition, a radical, independent-minded and ready for adventure; while the kind of man who was drawn to Japan was often a more retiring sort, in flight from the perceived aggressiveness of the West. So the girl, who wanted some wild, macho, Harley-throttling pop-star type, ended up, very often, with a man who had come to Japan specifically to escape the wild, macho, Harley-throttling pop culture of America; and he, drawn to Bashō or Murasaki, ended up with a girl who was trying to transcend the compliant surfaces enforced by Japanese convention. She wanted to see the world; he wanted just to settle down. Thus the woman ended up complaining that her partner was not wild enough, and the man that the girl was too wild; she, eager for the wrong man, found herself saddled with an unworldly Mr Right, and he, hoping for a poem, ended up with a would-be rock song. The only thing they had in common was that both were taken with a dream.

*   *   *

A few days later, Mark handed me a copy of Isaac
Bashevis Singer's *Spinoza of Market Street* and told
me to read the title story. Previously, in my ignorance,
I had always scorned Singer, imagining him somehow
to be an elderly taste. But as I began reading, I could
see why Mark had given the book to me, and why now,
with an unforced aptness that seemed a kind of gift in
him. For 'The Spinoza of Market Street' was shot
through not only with Singer's customary sense of wry
wonder but also with a kind of worldly uplift, an
exaltation in the face of earthly things, that I had not
expected. At its conclusion, a man, all his life a her-
mitic philosopher, gets up from his marriage bed and
looks at the moon and realizes that marriage has gone
against all his reason and philosophy, and yet has
somehow redeemed him beyond reason (and without
reason), with a logic all its own – a moment as moving
and transcendent as the same scene, more chillingly
evoked, in the new Springsteen song I had been
listening to in Kurama. Springsteen's faith was, of
course, very different in texture from that of Singer's
Spinoza-lover – it was a rougher thing, of the open
road and big cars, not philosophy and books – but still
it came to much the same thing: both characters had
given up what they held dearest, the very basis of their
lives – their *premises* – for a woman, and then had
found in her a kind of saving grace. They had opened
themselves up and, in the opening, found a transformation. In the pretty pun of C. S. Lewis, they had been
'surprised by joy'.

Increasingly, then, as I went on reading Singer, I
began to see that the great project of this closet pan-
theist was, quite literally, to build a rainbow bridge
between heaven and earth. Again and again, his robust
tales turned around men who wished to renounce the

world in favor of some unearthly, abstract love – a devotion to scholarship, or even God – and then, of a sudden, found themselves confronted with the presence of something less lofty that seemed to betray a higher source; again and again, his people were divided, their eyes on the heavens and their hands on earth. And invariably, Singer resolved the issue by showing that earthly love could be just the manifestation of heavenly love; that it revealed to us a radiance and a beauty that were otherwise concealed; that this was all we could know of heaven on earth, and all we would need to know. 'The more we know of particular things,' Spinoza had written, 'the more we know of God.'

Eleven

The following week, I met Sachiko early one morning and we set off together on another expedition: to Nara. Whenever she had the choice, I saw, she loved to go not to places she had never seen but to ones she already knew. Our trips, I sensed, were journeys as much into remembrance as freedom; and in visiting the places she had not seen since college, Sachiko was visiting, I sensed, the parts of herself she had not known since before her children and her marriage.

On the train through the countryside, I took out a fading twelve-year-old copy of Joni Mitchell's *Blue* and said that in the West, at least, such songs were very popular with girls. The sadness of the songs appealed to them, I went on; the complexities of boyfriends lost and babies missed, and lonely nights in lonely rooms. Perhaps it was not so different from Japan? Sachiko was silent as I told her this, but her face looked puzzled. 'I think people in your country very, very strong,' she said at last, reiterating her favorite theme. 'Woman too, very tough.' 'In some ways,' I said, reiterating my favorite theme, 'American women are often as tough as men. They work in offices and hold good jobs.' 'But,' she tried, 'when they go home, they all alone, very sad?' 'Exactly! And that's when they listen to Joni Mitchell and dream of boyfriend or child.' I dealt in stereotypes, I knew, in laughable cartoons, but I felt that nuances would only get lost between us and that I could not overdramatize for her the gulf between the world she knew and the one that she imagined.

When we got off the train, I realized that I was in for another surprise: we were not, it seemed, going to Nara at all, but rather to the nearby town of Asuka, the ancient city where Buddhism had arrived in Japan thirteen hundred years before and subject of some of the most haunting of old love poems:

> The mists rise over
> the still pools at Asuka.
> Memory does not
> Pass away so easily.

Outside the tiny country station, the obligatory school-children were lined up, scores of them, seated in rows in which they listened to the instructions shouted at them through megaphones: one movable feast of unified young humanity. But mostly, the villages and fields were quiet as we wandered along the lanes and up a hill, walking over rice paddies, and lost, for the most part, in our talk. The sun came out and disappeared; a mist rose above the mountains; the sky was slivers of blue in a gray porcelain bowl.

As we meandered along the quiet paths, Sachiko bent down to trace the flowers with her fingers, teaching me their names, and what they represented. This one, she said, was the cosmos, the harbinger of winter, this one the 'orchid' (she knew the English word because it was the favorite flower of Morten, lead singer of a-ha). This one was her grandmother's favorite; this one, she said, was me.

We walked through quiet lanes of little huts, and she motioned to a stream swishing through a ditch. *Seseragi*, she explained. I stopped for a moment and realized of course she was right: the silence was made musical by the gurgle of the water. This time to herself, she said, was very special, 'very fragile, like grass' (and now it was my turn to look confused, having forgotten her tendency to say *r* for *l*). 'Very fragile time,' she said again, ruminative. 'These days I always hold in my heart.' She paused for a moment on a bridge and looked into the running brook below. And I sensed that this chance to wander without plan called her back to something long hidden within herself like a temple bell.

Then, recollecting herself, she led me over more country hills, and as we walked, I taught her the English words I chanced to use – 'innocent', 'delicate', and 'subtle'. She looked up at me with searching eyes. 'You teach me what is in my heart?'

I chose to evade that, and asked instead if she was hungry. 'I forget,' she said dreamily. 'Time stop. My stomach hungry, but my heart very full.'

And so we straggled on some more, and later, in a village, stopped in a tiny shack for 'Fox Noodles' and '*Tanuki* Noodles', and then walked out, across the random fields. She told me how her nickname since girlhood had been 'Hime', or Princess, and how she dreamed now of going to spend a night with her best friend, Keiko, in Osaka, only a few minutes away from Kyoto, provided she could get her husband's permission. And gradually, as the hours passed, the day began to ease open, as if some catch had been unclasped. And as the sun began to set, our talk grew gradually more close. 'Sunset time very beautiful,' she mused quietly, 'but sad. Because children stop play, and I cook dinner, and all things finish. You are bird, I woman. You are hawk; you have strong heart, do anything, very easy. But I cannot. Then I only dream. Please you bring me world.' She paused, in a temple, in front of a painting of a monk seated before a ball of fire. 'This time dream time.'

Then, in the train going home, as she looked out on the darkening fields, I tried to cheer her up by telling her a story I had dreamed up as a boy, and as I did so, I realized, with a start, that somehow, without my intending it, this tale of white birds bringing dreams across the sea, above a silver 'moon path', was more apt – and more Japanese – than ever I had known. Even the raccoon story I had made up for her children, with its theme of a rescued princess, and the provision of dreams, did not seem quite so innocent any more. And yet, I realized now, there too, I had inadvertently gone Japanese by including two heroes instead of one, and so, somehow, providing a denouement that concluded not in marriage but in parting.

Finally, in the failing light, turning from the window, she summoned up all her English in a brave attempt to tie up the day. 'Thank you very much. You give my heart much imagination, much feeling. Thank you very much. I very, very fun. This magic time for me. When I little children size, I many times visit Grandma house. I dream very different life. But soon wake up: same me, same everything. Today I wake up, I feel new me. First time, I learn this feeling. Now I wake up – same bear with North Wind daughter. I think I bear, I have new heart.'

That night, back in Kyoto, I walked into Mark's room to find a middle-aged woman listening to a Grateful Dead tape and looking up at me with a stare of unnerving intensity – a capable New England matron by the looks of her, in sensible brown sweater and Seven Sisters skirt. 'Hello,' she announced, 'I'm Emily. I'm a pagan.' At that, Mark appeared from out of his crooked staircase, and the three of us found a cab, cowboys running around on a tiny pay-TV in front of us, spouting Japanese. As we weaved through the festive lights and crowds downtown, an ad on the screen showed a teardrop, silver, and a necklace on bare skin.

In the waiting express train, as we took our seats, Emily chattered away about the religious impulse and her belief in Seth and about a new image of the Goddess that should be associated not just with Kali but with the spirit of Fertility. Around us, Osaka sparkled like a jewel box in the dark: sapphire and emerald neon making dream patterns on the buildings, bright lights gleaming in the fresh-washed night. Off in the distance the shadowed, silent mountains, and a full moon rippling through the river below.

Getting out of the train, forty minutes later, we walked along moving stairways, up escalators, through corridors of signs, and out into a narrow lane of jangled colors. Under a bridge, across a tunnel of lights, stood an illuminated dome called Studebaker's. Inside was quite a scene: a blond American deejay was flinging his hands about at the front of a room and spinning oldies – 'California Girls', 'Twist and Shout', 'Return to Sender' – while four female customers in front of him, all in expensive, primary-color dresses, hair falling down their backs in identical styles, stood in a perfect row on the dance floor and went through elaborate steps, in perfect sync, to every song, a different step for every song, following the lead of the fast-talking deejay, never stopping, never sweating, just rolling their hands or twisting their hips or punching the air, impassive, song after song after unrelenting song. The whole place was done up in bright, Beach Blanket Bingo colors, pinks and Cadillac reds, and the waitresses, in perky ponytails, red miniskirts, and Laguna Beach sunglasses, danced as they went around the room, holding trays and jumping on to tables every now and then to do the twist, while the waiters, also sunglassed and fresh-faced, leapt on to the bar and strummed crazily away on unplugged guitars in a pantomime of fun, all of it meant to replicate some squeaky-clean, synthetic movie image of Redondo Beach in '64.

The tables were filled with businessmen and their pretty paid companions, the former apparently exulting in this walk on the American wild side, the latter smiling whenever required to do so. When asked to dance, they headed out on to the floor, in orderly groups, and, lining up in rows, serious as workers doing morning calisthenics, set about duplicating the deejay's every move. Here an arm to the right, there a finger in the air. The energy and the unity of the place were breathtaking. Below me, the four topettes were still boogying on cue, not one of their silky hairs out of place, not a trace of fatigue on their bright, unsmiling faces. They exchanged no looks or words or gestures as they danced, and when one of them went to the ladies' room, the others kept on dancing, leaving a blank space in the line for the missing girl to fill as soon as she returned. These girls, I assumed, must come here every night and go religiously through their motions. They did straight-faced surfing moves on 'Surfin' Safari', broke into a conga line for a Sam Cooke song, clapped through 'Locomotion'. Behind them, everyone else was equally punctilious, waving their hands about every time the deejay waved his hands about, bending their knees every time the deejay bent his knees, mimicking berserkness whenever the deejay went berserk, and some foreigner at my table, a Buddhist businessman from Staten Island, was shouting, exultant, 'This place is perfect! Just perfect for Japan! Everyone in lines. And following the American leader!'

Emily the pagan and a hippie girl, meanwhile, were arguing furiously about the nature of the fifties and the conformity of hippies, and around us the bouncy waitresses continued wriggling on cue, tireless as cheerleaders, and the four chic 'office ladies' jived, expressionless, through Motown moves. An Iraqi sailor from Basra sat alone at the next table, nursing his drink and shyly clicking away with his Instamatic. Several gray-suited American businessmen were led in by their eager-to-please Japanese hosts, and looked as if they would very much have liked to be elsewhere. Two goofy salarymen in their fifties got on to the dance floor with two American escorts, absurdly tall and elegant girls who must have been pulling down three hundred dollars apiece just for teetering over their dates.

All the while, Elvis and the Supremes and Ritchie Valens kept blasting on, and the guests on the dance floor went manic on cue, dipping their knees to '409' and hopping up and down to 'Jump' and banging their fists together on 'Hand Jive', as an old copy of *The Dancing Wu Li Masters* was passed around our table. Then, out of nowhere, the deejay spotted our group of aging foreigners. 'Hey,' he said, pointing a trigger finger over at us, 'this one is just for you!' And on came the one and only Top 40 hit from the Grateful Dead.

Two days later, at Arashiyama, along the western hills of town, everything was erased in the holiday sunshine. Boats meandering across a sunlit lake; teenage girls in kimono extracting disposable cameras from gold-lamé bags; bright crowds thronging across the Togetsu Bridge as in almost every Hiroshige print I had ever seen. Old men leading their grandchildren to stalls along the riverbank and coming away with ice creams or strange sweetmeats; ladies in kimono arranging themselves like flowers in a small, exquisite garden; families flocking in patterns through the bright, still air, as quiet as the trees around them.

It was, in fact, as much the people as the leaves that made the Japanese autumn: seated on low red-cloth tables under a canopy of colors, sipping tea and sitting silent, their talk, when it came, as soft as running water. The Japanese autumn was never wild or febrile, as in other tree-filled lands, but diffidently spectacular in its tidy, daily miracles, the air as mild as spring. And the people who came to inspect the scene were miraculously quiet, as hushed as viewers at some play. Having beautifully civilized Nature, made it orderly and trim, they fit themselves into its rhythms without ever making a sound. So even when there were crowds of people, as today, they were all so modest and self-possessed – and so fluently disappeared into the whole – that the purity of the scene remained unsmudged. At times like this, the observation of the seasons seemed akin, almost, to a playing of the national anthem; a solemn, silent act of faith.

Twelve

As more and more experiences began to crowd in on me in Kyoto, and my once empty room began to fill up with more and more presences, I was finding it harder and harder to keep clear. I had ended up, so it seemed, in a whirlpool of paradoxes, such as the one about what a sadist should do to a masochist. What does a would-be solitary do in the company of other solitaries – the very people, in other words, whose company he most enjoys? How does a Thoreauvian respond to a society of antisocial Thoreauvians? Was not keeping oneself open just a way of dodging all commitments?

And as my days in my new home began to turn into weeks, and my discoveries into day-to-day occurrences, I found, inevitably, that I was beginning to domesticate the dream, to know my way around the marvel and superimpose upon the map of Kyoto's streets my own particular homemade grid: this was the restaurant where I could find the most delicious *chai*, made by a Japanese woman who was a devotee of Sri Chinmoy, and this the coffee shop that had the best 'morning service' (not, as it happened, a religious rite but a toast-and-coffee special); this was the bus that took me to the smoky jazz bar where polite longhairs served up baked potatoes mysteriously attended by slices of lemon and chopsticks, this the one that took me to the latest issues of *Sports Illustrated*; this was the temple where I did tai chi on early Sunday mornings, and this the one where schoolgirls never came.

Often, moreover, as a resident, I did not have to go out to find Kyoto, for Kyoto was all too ready to come in to find me. One day, I was sitting inside my room, deep in Peter Matthiessen, when there came a knock upon my door. Outside, in the corridor, stood an elegant, gray-bearded man in a suit, accompanied by a sweet-smiling popette. They looked like the host and hostess of some morning talk show.

We bowed in all directions at once, and the man quickly pursued his objective. 'What country do you come from?'

'England,' I said (hastily riffling through alternatives).

Digging into his briefcase, he presented me with a brochure advising me not to fret; God had guaranteed happiness for us all. This made me happy. Then he followed up his advantage. Would I like a Bible?

No, thank you, I told him in a Japanese that apparently afforded him some pain. I had been to a Christian school in England and had had ample opportunity to read the Bible there. Looking unhappy, he bowed. I bowed. The girl bowed. I bowed again. Then there was more bowing all round, and the threat moved off to another room.

Two nights later, I was just hurrying home through the rain, a hot box of Kentucky Fried Chicken in my hands, when suddenly a boy loomed out of an alleyway before me. He asked me a few questions, and I, assuming he wished to try out his English on me, grimly replied in ungracious Japanese. Then he asked if he could bless me. This did not seem like an offer to refuse. Dutifully, I put down my box of two legs and a thigh (original flavor) and stood before him in the drizzle. Putting his hands together in prayer, he asked me to the same. Then, eyes tightly closed, he recited three times something along the lines of 'Oh, please, great spirit, bless this *gaijin*, thank you.' Then he asked me to cradle my hands in front of my stomach and close my eyes for two or three moments while he did some extra petitioning for my soul. This I did, in the midst of the rain, my chicken growing colder and wetter by the minute. Finally, he gave me permission to open my eyes, and *kuriingu* complete, I was free to go home with my soggy dinner.

The next day, therefore, when a man in the laundromat turned around and started to engage me in conversation, I was all set to close my eyes and get a few extra credits in the heavens – until I realized that he really did just wish to tell me about his honeymoon in Disneyland. A little later, though, when I went into Shakey's with an American student of Zen, a waiter hurried up to us, blocking our way and motioning for us to leave. The place was full of happy diners at the time, conspicuously consuming their corn-and-pineapple pies, while a voice on the public-address system declared, 'This is Mr Tender Juicy Chicken, a spokesman for Shakey's . . .' When we tried to move closer to the salad bar, however, the employee panicked, shaking his head furiously. 'But we only want to eat some salad.' 'Salad?' He looked thunderstruck. 'We're only here to eat.' 'Eat?' He stole a terrified glance at the copy of *Time* I was carrying, with its cover shot of Arafat. Apparently, he had thought that these foreigners had come here to convert defenseless pizza-eaters to some messianic figure in a kaffiyeh.

Mostly, though, I was free to wander around alone, in the company of the autumn. The smell of fresh-baked bread on the Philosopher's Path, on a shining afternoon, and the solemn tolling of a gong across a wall. A flash of gold on the wrist of a temple maiden. Men with jackets on their arms swaggering past in loosened ties, practicing English sentences: 'When you are middle-aged, you must take care.' A girl in Porsche sunglasses and blazing scarlet trousers trying out 'Where do you come from?' Middle-aged gentlemen standing rigid as statues while harassed photographers waved them back into the sun.

Stopping off one morning in Shisendō, the Temple of the Poet Hermits, I sat on the veranda, looking out on to the garden. A lady, very beautiful, her face the faint pink of pearl, came and sat down by my side. A light, light rain began to fall, so light that I had to strain my eyes to see it and knew that it was raining only because the bark on the trees was growing browner. Another Comme des Garçons girl came in and slid down on the floor beside me, her head on her cashmered shoulder, as she looked out at the dreamy rain. Occasionally, a drop trickled down from the rafters. The leaves were scarlet, green, and burgundy. The drizzle was softer than a silk still life.

A little later, I gave Sachiko a call, and we arranged to go to Kobe, the shining, broad-avenued port that had always been, of all Japanese places, the one that was closest in spirit to a foreign town. As always when we met, the day was all sunshine and light drizzle. But the rains began to lift as we got on to the Kobe train, and by the time we arrived, the sky was blue above the silver sea.

Drifting along through the huge antiseptic spaces of Kobe's lonely de Chirico streets, we chatted leisurely about Bjorn Borg and Victor Hugo, Holden Caulfield (whom she loved) and Jacky Chan (whom she admired for his 'child's eye'). Then, coming upon a bench, she suddenly sat down and began fishing out presents from her knapsack, handing them over to me in sequence: a pretty drawing, in crayons, of the story I had told her ('I'm sorry. In my heart, very beautiful, but paper not so good'); then a sheaf of autumn photos – yellow light streaming through the ginkgo trees, and maples rusted against the blue; then, out of nowhere, a monkey-decorated telephone card (a woman's gift, I thought, and a Japanese woman's gift, obliging me to call her).

Making our way towards the port, we looked out at the ocean liners, black in the chromium light, and sitting down on a log, the wind blustering all about us, we fell into our usual patter, she telling me how America was the land of the free, I telling her how much of what I saw in America was loneliness. And every time I ventured some generality that even she could not assent to – that the Japanese were close to their parents, say, or that thirty-year-old Japanese had the hearts, very often, of fifteen-year-olds (where in America it was often the reverse), or that Japanese women half expected their men to take on mistresses – she simply nodded and answered sagely, 'Case by case.' A gentler putting-in-place I could scarcely imagine.

Then, through the wide boulevards of the town, we walked up Tor Road, up into the hills of Kitano, and the small cobbled streets of the foreigners' quarter. Surrounded by white stucco villas scattered along the winding roads, the sea below, the sky all blue above, I could easily imagine myself in the canyons of North Hollywood. Across the street, as if by design, the name of the ice cream store was Santa Barbara.

And so we drifted in and out of foreign dreams: in a Peter Rabbit store, she wound up a music box and put it to my ear – I heard 'As Time Goes By' and then a song she identified for me, whispering, as 'Lili Marleen'; at the English House, commemorating a foreign way of life, she lingered in the pretty flowered bedroom, gazing at it dreamily and talking of Emily Brontë.

Wandering along past restaurants called Lac d'Annecy and Café Chinois, she asked me what Rob Lowe was like and why I did not think that Cyndi Lauper was cute. As we talked, I taught her a few new words: 'soul' and 'clear' and 'fascination'.

Then, when least I expected it, I looked up to see that we were standing outside a restaurant called Wang Thai, the only Thai restaurant in this part of Japan, and something I had despaired of ever finding. This, too, seemed an augury, a present from the fates, and so, without a pause, I bustled poor Sachiko in and ordered her a spicy chicken soup. Soon she was daintily choking over her bowl, while trying, with typical courtesy, to find something positive to say.

Once she had laid the poisonous broth aside, and the second course arrived, she tucked her fork, delicately held between two fingers, into the rice and offered brightly, 'I like Kali.' I was wondering what kind of demon I had roused within her to get this demure lady to champion the goddess of destruction – a less useful figure, I recalled, than the spirit of Fertility – when she repeated, with more heat, 'Kali, I like very much,' motioning to her plate, and I realized that it was only the curry she was extolling.

Yet for all these customary hazards, Sachiko seemed to be drawing closer as the meal went on, and towards the end, as she leaned towards me, oblivious suddenly of the stylish *Ramayana* murals all around us and the dreamy Thai pop music on the system, I realized that she was working around to some confession. Still, it was, as always, a little hard for me to follow what exactly she was saying. 'With you,' she began, 'I have clear heart. I talk my heart, very easy. But I very shy.' She smiled and hid her face in her napkin, and it was harder still to guess what she was trying to convey; I could tell it was important only by the diffidence with which she brought it forth. 'When I meet husband, I little teenage size, nineteen. First time I together man. We talking bluegrass music – very easy, very fun. I expect soon marry. Before many times, I talking brother. Very close feeling. But his wife soon little sad, maybe little jealous. So long time, I not talking him. But now my heart very different. With you, talking very easy, very fun. You have clear heart. No dust on your mirror.' She stopped again, and I held my breath. 'I have two heart,' she continued slowly. 'I like children very much. I like you. But different. With you is dream world.' I was getting a little confused at all this. 'You have found young heart in me,' she said. I said that I sensed as much but I did not know if her two hearts were in collision or in sync.

'I very shy,' she went on. 'But I say true. If not good, please you say. I not want bad.'

'I'm really happy to be with you.'

'Really?' She sounded incredulous.

'Yes, really. Thank you for your friendship.'

'You're welcome,' she said with a bright light, tilting her head on her shoulder and flashing me her prettiest smile. 'My pleasure' – she tried out the phrase I had taught her.

Thus we struggled on through a curious discussion. Her wavering, heartfelt nonconfession seemed to mark the crossing of some threshold, and now, of a sudden, she opened up with a flood of foreign images. She imagined my mother in a deep-blue sari, with a golden border, she said, and she would wear a sari for me on my birthday, even though she did not own one. She had always dreamed of India. She liked above all Thai reds.

'Art, you mean?'

'No. Red!'

Then she went on to tell me a Inoue Yasushi story

141

about a man who quit his country to seek out the moon in Tibet, and I reciprocated by telling her about my readings in the Zen traveler and poet Issa. And so we wandered out into the Californian hills, past girls in 'SANTA BARBARA: High Fashion Dreaming' shirts, along chic cobbled streets, a theme-park vision of gentrified Victoriana, with Sherlock Holmes alleyways and olde England streetlamps. This shiny local version of foggy London was called 'romantic Kobe', she informed me. 'Many, many Japanese woman like come here this place.' 'For shopping?' 'Also for romance!'

We sat down on a wall, and in the minutes before twilight, she laid her head upon my shoulder. I could feel her perfume all around me, and as we watched the clouds catching the last of the light on the city below, she sighed, and a chill came into the air. I had never seen eyes shaped like hers before, with ocher eye shadow and folded lids, and when she looked up at me, I felt a shudder. 'Time stop,' she said. 'Why clock not stop moving?'

Then, smiling, she took my hand in hers, and hanging on to my arm, a skipping girl again, she walked me back to town.

At the station, as we waited for the train, she pulled out a scarf and tied it round my neck. Then, as we got in, taking seats by the window, I could feel her sadness building as we rode back into town. Squashed together in the crowded compartment, I improvised a story for her then, a story of a lady and a monk, and when I got to the end, I saw her eyes fill with tears. She looked down, embarrassed, and hid her face in my jacket. 'I'm sorry. I very sad. Sun set. And train go back Kyoto. I understand your story. Very sad.' 'But Japanese people like sad stories?' 'Yes,' she said. 'Maybe you catch true Japanese heart.'

Then, brightening abruptly – as if she had quite

literally taken a grip on her errant self – she looked up smiling and offered me a pastry she had bought from a German bakery. 'This baker's name is the German word for "friendliness",' I said, trying to lighten the atmosphere. She beamed. 'You two kind bird. Hawk – and owl. You give me much input. Thank you.' And as the train drew slowly into Kyoto station, she covered my hand with hers. 'Now,' she said, 'I little catch bird.'

There was once a beautiful lady who lived in a village near the ancient city of Kyoto with her husband. One day in late summer, as the crickets began to fall silent, the man fell ill; and by the coming of the autumn, the woman could see that he was almost gone. All night, she sat patiently by his side, tending to his needs and listening for his breath; and as the light came up, she felt his heart, and knew that he was gone.

She loved him still, she knew, but the woman was too strong to let her own life wither. So, each day, in her black kimono, through flurries of falling leaves, she went back to the local temple, to lay scarlet flowers on his grave.

Now it happened that the guardian of this temple was a monk who had inherited it from his father in his youth. Seasons had passed, and the monk had grown sturdy in his faith; impervious to the world, his mind was fixed on Buddha. Yet when a member of the village died, it fell to this monk to perform all the rites for sending the soul on its way. So when the young lady came each day with scarlet flowers to the temple, he sat beside her and told her of the Buddha's teaching, she in her black kimono, he in his black-and-golden robes.

As time went on, the woman began to return more and more often to the temple, and the monk, though

143

lost in meditation, could not so easily keep his mind in focus; even in the meditation hall, he could see a flash of red, could hear the rustle of kimono. The forty-ninth day of the husband's death came and went, but still the woman kept returning, as if she could not put the memory away. And even when he said his sutras, the monk found that his mind was filled with the image of the long-haired woman in the garden, red flowers in her hand.

One day, as the first bite of winter chilled the air, the monk decided that he must barricade himself against such distractions and recover the strength of his faith. He caught her fragrance in the hall, he sensed the lady everywhere. But all day long he kept his face turned towards the wall. And when at last he returned to his room that night, he found a single red flower laid outside his door.

And so it continued each day for a week: not once did he open his eyes to his visitor, but each night, when he returned to his room, he found a flower by his door. When his teacher, a head abbot from Kyoto, came to visit, he saw all that was happening, but he knew that there was nothing he could do: the monk would have to face this challenge by himself.

Finally, one cold and brilliant day, the monk decided to wait in his room to watch for the lady's visit. He saw her arrive at dawn, shivering in the winter chill, and even as he recited his sutras, he saw her waiting there all day, eyes smarting in the cold. As he watched her standing there, the monk felt shaken out of words: here, he thought, was a purity and singleness even truer than that he gave to Buddha. Here, in fact, was the meaning of devotion. As darkness fell upon the garden, and the woman got up to leave, he suddenly called out to her.

'Please wait,' he said. 'I saw you standing here all

day, hardly moving save for cold. Please drink some sake before you leave.'

When she saw him, the woman turned pale, till her face was ghostly white; but as he pulled back his screen, she slipped off her sandals and entered the incense-filled space. Sitting together on the tatami, they watched the full moon rise above the eastern hills.

That night was the coldest of the year, but neither the monk nor the lady knew it. And when the monk went to prayers at dawn, his bare feet tingled on the frost.

That morning, when the woman returned to the temple, the monk was nowhere to be seen. And so it was for many days, she returning to the chilling temple garden, red flowers in her hand, and he alone in his chamber, silently aflame. Finally, when she arrived one morning, the lady found a white flower placed outside the monk's door, inside of it a letter.

'You have given me,' the letter began, 'all the warmth and color of the world. I want to keep my image of you as clear as running water. Please take this flower as a memory of our friendship. And know that, though we should not meet again, it is you I always think of.'

The woman took the letter and the flower, and the monk never heard from her again. But next morning, when he rose to say his sutras, there, on his doorstep, was a red flower, and a black kimono, scented with her fragrance, and the first faint touch of spring.

And as the leaves began to fall, I really did begin to feel that something was flowering in Sachiko, as if — though I feared to say it — she really was a kind of sleeping beauty awakened by romance, or at least its distant shadow. And for all her composure and supercompetence as a mother, for all her chic and self-possession, I could tell that hers was a heart more than ready to take flight and soar out of her control. And

145

even though I had often been abroad, and often been faced, therefore, with the issue of what to do with foreign dreams, whether to try to encourage fantasies of abroad, or simply damp them down, I still had no sense of how much she was interested in making her visions reality, or whether, as a good Japanese, she was content simply to maintain another world that she could visit in imagination.

At times, in fact, I wondered whether, in encouraging her to express her dreams of flight, I was falling prey to the temptation I had already noticed in some of the more softhearted of the foreigners in Japan: the urge to give the Japanese a glimpse of the world on the other side. When she had attended her first tea ceremony, Siobhan had told me, she had found herself, this radical feminist pagan from the Haight, surrounded by elegantly prim young housewives-in-the-making, getting their training in all the ladylike arts. The school play, she could not help but notice on a nearby bulletin board, was *Cinderella*. And seeing all of them preparing for a life of simple self-denial, she had started inviting some of what she called 'the good girls' back to her hippie commune, to get a taste of forbidden freedom. Later, she said, she had heard them excitedly telling their friends about their 'wild night of sin'.

I wondered, too, whether in encouraging Sachiko to indulge all the hopes that Japan so strenuously teaches its children to suppress, or to enjoy only in specific, and very circumscribed, conditions, I was schooling her in desires she could never fully realize. Encouraging people to realize their potential was an especially dangerous occupation in a country that taught them to fulfill their duty instead.

Most of all, I wondered how deep the ambiguities between us really reached. For even in the same tongue, we were rarely speaking the same language. To begin with, of course, she was married, and I did not know what exactly that betokened – especially in a culture where marriage was often nothing more than separation by another name. Much of the time, Sachiko functioned as if she had no family at all, using her society's sense of extended ties to find parents or friends to baby-sit for her, and tuning out her marriage as if it were just a distant radio station. It was almost as if being a mother and a wife was a role to her, and thus a self she could shrug off as easily as her mother's clothes or voice; she seemed, in fact, less fettered – or more resourceful about slipping free of fetters – than most single people that I knew at home.

She, in turn, of course, knew little of foreign codes of friendship and how to translate them into terms she knew. So every time she said, 'My children little want see you,' I did not know to what extent that meant that it was she who wanted to see me. And every time I replied, 'I want to see your children,' I did not know if that just meant that I wanted to see her. And even though traveling had schooled me, I had thought, in the seven types of ambiguity, and more, I still had to admit that Sachiko was the end of the line in this field, the state of the art: for Japan itself was firmly based on people's not saying what they meant and on the accompanying assumption that what was meant was rarely what was said. And women in particular were encouraged – even trained – to project an air of charming acquiescence that suggested everything and meant nothing. In a land where language itself was a force of separation as much as communion, where foreigners were invariably treated as symbolic carriers of abroad, and where everything was turned into soft focus – surrounded by an all-embracing vagueness – it all added up to the most troubling of riddles.

Thirteen

As autumn deepened, bringing with it new intensities,
I took myself off one morning to Nara. After listening,
in silence, to my story of the lady and the monk, Mark
had lent me a tape of Laurens Van der Post delivering a
lecture on the unlikely, even unpromising, subject of
'The Unwritten Literature of the Bushmen'. And as I
got on the train, crowded now with tidy, festive families,
old couples going on temple tours, a young monk
shyly turning his face from tourist cameras, and packs
of schoolgirls on their way to Dreamland (the modern
amusement park that was now the most popular attraction in the ancient capital), I turned on the tape and fell
into the rhythms of the old Dutch farmer's swelling,
bardic cadences. Birds, he was saying, in every kind of
folklore, stood for the world of the heavens, emissaries
from above. Birds were messengers from the gods
bringing inspiration to earthbound men. That was why
among the American Indians, and the tribes of Africa
too, chiefs traditionally wore crowns of feathers, as if
their heads were flocks of inspirations. That was also
why Plato called the mind a cage of birds.

I thought of this as we rolled through the countryside, and of my own story about birds, and of how
Sachiko always referred to me as a winged ambassador from abroad. I thought of how much I wanted to
share this thought with her, so sonorously phrased, by
a disciple of her brother's guru, Jung, and how strange
it was that stories and images that had come to me

unbidden seemed much more pointed than I knew. And as the train rolled into Nara, I was jolted from my daydreams by the Buddhist capital itself, where a local department store was offering a cup of gold-flaked coffee for more than three hundred dollars, and posters of Madonna fluttered from the souvenir stalls.

Inside the famous Deer Park, though, one was back inside a more changeless Japan. Families were enjoying picnics on the grass, deer grazing at their sides as in the Oxford college where I had cavorted as a boy. Ladies strolled through galleries of red, papers held up to their ashen faces to shield them from the sun. A group of smiling elders sauntered through a reception line of blazing orange trees, the sun catching the copper in the women's hair, the men framed by an extravagance of gold. Now and then, the tolling of a distant bell summoned us back, so it seemed, to a higher time and self.

Making my way up to a temple terrace, I leaned on a railing and watched the blue hills in the distance, half shrouded now in wood smoke. Coins clattered in the collection box behind me, and an old woman grabbed the clump of white and red and orange ropes and rang and rang and rang the temple bell. An aged couple asked me to take their picture, framed against the falling leaves. Around us, the sun came down with the cleansing intensity of mountain light.

In Nara, I saw a shrine with statues of moonlight and sunlight, three thousand lanterns bobbing above the moss. Across town in the Hall of Dreams, I visited the famous Korean Bodhisattva, salvaged, like so much else here, by the visiting American Ernest Fenollosa. Outside the Great Buddha, commanding the largest wooden building in the world, I saw a wandering mendicant, a mountain monk, in white robes and straw sandals, standing stock-still, swathed in a

149

curious mix of animal skins and bells, muttering shamanic chants.

In Nara, the temples were more hidden than in Kyoto, left to themselves, with room to breathe. To get to them, one had to change trains twice, at sleepy country stations, walk for many minutes through crooked, nameless lanes, ascend unforgiving flights of steps; one had, in short, to earn the temples, and travel away from the workaday world – and self. A visit here could only be a pilgrimage.

Later, returning in the falling light to Kyoto, I descended once more into Van der Post as he spun out Bushmen tales of how a man had spent his whole life pursuing the reflection of a bird he had once seen, and only grabbed a feather on the day he died; and another of how a man had caught the goddess of the moon, but then, through looking in a casket full of starlight and seeing nothing, had lost her too. By the time the train pulled into Kyoto Station, I was lost in the world of the storyteller's flights and, loath to hurry home, began to walk through narrow lanterned streets and along the Kamo River, lit by a trailing series of red lights.

As I walked, past houses lit up by a brilliant moon, I thought how much the Japanese were a people of the moon, the central image of the first Japanese story I had ever heard. And though they traced their lineage to the Goddess of the Sun, the sun was mostly used now to describe the modern or the public world – the Sun Plaza American-style convenience store, the Sun-flower Hotel, and rows of Sunny cars were all five minutes from my home. The moon, by contrast, was the part they kept jealously to themselves. In their hearts, I thought, the Japanese were still a people of the Rising Moon. And just as I was dwelling on this, and recalling how Kyoto itself had once been known as 'Moon Capital', I turned on the tape again and – out of

150

nowhere – heard Van der Post talking about how the moon in Japan was always three times larger than in any other place and how the Japanese had a deep affinity with the moon, renewing themselves, after earthquakes or wars, as cyclically as the moon.

The moon, I recalled, was the one possession that even monks did not renounce. When he lost his house in a fire, the Zen poet Masahide wrote, he found occasion for new hope: he now enjoyed a better view of the rising moon.

When next I visited Sachiko's home, for dinner, she sat me down and put on a tape of *Howard the Duck*. Gloomily I surveyed Duck magazines, Duck TV shows, and a host of lame Duck jokes. 'I much love George Lucas,' she averred. 'Spielberg too. They have very innocent child heart. Coppola little different feeling; he more big brother heart. You see this movie *Goonies*?'

I shook my head no.

'*Gremlins*?'

'I'm sorry, no.' She looked disappointed. 'But I do like Kurosawa.'

She now looked very grave. 'Japanese person not so like this man,' she said. 'Foreigner person like, no problem. But Japanese not so like. Little show-biz feeling.'

The next thing I knew, though, she had slipped into her other, deeper self, drawing out her guitar and breaking into a series of piercing, lovely lullabies. I could see her eyes as she sang begin to glitter at their corners; I could hear a quaver as she hit the high notes. She sang another wistful ballad, then, about a man looking at the pressed flowers that his lover had left for him, and again, as she sang, her eyes filled with tears. *Mono-ganashii*, she explained, the beauty of what's fleeting.

In terms of everything I knew, things were fast becoming more and more slippery and strange. When

I gave her a couple of poems I had written for her in Nara, she looked up at me with a kind of melting intensity and said, 'Me too.' And when she showed me an album of her wedding photos, and I admired the loveliest one of all, of the bride in a white veil, caught in golden light, she simply peeled it out and handed it over to me. Now, I felt, I was not only gate-crashing her marriage but actually taking possession of her memories.

Whenever I tried to ask her about her husband, though, or his family, she never said anything except, 'My husband very good man, but weak heart.' If ever I tried to get anything more out of her, she just laughed it off, and said, *'Chotto muzukashii'* (It's a little difficult). Her husband, in the telling, was nothing more than a kind of spectral, distant authority figure on the margins of her life, spoken of in the terms that people in a large company might reserve for the CEO. So I never really got a sense of his features, his preferences, his self; he was just a kind of shadowy bogeyman who, like many a Japanese man, dutifully did 'family service' on his one day off a week, filled up his spare hours with jigsaw puzzles, and was too scared of foreigners ever to meet me or any of his wife's other foreign friends.

Then, finally, seemingly heavy with emotion, she tried to put into words why we should not meet in Kyoto. 'I'm sorry,' she began, 'my heart much change,' and I got ready for a brush-off – a prudent one, I thought, in the circumstances, and one in which I almost wanted to assent. 'Before, talking very fun, very easy. But now . . .' she went on, and I did not have a clue in what direction her heart had changed, when this had happened (since past tense and perfect were elided in her English), and whether she now felt closer than before or more distant.

I was also beginning to realize how treacherous it was to venture into a foreign language if one could not measure the shadows of the words one used. When I had told her, in Asuka, *'Jennifer Beals ga suki-desu. Anata mo'* (I like Jennifer Beals – and I like you), I had been pleased to find a way of conveying affection and yet, I thought, a perfect distance. But later I looked up *suki* and found that I had delivered an almost naked protestation of love. Often, too, I would use the particle *ga*, never remembering that it could be both nominative and accusative. And both of us, in other ways, were forever confusing subject with object. So she would say, 'You help me,' and it was a long time before I realized that she meant, 'I'll help you' (and not just because one good turn deserved another). Thus both of us ended up like children in the dark, flinging around pronouns at random till it was utterly unclear who was meant to be doing what to whom. When we got to sentences like 'I'll call your house', the ambiguities became positively disabling.

Worse still, of course, matters of causation were invariably scrambled and Humpty-Dumptified, since the Japanese put their 'because' in the opposite place from where we do. Thus I, in essaying 'I like you because you are kind,' would come out with the equivalent of 'You are kind because I like you,' and she would look back at me, frowning more than ever. Noticing that she still tended to use the Japanese word *dakara* in every sentence, even when speaking English, I thought I was doing her a favor by teaching her 'therefore'. But this only vexed the chaos further. 'I little sad, therefore you are leaving,' she said, and I recalled – too late! – that *dakara* could mean 'because' as well as 'therefore'. And she often used 'yes' where we say 'no' ('You're not cold?' 'Yes!').

And just as Sachiko, I could tell, became franker and

bolder – more direct – when she was speaking English, shedding her inhibitions in translation, so I began to see that I too was probably more daring, more intimate, more reckless with myself, when I ventured into Japanese, throwing around terms I had found in Rexroth's love poems without ever really knowing the nuances they carried. Meanwhile, of course, nearly all her shadings were lost to me, and I felt sorry for her having to box her feelings into the few adjectives she knew, throwing heavy terms over subtle, fleeting nuances – like the loose and flabby U.S. Army jacket she wore over her tiny body. Once, when I had to leave her house ten minutes early, she said, 'I very sad,' and another time, when I simply called her up, she said, 'I very happy' – and I began to think her unusually sensitive, or else prone to bold and violent extremes, when really she was reflecting nothing but the paucity of her English vocabulary, all the more frustrating, I imagined, for one accustomed to a language that so finely distinguished between melancholy and mournfulness, wistfulness and sorrow. Talking in a language not one's own was like walking on one leg; when two people did it together, it was like a three-legged waltz.

Yet in the end, the fact that we were both speaking in this pared-down diction made us both, I felt, somewhat gentler, more courteous, and more vulnerable than we would have been otherwise, returning us to a state of innocence. In speaking a simplified English, we were presenting simpler and clearer accounts of ourselves, edited down, with the rough spots filtered out. Reduced to essentials, in fact, and bare declarative sentences dominated by basic adjectives, we ended up speaking with a little of the clenched, suggestive clarity, the clean simplicity, of Japanese poetry. And since she spoke always in images, and I tended to mirror her speech, our conversations grew more and more lyrical, and more so still, since the Japanese words I had learned, I had largely learned from the poems of Yosano Akiko.

I knew very well that this kind of lyricism was offhand, and almost second nature in this country, and that it reflected in part just Sachiko's limited command of English; I knew, too, that this kind of phrasing, which sounded so poetic to me, could often be formulaic in a land where people thought in images (Saikaku had once composed 23,500 *renga*, or linked verses, in a single day; even the future prime minister had composed 2,000 haiku). I noticed too how every English metaphor I explained to her – 'raining cats and dogs', being 'the apple of my eye' – struck her as ineffably poetic. Yet still I could not easily resist the sustained delicacy of the terms she used and the sense of moment, as well as depth, she brought to every meeting. Her emotions seemed as exquisitely worn as her seasonal bracelet or earrings, and the words she used had a kind of other-worldly, romantic Zen flavor – or, at least, a sense of clarity and calm that seemed to cut to the heart of Zen and to the very notion of depth in Japan. She made our friendship seem a sacrament.

And all the while, the brilliant blue-sky afternoons kept coming, day after day as clear as road reflectors, and the hills of Kyoto began to blaze with reds, the trees along the canals to light up like gold. And on these shining days of autumn, the sky shifting from milky white to blue, the trees a rhapsody of colors, I felt the brightness of the Japanese autumn was like nothing I had ever seen before: such hope and stillness in the air. Tingling mornings in shiny coffee shops, dazzled afternoons among the white-robed priests: singing Handel days of rapture and precision.

Fourteen

As autumn drew towards an end, I found myself returning one day with Sachiko to Kobe, and on the train, as we sat side by side, she reached up and unclasped, for the first time ever, her mother-of-pearl comb, letting her hair fall in a rush down the right side of her face. The suddenly loosened sensuality hit me like a shock. 'This year,' she said, 'Autumn more more beautiful. I see beautiful color, and many flower, and cosmos flower, little messenger of winter. But sometimes I sad. I thinking moon soon full, then small again; my heart little same. Now full. But future, I don't know. Maybe very empty.' In response, I told her Van der Post's story of how the moon renewed itself.

She nodded slowly, with determination. 'I want build strong heart. Please you help. I want very strong, so when you go, I not so sad. Sometimes I little fragile' (she had learned the word from a Sting album). 'But now I more confidence. Before, I say, "Be careful! He bird! He stay in Japan only one year." But now heart control, very difficult. I open window and you give me sunshine.' She smiled at me warmly. 'Santa Barbara sunshine.'

Already, I could tell, she was savoring the poignancy our walks would have in memory, smoothed down and elegized by its sepia tints. Already she was composing – and relishing – her reminiscences. And yes, with half her mind, wondering whether a happy

Western ending might not be better than a melancholy Japanese one.

In Kobe itself, city of foreign romance, we made our way, in the blithe blue morning, to the silent modernist spaces of Port Island, walking through avenues of glass. When once she saw a piece of litter on the spotless walkway – the first blemish I could remember seeing in two months in Japan – she could not hide her shame. 'I'm very sorry,' she said, bending down to snatch it up. 'This place very dirty. Japan not so clean place.' I could not explain to her that it was far and away the cleanest place I had ever seen, and so we went on talking, and walking, amidst the glinting high-rises and Californian plazas of this spacey world, the stores called Printemps and Los Abrigados and Orso. She asked me which of Vivaldi's Four Seasons I liked, and told me how much she loved Goethe's *Faust*, which she had read three times. Once, she explained, she had been fascinated with the Tarot too, but then had chosen to put it aside, after foretelling some uncomfortably dark truths about her cousin. She went on – though Paul Kennedy had yet to hit the best-seller list in Japan – that every country had to go through its cycle of power, as Egypt, Greece, India, China, England, France, and America had done. 'Now Japan Number One,' I said, and she was bemused. 'Soon,' she replied, as all Japanese did, 'Korea more more strong.' Whether this was fatalism or a spur to greater effort, the Japanese seemed alone in the world in assuming they were about to be overtaken.

Later, as we walked, she talked about her love of 'macaroni Westerns' and explained how Diana Ross had changed her look to appeal to whites; and then, of a sudden, how she had won a school oratory contest with her heartfelt account of the Hiroshima bombing, which had left her aunt sterile.

At times, I realized, it was easy to interpret too much – as well as too little – from the way she had to fashion elaborate English packages, wrapped up in images, analogies, and parallels, to get her meaning across to me. Yet still Sachiko's words rang out like music after the more familiar Californian diction of 'coping' and 'sharing' and 'parenting'. I was falling in love, in a sense, with the fairy tales she made of even the smallest of our encounters – 'If you not here, then flower not open,' or 'Where your white horse? I think you prince'; she not only quoted but lived out the ancient poems I had always sought.

Then, walking into the Portopia Hotel, we came, unexpectedly, upon what resembled a Japanese production of *Gatsby*: the whole yawning lobby was taken up with men in black ties and tuxedos, girls with Isadora Duncan hats above black flappers' dresses.

'Is there some kind of marriage going on?'

'No marriage,' she said soberly. 'These lady little hostess feeling. Not real people.'

'But this is a hotel. And these men seem to belong to some company.'

'This Japanese system,' she went on. 'If company have party, many hostess here. Wife must always stay in home. If man introduce wife, very terrible feeling. Then company give little hostess.'

'But isn't this very expensive?'

'Very expensive,' she said solemnly, stealing a glance over at a hostess as she might at a gangster's Rolls-Royce. 'Night-world person, very sad eye,' she whispered, with a faint tremble that suggested she would like to turn to other things. 'Please we go upstairs?'

Upstairs, in the coffee shop, she was a bouncing girl again, excitedly explaining how this was the very hotel where she had stayed a year before, stealing away from her husband for the first time ever and buying an a-ha ticket for several times the forty-dollar price, and then, after the concert, coming by chance upon her heart-throb Morten. The moment still glowed inside her like first love. When she had met him, she said, in the elevator, she had given him a present: What did I think it was? Flowers? No. A ring? No. A record? No, a book. Oh, Inoue Yasushi? No, a book about Zen. Because, she explained, she had read that he was a devout man who had almost become a priest. And this book was the best way for a foreigner to get to the heart, the very soul, of her country.

Just as I was about to wonder about her judgment, though, she took me, as ever, by surprise. 'But I not want visit this man's house in London,' she went on. 'On stage, I look him, very easy, very fun. But in his life, I not want talk. I think he not remember me. Maybe he never read book. He not know my name. But not important. I always keep him in my heart.' The quintessential Japanese balance, I thought: to surrender all of yourself to an illusion, and yet somewhere, in some part of yourself, to know all the while that it is an illusion.

Meanwhile, Sachiko was meandering again into an account of her life and telling me about her fear of the sea, and how a carp would suddenly bob up and pull her down, down into its mysterious depths, where it was bottomless and dark. The sky was all right, she said, because it could not exert such a pull on her, and the jungle was OK, though she feared its central darkness. She told me, too, how Madonna was traveling with a fourteen-year-old boy, because of her conviction that in an earlier life, she had been a boy who died at fourteen.

'Madonna is like an elephant,' I said facetiously.

'Very different,' she answered quietly, and grave.

'She jaguar. Very beautiful, very dangerous, man-eating jaguar.'

I, for my part, told her about malls in California, and Valley Girls, about gay waiters, and husbands who did the cooking. All this she seemed to find remarkable. 'Why? Whattt? True??' I told her that trains were not invariably on time in America, and she could not even digest this kind of aberration. 'Why? How? Not possible, I think.' 'Well,' I began, Reaganesque in my evasions, 'sometimes they are broken.' 'Really? *Hontō ni*? Why? How possible?' 'Well, maybe it is an old train and not perfect.' 'Why? How?' She frowned uncertainty back at me. 'I not understand!'

Later, as the afternoon went on, I taught her some new words – 'clever', 'bright', and 'precious'. 'Thank you for a precious day,' she dutifully sang back to me. And when the sun got ready to set, I could see the sadness in her eyes. 'This day,' she said slowly as we took our seats on the train, 'I open door of heart. Then put memory inside. Then close.'

'Like a safety box?'

She nodded sadly. 'Safe box. And when I have "myself time", then I open and look.'

She paused again, falling silent as we drew towards Kyoto. 'Sometimes I want wing, fly away.'

'For a day or two?'

Nodding solemnly, she smiled in shame.

Meanwhile, my occasional dabbling in Zen straggled on. Often, I asked Mark directly about the Zen experience, but more often he gave me glimpses of it when I did not ask. Left to his own devices, he rarely seemed to talk about either his painting or his training. There was, in a sense, no seam in him: cut him in any place, and he was the same. His doctrine was his being as surely as his being was his doctrine.

When I asked him about this reticence one day, he said quietly, 'That's my teacher. He believes that the first thing you must do is get yourself together as a person. The painting's really just an act of discovery; it's so direct that it becomes a way of seeing yourself. So, in *sumi-e*, there's really no difference between the state of your mind and the state of your art. My teacher, for example, has two altars in his house – one devoted to Shibayama and one to Bashō: the abbot and the artist. And he has his own temple on Awajishima. But for him, I think, his painting is a form of meditation.' He fell silent. 'Usually, I wouldn't use that kind of word around foreigners, because they haven't got a very deep sense of meditation. They think it just means mindlessness, emptying out.'

'Whereas in fact it means mindfulness?'

'Yeah. And emptying out, but with awareness. It's hard to understand unless you've done some sitting. Some of these guys, they're just incredible. I remember one group of monks that did *zazen* for forty-nine straight days after their head monk died. I was amazed, but when I thought about it, it really wasn't so strange. Their teacher just believed that *zazen* was the only truth and that was the way to go.'

In *sumi-e*, he said, as in haiku or in any Zen training, the aim was to develop a discipline so sure and a spirit so true that one could afford to be utterly spontaneous; to get into such a state of deliberateness that as soon as one put pen to paper, one would produce something powerful and true (like Shakespeare, perhaps, never blotting a line). Thus a *sumi-e* painting should be quick and direct as an ax cutting wood (akin, I thought, to Shelley's definition of poetry as 'a sword of lightning, ever unsheathed'). Instantaneous in its execution, a *sumi-e* painting should catch the moment before it fled; and let the moment speak, unclouded by hesitations or revisions. And though this sounded strange to me at first, I recalled how, whenever I had tried to record dreams, I had had to transcribe the instant before the moment fled, without thinking or even realizing I was writing. If I waited even a minute, the mood was gone and the images would fade; if I waited any longer, it would soon be impossible even to remember that I had ever had a dream.

The most eloquent aspect of Mark's explanation, though, was simply his example; he lived Zen a good deal more than he talked about it – indeed, one sign of this was that he spoke very little at all, and then only with a slow, and prudent, settledness. And whether this was the cause of his feeling for Japan, or its effect – or, more likely, both – he seemed to know exactly where he stood, and so had found the self and life he wanted.

As I read deeper in the Zen poets, I soon stumbled upon Ikkyū, the fifteenth-century sword-wielding monk of Daitokuji, who had entered a temple at the age of six and gone on to express his contempt for the corrupt monasteries of his time in famously controversial poems. Like the Sixth Dalai Lama, in his way, Ikkyū had been a patron – and a laureate – of the local taverns, and of the pretty girls he had found therein; and like his Tibetan counterpart, or John Donne in our own tradition, he had deliberately conflated the terms of earthly love with those of devotion to the Absolute. The very name he gave himself, 'Crazy Cloud', had played subversively on the fact that 'cloud water' was a traditional term for monks, who wandered without trace, yet 'cloud rain' was a conventional idiom for the act of love. His image of the 'red thread' ran through the austere surroundings of his poems as shockingly as the scarlet peonies of Akiko. And in his refusal to kowtow to convention, the maverick monk had turned every certainty on its head: whores, he said, could be like ideal monks – since they inhabited the ideal Zen state of 'no mind' – while monks, in selling themselves for gold brocade, were scarcely different from whores. Many of his verses trembled with this ambiguity. One couplet, taken one way, was translated as 'Making distinctions between good and evil, the monk's skill lies in knowing the essential condition of the Buddha and the Devil'; taken another way, it meant: 'That girl is no good, this one will do; the monk's skill is in having the appetite of a devilish Buddha.'

So the Zen practice of dissolving all distinctions was taken to its most unsettling extreme in Ikkyū's 'wild fox' Zen, and the lingering sense that Zen addressed every problem except that of men and women was confounded by the unorthodox monk who explicitly sang of his love for girls, and their private places:

A beautiful woman, cloud-rain, love's deep river.
Up in the pavilion, the girl and the old monk sing.
I find inspiration in embraces and kisses;
I don't feel at all that I'm casting my body in flames.

A couple of days later, she called my guesthouse again, beginning, as ever, with phrasebook propriety – 'Hello, my name is Sachiko Morishita' – and then, almost instantly, leaping into a tone of whispered intimacy, her voice, as ever, like that of an awestruck worshiper. 'Today I write poem about wind. I much like wind. Very free feeling. When I children size, I every day talking wind. Now too. Last night,' she went on softly, with her air of explorer's wonder, 'I little wake up four o'clock. I want see star.'

In response, I began to tell her about the light nights I had seen just a few months earlier in Iceland, and she replied that she knew this *thema* very well and, in fact, that she had seen the movie *White Nights* and it had changed her life. 'I see this movie, I much much love. Much cry. Then I see Mikhail Baryshnikov, Osaka Festival Hall. *Giselle*. First time ballet. No words, only music – but verrry beautiful. I more more cry. Then I see Gregory Hines, Osaka Kintetsu Hall. I have best seat, I shake hand. After, I take Yuki classical ballet class. Before, she three years old, she learn modern dance; now, two month ago, she start classical ballet. So' – she giggled sweetly – 'this movie little change Yuki life.'

All this brought home to me again how strongly the quaint Victorian notion of feminine accomplishments still held in Japan, and perhaps especially in Kyoto, and how often women here still seemed to belong in some polite and proper Austen drawing room. Here was a fairly typical young woman – a normal, middle-class woman of limited means and opportunities – who routinely drew, wrote poems, made kimono, painted watercolors, played the koto, sang foreign folksongs with guitar, could hammer out a couple of melodies on the piano, played the banjo, was an expert at aerobics, knew *kendō* and kung fu, and was mistress of all the other traditional arts – serving tea and sewing, acupuncture and *ikebana*; her five-year-old daughter, no less typical, was already cultivating Chopin on the piano and learning to dance *Giselle*. And as in an Austen world, women lived so much in the parlor that even the slightest encounter with the world outside had the capacity to thrill or shock.

The next thing I knew, though, Gregory Hines had set her off on other tangents, and she was asking me what I thought of the movie *Soul Man*. After I gave a suitably evasive reply, she said, abruptly, 'Sometimes, I think, we talk telepathy.'

164

'Telepathy?'

'Sometimes I alone, I talking you, and then I hear you talking. Please we always have telepathy?'

'Sure,' I said, though, as ever, I had not a clue to what I was assenting.

'Please you wait,' she said, and a few seconds later, I heard a music-box lullaby over the phone. Then her soft sigh. 'Usually, this style, many time, I think not good.'

'I understand,' I said, though really I didn't.

'Usually not so fun.'

'That's OK,' I assured her, assuming that she was trying to keep me at a distance. I could imagine the strain of trying to shuttle between lives, across a gap as wide as the Pacific.

'Now sun set, and I together children. Very different life. Big heart control, little difficult.' I took this at first to mean 'damage control', as it did, but then I saw that she meant something more.

'This year,' she went on, 'autumn more more beautiful. But I look leave, then I think, next year, you gone.'

That night, I had a whole series of bad dreams: that someone was advancing on me with a gun, that I felt a paralyzing chill, which stopped me from moving, that I was looking for a man called Wisdom but stumbled on to Wimbledon instead. All night the dreams spun on, about oversleeping, about missing something, about threat.

Fifteen

And just as it is common to hear how, when one is in love, anything one sees reminds one of that love – our feelings remake the world in a secular equivalent of the faith that sees the hand of God in everything – so I began to find that when one is thinking on a theme, everything seems to reflect on it. Suddenly, everything I saw or read, in this girlish city of temples, seemed to take me back to the theme of the lady and the monk.

When Sachiko gave me a translation of Inoue Yasushi's *Roof Tile of Tempyō* to answer some of my questions about the spread of Buddhism to Japan, I found myself again inside the same struggle, of doing and being, and the same question, of whether the products of a life could be its absolution. Inoue was no more analytical than any other Japanese writer, and his pale, ink-wash style refused to deviate from narrative. Yet still, with its tale of Japanese monks devoting their lives to protecting and transcribing Buddhist scripture, his story set up an array of troubling questions. What avails monastic aspirations when, as Mark had said, religious geniuses were born and not made? Could not renouncing the world be a form of self-indulgence? Was not monasticism, in the end, as much an act of cowardice as courage?

Then I picked up a copy of *The Slave* by Singer, and again the theme that impressed itself on me was the same. As the hero, Jacob, tried and tried to parse the Song of Songs, to unriddle the relation of spirit and sense, and the presence of murderers and whores in a God-created world, he was tugged at by Lilith, who was, in some sense, a Polish version of a *tanuki*, going abroad at night to lure men to their doom. In the end, Singer concluded, 'everything comes from God – including lust'. There was a point to everything, and everything justified itself; we could doubt it, or fail to understand it, but still it continued to exist, indifferent to our uncertainty, and we could do nothing but accept it.

I was just musing on these issues – the lady at the temple gates – when I met a former monk called Rick, and when I talked to Rick, the image became even more poignant simply because Rick was so clearly torn by it, and living with its legacy. Rick's story, as Mark had explained it to me, was at once remarkable and perhaps archetypal. Trained as a conservatory student at Oberlin, he had suddenly abandoned family and career and come to Kyoto to serve as a monk. For seven years he had lived in Daitokuji – Ikkyū's temple – together with his best friend, Ray. But like his meditation mate, he had never managed entirely to break with the world, and like Ray, he had often stolen out at night to visit a girl. And when his girlfriend had borne him a baby – as had happened to Ikkyū's principal disciple – Rick had felt obliged to quit the temple to join her. With nothing in his hands, he had walked out of the place and across town to where his girlfriend lived, together with his nine-month-old daughter. But the temple, of course, had prepared him for everything except living with a woman, and soon thereafter they had ended up having terrible, screaming, plate-throwing fights. Finally, he had left her – only to find himself totally isolated: his girl, now his wife, enraged that he had left her as a fallen woman, in charge, moreover, of a half-caste child; the monastic community outraged at his defection; and all the foreign community gathered in one clucking chorus to condemn a man – a monk, no less – for seducing a Japanese lady and then abandoning her. The final, implausible climax had come when Rick's wife and his abbot had actually joined together in their disapproval and, bound tight by a common adversary, had become partners of a sort. Rick, meanwhile, had fled to Kobe, and then to a run-down hotel in New York City, and at last to San Francisco.

When I met him, Rick, now working for a computer company in the Bay Area, was returning, on a business trip, to the city he had left in disgrace seven years before. As we drove through the country lanes, the mountains sharp in winter light, he simply kept repeating, *'Natsukashii!'* (It's nostalgic), and I could sense that it was too intense and charged a homecoming for him to begin to articulate.

We went to an Indian restaurant in the countryside – I was no longer surprised to find so many Japanese hippies here, or so many of them experts in reproducing the subcontinent – and as we sat, drinking *chai* and munching hot cashews while an Indian woman sang *ghazals* on the sound system and people drifted in and out of the red-and-yellow mirrored curtains, I was almost mesmerized by Rick's quiet intensity. He was always right there, this short fellow with the bald egghead and the shambling simian gait, now in his late thirties: his eyes arresting, his voice softly purring, all of him buzzing with a quiet fire. Even here, talking in a disheveled restaurant about the tricks of self-presentation, he blazed.

Rick was full of good stories about his years in the monastery: about sitting for ten days before the temple gates in order to gain admission; about covering his face with a wicker hat and going on his daily rounds of begging through the red-light area (where his American friend from Stanford was living, as the first non-Japanese geisha); about learning to sweep the maple leaves into a circle, because Zen teachers believed that if you could sweep them into a perfect circle, without bending down, it meant that your mind was as whole and fluid as a circle. And though this sounded strange to me, I could understand the way Zen worked by thinking of the calm I sometimes felt in washing dishes, and the pleasure of seeing a once filthy plate shine.

'Growing up in Ohio must have hardened you a little to the Kyoto winter.'

'Shit, no,' he replied. 'Not in the monastery. I had to stand out there in the cold, before dawn, in bare feet, shivering. It's hard, man; you don't know how hard it is. In summer, you sweat; in winter, you shiver. Every day in the monastery you're facing some kind of pain. And those old monks are killers, man; they really whack you with those sticks!'

'What took you to the monastery?'

'Well, I was learning to be a professional trumpet player. And then I began reading some books on Zen. And one day, on acid, I read Daisetz Suzuki to see how it measured up, and it was an awesome experience – a kind of awakening, almost – and it reminded me of that line from the mystic Heinrich Suso: "I felt like a vase that had contained a precious ointment and now all that remained was the perfume." So I sold all my trumpets and stuff, and came over. Went into training for the monastery.

'After I left the place, I found this amazingly elegant woman in Kobe. But her father was really uptight, hired a private detective and shit to follow me everywhere. So I went back home and became an interpreter in the Catskills' – the Catskills! – 'working

169

with this monk, a Living National Treasure, who had unified an entire sect of Zen for the first time in its history, and then, just as suddenly, left the temple. He just stripped his robes and spent three years going from temple to temple, challenging monks with koans and then, when he beat them at their own game, stripping them of their robes, and tearing them up to be used as diapers.'

Later, we sat around Mark's low table, under the bamboo lantern, and Rick played the *shakuhachi* bamboo flute – Ikkyū's instrument – with a kind of piercing intensity that sounded like the voice of Zen itself.

The next night, we went to a party together, and it turned out that the host, a complete stranger, was someone with whom Rick had shared a writing class in Vermont many years before – someone, indeed, who had come to Kyoto largely as a result of hearing Rick's haunted memories of temple life. As the evening wore on, the former monk took to washing dishes, and again I saw his spotlessness and the simple severity of his monastic discipline. Later, when we walked out into the street and piled into a cab, Rick began talking again, hypnotically. 'I'm thirty-nine now, but I really feel as young as ever. Shit – God, I don't know why I'm using that word so much; must be because I'm near the monastery again. Anyway, I feel all my life is ahead of me. Sure, I feel more aches and pains than I did fifteen years ago, but basically I feel as young as ever. There's this guy called Stephen Chang, a doctor in law, in medicine, from Chinese universities, master of tai chi, acupuncture, all this stuff, and he has this book called *The Tao of Sex*. In the West, you see, we've got all fixated on the orgasm. Usually, you go for that, and, bang, it's over – with the woman usually not quite satisfied and the man totally exhausted.' What was this ex-monk talking about? 'But this thing is all about conserving male seed, male energy. So you don't bother about orgasm but use this energy for higher things, send it to the sixth *chakra* or wherever.'

'And you've been using this?' The taxi was whizzing past pachinko parlors, video arcades, coffee shops – all the high gloss of a Kyoto winter night. And the former monk, as taut as a violin string, kept talking about girls.

The very next day, I experienced a strange kind of inversion of my encounter with Rick when I met a group of foreigners at a Thanksgiving party. None of them had any connection with Zen, yet for all of them, everything they did, it seemed, was a meditation. I talked to a flighty California girl who worked in collage. 'For me, tea is a kind of meditation.' Beside her sat her husband, a bearded Bay Area writer. 'Yeah, the thing about kite flying is, it's a sort of meditation.' Even as the Zen monk was mastering the tongue of Don Juan, these wanderers seemed to be talking the language of Zen.

'I've been studying tea for three years,' the woman went on. 'See, the thing about it is that it combines calligraphy, lacquerwork, scrolls, flower arranging, all the rules about bowing and manners. So everything's right there; tea's like a compilation of all the Japanese arts.'

'But to a typically uninitiated viewer, it's a little hard to see the subtleties.'

'Sure, but they're *incredible*. Believe me, they are *amazing*. Like, in pouring the tea, you've got to curl your finger into this exact shape' – she curved it prettily – 'which is meant to be the exact shape of the moon two days after it's new. No way you can do the second-day moon, no way you can do the fourth.

You've got to make it the third. And there's a different tea, not just for every season and every month, but for every week! So you have to have this amazing concentration – like aikido too.'

'Do you enjoy it?'

'Yeah. But I kind of think it's time to quit. The truth is, the longer you do it, the more you see what you're supposed to be doing. You get more self-conscious, more uptight – more Japanese, I guess. I remember one day I had been doing tea for two hours, and then I was arranging a flower, while looking out a window. Nobody could see me. Nobody! But this lady came up to me and told me I was sitting wrong. I felt like saying to her, "Fuck it! Who cares how I'm sitting if nobody's here?" But you can't do that. So I had to sit the right way, and there's no way I can sit the wrong way again. I've got to be self-conscious even when I'm fucking sitting down! When I first came here, I was just like this kind of happy idiot, stumbling over everything: a real bull in a china shop. But the more sensitive I became to the Japanese, the more self-conscious I had to become. I think I'm burned out.'

Another person at the party, a quiet-minded teacher who had lived for years as an editor in San Francisco, tried to explain to me what had drawn him here. 'All my friends in the Bay Area thought I was completely crazy. "What do you know about Kyoto?" they kept saying. "What makes you want to go there?" "I dunno," I'd say. And I'd look in the papers and see things like "Moon Viewing in Oakland Botanical Gardens", and I'd go along to that, and my friends would say, "Why? How come? What's the point?" And I'd go, "I dunno." It's just like this mountain I kept on seeing, and I had to go there. So then I came. I gave myself a year to stay, with an option on another year. And I knew nothing about the place – *nothing* – when I came over; I thought it was just a small town.

'I got a job teaching at a university, and there was this girl who worked in the office there. Anyway, one day, she sent me a card about a play I had produced. I went back to California for ten weeks. And when I came back, I just answered her card. That was in April. In May, we went on a date. In October, we began living together. By February, we were married. Now she's expecting. It was just one of those things, you know – I thought I was going to leave after one year, and there was this girl saying "You're not going to leave." Now, of course, I think that *she* was the mountain I had been seeing all that time.'

Two days later, Mark and I went for Thanksgiving dinner to his friend Etsuko's house, a fairy-tale mansion in the Japanese context, its intercom-activated gate leading into a garden softly lit with lanterns, its large wooden doors giving on to an exquisitely appointed living room – a museum in miniature – lined with Chinese scrolls and ancient Javanese puppets and books about the art world, in Japanese and English. Bach was floating through the room on a Deutsche Grammophon compact disc, and for appetizers, our hostess placed before us a couple of almond and horseradish wafers.

Etsuko's situation was more or less typical, so it seemed. Her husband lived in Tokyo, roughly three hundred miles away, and she saw him only occasionally, on weekends, if at all (in all the years he'd known her, Mark had talked to her husband only once, very briefly, on the phone). She, meanwhile, devoted most of her energy to raising her teenage daughter. But what time and attention she had left over, she threw into a flurry of activities, setting up charitable organizations, helping to run an English-language magazine for visitors, representing her husband's family at social ceremonies and conferences, and, for the most part, running intercultural institutions aimed at introducing Japan to foreigners and vice versa. Having spent almost half her life abroad, she sought now to act as a kind of ambassador from each world to the other, trying to repair diplomatic relations which were always frail as china.

Serving us the sweetest grapefruit juice I had ever tasted, in cut-glass tumblers, she patiently fielded my questions, explaining how the Japanese had different colors for each wind, as well as for every season, telling me the different words for moonlight on the water, spelling out the name of the insect that was virtually synonymous with dusk. Many of these words, she explained, were suffused with a sense of nostalgia, harking back to the age of Asuka and the versatile Nukata no Okimi, once Empress of Japan; and only then did I realize that on the day Sachiko had taken me to Asuka, she had in fact been introducing me to a woman's sanctuary, a private, forgotten place charged with the memory of this famous poetess.

Then, with a graceful bow, Etsuko ushered us into her dining room, ringed with beautifully arranged blue cups and a gallery of china plates. She served up chrysanthemums in tiny blue bowls, and fine, rare mushrooms; then, in honor of the day, a huge Thanksgiving turkey; and then, for dessert, sustaining the seasonal motif, a delicate sweet shaped like a chrysanthemum. Over tea — made from a host of Fortnum's selections, with a separate china cup to keep the water hot — I learned a little more about this unlikely housewife, professional gerontologist, and former student at Edinburgh, who could speak, without strain, about *quattrocento* churches in Florence, Mozart pieces (identified by Köchel number), and the early writings of Fosco Maraini. She was going to Tuscany soon, she went on, to see various chapels whose art reminded her of a certain style of Chinese painting – 'blasphemous though that doubtless is.' She spoke, in French, of her studies at the Sorbonne, of the three years she had spent in Kathmandu, of Keats's 'Ode to Autumn'. She described the latest holdings in the Musée d'Orsay. And I, many fathoms out of my depth and amazed to see someone move in this almost Jamesian aura of refinement, realized anew how, whatever role the Japanese played, they played it so well and took it to such a pitch of excellence that one could never wish to see the part played again. A Beatles freak here was a freak to end all freaks, with five hundred albums in his collection; a gardener was a wholehearted purist who gave all his life to developing a single perfect flower; and a woman of culture was so accomplished at her role that she made her counterparts anywhere else seem puny by comparison. The Japanese played themselves as Gielgud, Hamlet.

A few days later, as the month drew to its end, I awoke at dawn to find my window all fogged over: the first hard frost of winter. Longing to share the moment with someone – I had not experienced winter for three years now – I hurried out into the mild invigoration of the morning to visit Mark. It was a joy undiminished to awaken in the cloudless blue and see the mountains sharp in the distance, to feel the briskness of a winter morning in the sun. The whole world felt uplifted and refreshed: the narrow lanes alive with oranges, old women chattering away below the muted sun, and everywhere a sense of purpose.

My only disappointment, I told Mark as I came into his house, was that I would not be able to see the *hatsu-yuki*, or first snowfall of the year. I would be

175

leaving Kyoto the following day, not to return for a month, and I knew that I would miss the winter's first moment of silent transformation.

The next day, my last day in Kyoto, Sachiko came to my room again, bringing with her a book by A. A. Milne and a textbook for an English lesson. I led her up to my tiny space, and there, in the winter dark, I tried to teach her again the words that she might need. We sat on cushions on the tatami, the dark room lit by the glowing orange bar of my single-element heater. Often, in explaining the terms of my own language to her, I felt as if I were explaining them to myself. As I began, slowly, to speak English as a second language, my own tongue came to seem as new to me, and mysterious, as Japanese.

Patiently, sometimes frowning over the words and muttering *'Muzukashii!'* sometimes giggling away the difficulty, she stumbled through a text about fishermen in Holland. When we were through, she looked at me, there was a long silence, and I stood up in the darkening room to make some tea.

As she wandered round the tiny space, inspecting the *gaijin* in his native habitat, I tried to divert her with some questions. I held up a Christmas card. 'Ah, Monet!' she cried. Then a postcard I had bought in a museum. 'Rodin!' Then a paperback I had found downtown, in Sony Plaza. 'Paddington Bear!'

After the kettle had boiled, I put down two mugs on the table and knelt down on the tatami to show her some earrings I had bought for my mother. She leaned forward till her hair was tickling my face. In the winter darkness of the tiny room, the fire glowing, I brushed back her hair, felt her lips touch mine, her body shaking as if electrified.

Later, we walked along the river in the dusk. Turning, we saw the eastern hills, thick with orange trees, glowing in the dying light. Then, sitting down beside the red-lit river, she sang me a melody from *The Sound of Music* – 'Something Good' – about Maria's escape from her abbey, in a quavering, high, but steady voice. 'When I little children size,' she said, 'this song my favorite. But I never think I find this feeling. I think I cannot. I always "lost lady". Now I feel this song more more. Thank you very much.'

There was a long, charged silence on the riverbank. 'Autumn now ending,' she said, as we watched the last light leave the hills. And that night, it snowed.

Winter

Our old older, Our new newer,
Our kind kinder —
Welcome to Japan.

—THE SIGN OF MAKITA POWER
TOOLS, GREETING ARRIVALS
IN OSAKA AIRPORT

One

It was the smells that hit me first: smells of cooking, smells of rotting, smells of people being people – all the smells I had not smelled for months in exquisitely deodorized Japan, where only pleasant fragrances are permitted: the lemon scent of air freshener, the costly glamour of French perfume, an occasional hint of incense. The minute I set foot in Taiwan, I was assaulted by smells, sultry, piquant, and strange: assaulted, too, by spitters and shouters, by offers, importunities, cries of 'Why you no buy? Best price for you!' Waiters dropped plates on my table as if they were hot (which they never were), men whispered, 'Dollar, dollar,' crowds pushed and shoved and squawked. There was the sudden shock of car crashes in the light-dizzy streets, of winking cabbies, of women in blinding pantsuits who caught my eye and held it.

Three days later, landing in Southeast Asia, I felt again, in a rush, all the things I had been missing in Japan, not so much the roughness now as the spiced softness, the seduction of kerosene lamps and unlit back lanes, the lure of night-market meals and clove-scented villages; thronged festivals, black markets, a flash of white smiles among the trees. The whole whirl of tropical sensations hit me like a fever dream: the darkness full of spirits, and whisper-soft girls in off-the-shoulder dresses; the sound of gonged instruments in the night. None of the hard, purposeful austerity of Japan, but stronger, darker forces in the hot tropic air;

181

here again one was in the realm of the subconscious.

My very first night in Thailand, I found myself standing on the Golden Mount, talking about water buffaloes with an irresistible shaven-headed twelve-year-old monk in saffron robes and sandals, as together we watched the full moon rise above the diamond capital; half an hour later, in the midst of crowds, I was being befriended by two sidelong-glancing, strangely affable transsexuals. Even the Japanese department stores here, all video smarts and squeaky-clean announcements, were lit up from within by a blast of Thai warmth and laughing dishevelment; and even aseptic Singapore, an aspirant Japan, seemed ripe with the promise of adventure, a veritable Marrakesh after Kyoto, with its unkempt bands of ricksha men, shirts cracked open to their hairless chests, and sharp-faced, lipsticked hookers, brazen in their scarlet shirts. Suddenly, the imagination was given something rough to chew on, a world unedited.

At times, of course, I grew so enamored of my thesis that everything confirmed it; how dowdy were the Chinese, I thought, looking at a group of revelers, gawking clumsily, in my Taipei hotel; how different from the elegant self-possession of the Japanese. And then the people began to speak, and their language – of course – was Japanese.

Yet still, I had hardly left Japan before I could better see how the Japanese regard all the world outside as barbarous and crude, undeveloped in every sense of the word, and terrifying too. So sheltered had my life become in Kyoto – so sanitized of danger or alarm – that I had all but forgotten that another world existed; and now it was a shock to enter a stage where tempers were lost, things went wrong, the surface snapped. And if even I felt this, after only ten weeks in Japan, how much more unnerved must a Japanese be, suddenly propelled out of his cozy home and into a world of disruption and threat. Mother Japan prepared its children only, and ideally, for Japan.

Coming from Kyoto – quasi-Japanese myself now – I found myself at sea abroad, forgetting to leave tips, reluctant to jaywalk across empty streets, recoiling like a child whenever men approached me on the streets with offers of hotels. I stood outside taxicabs, waiting for their doors to open automatically, and then, once inside, fell into broken conversations – how many children do you have, how many hours do you work? – in Japanese. When once, returning home, I put my shoes on inside my room, I felt as surreptitious, as sacrilegious almost, as if I had worn a Walkman into church.

Abroad, as unguarded as a Japanese now, I left my things unattended and my room unlocked, and wandered round with $170 in my pocket (Japan was, perhaps, curing me a little of materialism, though not in the way expected). Whenever I bumped into someone in the street, I said, reflexively, '*Sumimasen*,' and when I returned to California, I startled teenage shopgirls with my earnest *Sō, so, sō*s. On my way home from Los Angeles Airport, a Mexican in a gas station rushed up to me in relief – a compatriot, so he thought – and pressed me in Spanish for details on the way to Calexico. '*Hai, hai*' – I nodded briskly – '*Demo kochira wa . . .*' and looked back to see the poor man terrified.

After Japan, even Harrods looked a little declassé, and when I bought a cup of tea at the Singapore Hilton for $2.20, I could not believe the bargain. I was Japanese enough now to shiver when I saw a man kiss his girlfriend in a Bangkok restaurant. And at home, in California, I felt Japanese enough to appreciate, for the first time ever, the lavender blush of hibiscus in the mild December days and the piercing clarity of Venus in the denim sky. Japanese too, I could see now, for the first time ever, the true beauties of California: long hours and long horizons.

But I felt a little closer to Japan now in some deeper sense as well, in affiliation as well as habit. Whenever I saw groups of JAL-packaged tourists being herded through the Grand Palace in Bangkok, or pairs of frightened-looking girls in khaki shorts, deep in sidewalk negotiations with some local con man, I felt, mysteriously, a pang of sympathy and kinship; abroad, the Japanese looked so lost to the world, so far from the reassurances to which they were accustomed. They looked to me as vulnerable as shy teenagers alone, in a corner, at their first real cocktail party – not just afraid and disoriented, but anxious to combat self-pity. And whenever foreigners fell into the usual litany ('But the Japanese are so strange, so neurotic, so hard to get close to'), I found myself rushing to their defense: 'But they're so innocent, so thoughtful, and so kind.' Taken on any terms other than their own, the Japanese did, to be sure, seem tough negotiators, industrial spies, and torturers of whales, playing life to win; but now I was able to see them a little more from the other side, in terms of which everything they did made perfect sense and the world they produced was hard to improve upon. In a sense, in fact, it was that very perfection that removed them further from the world at large (as a concert pianist has that much less in common with a garage band) and made the world at large seem that much more menacing and dark. Watching the Japanese circling around Asia in a kind of see-no-evil, speak-no-evil, hear-no-evil spell, taking in everything with polite enthusiasm, screening out disease and dirt

184

– exemplary guests as well as hosts, as good at receiving pleasure as at giving it – my heart went out to a culture bound, and perhaps determined, to be misunderstood.

Abroad, in fact, it was even clearer that Japan was taking over the role of America in the fifties. In Japan itself, it was easy to see its affinities with the Eisenhower era, in its nuclear families with their clean suburban homes, placid and a touch complacent; its identically dressed commuters on their trains, men in gray flannel suits dreaming of golfing holidays; its almost science fictive world of gadgets and consumer goods and a conformity so absolute that it gave rise to the intertwined notions of the affluent society, the organization man, and the lonely crowd (and, in response, of Ginsberg howling poems in Kyoto streets). Abroad, however, the likenesses were even easier to see. For with the dawning of the Japanese Empire, the 'Ugly American' of thirty years ago was fast being replaced by a new focus for the world's envies and fears. Now it was the Japanese who were traveling around the globe in groups, like conquering armies on the march, dressed in Hawaiian shirts and Bermuda shorts, cameras slung around their necks, marveling at how everything was smaller – and better – at home. Now it was Japan that seemed the role model – and the hated archrival – of many developing countries, even such unforgiving former colonies as Korea. Now it was Japan, indeed, that seemed the Land of Opportunity, and to Japan that foreigners came in search of new lives for themselves, and new identities, in a land of promise and abundance – in search, in fact, of the American Dream. And now it was America that seemed the funky, disorganized, low-budget slice of exotica that the Japanese delighted in inspecting whenever they wanted a taste of primitive wildness.

Whenever I visited expensive hotels (or expensive countries, like Bhutan), nearly all the tourists I saw were groups of wealthy, retired Westerners and youthful Japanese. It seemed a natural pairing.

It was only when I returned to the world at large, moreover, that I realized how far away I had been in Kyoto. It was not just that Japan occupied a different kind of universe, which rarely made contact with our own; but, more, that this island was – by choice as much as circumstance – psychically as well as physically removed from the world at large. The analogy here was not so much with Gulliver as with Alice; in Japan, one felt as if the world had been turned upside down and inside out, all its values and assumptions turned on their heads – as if, one might say, the force of gravity had been so radically altered that one had ended up on another planet. It sometimes seemed – and Japan liked to make it seem – as if Japan had a different epicenter from the rest of the world, as if, indeed, all the rest of the world inhabited a Copernican, and Japan a Ptolemaic, universe; and so, where much of the rest of the world traditionally looked to America as its center, Japan looked only to Japan. America might be a fashion accessory, a collectible, a sign of imported glamour; but it was not the end-point of most aspirations here. America was an alternative to Gucci, not to Bushidō or Emperor-worship or Japan.

Besides, Japan's strength was only growing as America's declined. It was morning in America, but in most parts of Asia, especially in Tokyo, it was already the next evening. And the notion of a Japanese take-over was gaining an almost literal significance as the Japanese bought up hotels and companies and entire downtowns; the sluggers of the major leagues, the diamonds of Tiffany's, the canvases of Van Gogh. Even

Monet's 'Soleil Levant' had been spirited away, by *yakuza*, or gangsters, to Japan (the Rising Sun itself was going East). Meanwhile, all the news from America was bad: AIDS, crack, Irangate; an aging president, a collapsed economy, a clergy double-crossing itself with scandal. And my sense that America was beginning to look more and more like an underdeveloped country next to Japan was only eerily confirmed when, my first night back in California, a thunderstorm began to shake my hillside house, rattling the windows and pounding the walls all night, like the ghost of a monsoon, until, of a sudden, we were plunged into darkness, powerless for twenty hours while the wind howled all about.

Ambushing Japan from afar, I was better able to see what I liked about it. Bangkok, for example, bustling by day and dazzling by night, alive to business and to pleasure, struck me as the ultimate urban intoxication; yet it also seemed to encourage the abandoning of vision for mere fantasy. It was hard to imagine reading there, or thinking, or leading any kind of life that would engage the deepest part of one. The place invited one to surrender to reality, not to lead a life so much as to be led by one. And where people came to Japan, very often, to pursue something, they came to Bangkok – or Bali, or Sri Lanka, I suspected – not to do so. Thus spicy, sultry, vivacious Bangkok sent me back with renewed affection for Japan. Thailand, I thought, was the girl at the edge of the temple, beckoning one away with a smile.

Two

I had not even set foot in Kyoto on my way back to
Japan before enlightenment and seduction – and the
intertwining of the two – were all about me once again.
On the plane back from L.A., I found myself next to a
glamorous young Korean who was all fluttered
eyelashes and whispered invitations, until I exposed
her, in midflight, as a Mormon practicing her mission-
ary positions. And when the plane got stranded in
Seoul, I found myself sharing a room with a tree
planter from Sonoma County, who was, he said, on his
way to India to spend twelve hours a day, for one
hundred eighty days, meditating in a cell. I said hello
to him, and he raised his hands in prayer and said, 'I'm
so grateful to meet you, sir'; the airline representative
gave us vouchers for our breakfasts, and he said, 'I'm
so very grateful for your gift, ma'am.' I asked him how
his flight had been, and he smiled, beatific. 'At first,' he
began, 'I couldn't sleep because I was next to these two
kids, and they were crying. It was beautiful that they
had to cry' – he smiled forgivingly again – 'but it made
it kind of hard to sleep.' Then he addressed his
spiritual life. 'I used to be into this guru thing,
Rajneesh and all that stuff. But I suffered a lot of
alienation. Now I just want to find this quietness inside
of me, and be of service to humanity. After a while,
you know, when you're meditating, you just get into
this state, and all your sexual energy disappears.' A fit
antidote to Rajneesh, I surmised.

'Sure,' he said, looking out upon the sleek neon blocks of Seoul. 'Meditation and relationships – those are the ways to do it, I guess.' He thought a little more. 'Relationships, I guess, are the fastest way.'

That night, I had strange dreams of Kyoto: of huge boulevards and people sitting in the streets; of standing on large intersections late at night, not knowing where I was, and groups of Japanese terrifying me in their clowns' costumes, painted red faces dreamlike in the dark.

My first night back in Kyoto, the city was indeed a dream to me again, as I wandered through its dizzy streets, in and out of waving crowds, past megaphone voices and floodlit stalls, a fairy world of Pierrot faces. A surge of kimonos everywhere, streaming through the reeling lanes, in and out of noodle stalls, snapping up octopus pancakes and New Year's tofu, features all invisible in the dark, then shockingly lit up by passing lanterns. Shadows gliding through the temple corridors, billowing white banners above their hooded entrances; figures collecting fires from a central roaring blaze; and then, at midnight, the great bronze bell of Chion-in, tolling and tolling in the new Year of the Dragon.

Jet-lagged on New Year's Day itself, I arose before dawn and hurried out into the phantom streets, where the dark blue was beginning to clear above the lowering mountains and silver the city's canals. All the commotion was gone now, and all noise vanished: just unlit lanterns in the street, deserted stalls, silence and debris. A few students observing the year's first sunrise; a girl in blue kimono and white stole, hugging herself in the dawn, condensation escaping like a whisper from her lips.

Inside the Heian Shrine, the new world was just beginning to stir. White-robed priests in conical black hats stood under orange pillars, ceremonious in the cold-breath morning. A gray-suited man bowed before an altar, the young light shining off the polished wood around him. A flock of white priests, unearthly in the early light, shuffled in slow processional along the corridors, sticks of incense held in front of them. Smoke rising off the dying fires like communal breath in the dawn.

Later, very slowly, the open courtyard began to fill up, patient as a painter's canvas: women in flowered kimono, snow-white fur stoles around pale necks, clopping on wooden clogs across the sunlit gravel, the sun spreading warmth across the yawning space; worshipers tossing coins into boxes, clapping their hands and, eyes closed, murmuring the year's first prayers; then receding again into the day's perfection. In the shining winter light, families took up positions on low wooden tables spread with indigo and scarlet cloths; lovers lingered round sun-dappled streams; pedigree ladies led pedigree cats in warm leather jackets across the shrine. A gong, slow and solemn, tolled and tolled, and little girls with flowers in their hair joined hands with beaming fathers in flowing black kimono.

Walking home, through the sun, flowers placed on doorsteps and futons draped over balconies, I felt as if I had landed in some matter-of-fact utopia. The high cries of children playing hopscotch in the lane. Householders polishing their bikes in the quiet sun, unloading furniture from houses, silently hosing cars. The rites of everyday life polished till they shone like glass. In Kyoto, every day felt like New Year's Day, so deft were the Japanese at remaking themselves each day. For a foreigner at least, able to enjoy all the conveniences of

190

this world without having to pay the price in terms of obligation, there was a sense of airy weightlessness to life here that seemed to suspend harsh realities. Coming back to the sharpened air of Kyoto after a few weeks away, I felt as clean as a small town after heavy rains subside.

Later that morning, New Year's cards were hand-delivered to everyone in the land, and I found myself with a bouquet of lyric offerings: from Sachiko, a pretty snowdrop, inscribed with her own calligraphy, above a printed message that said, 'She has a floral word meaning "a solace"'; from the Buddhist priest who had taught me executive's Japanese in California, a hand-drawn cartoon of two happy alligators, one bestriding a pair of scales, the other cradling a baby, a soccer ball between them, and the greeting 'Happy Rew Year' (*rew* – or, more properly, *ryū* – means 'dragon'); from Mark, a *sumi-e* dragon, all Buddhist power and coiled strength; and from an American businessman in Tokyo, a photograph of himself.

A letter had also arrived from Nagoya, home to no-one I knew, and when I tore it open, I found a long and penetrating inquiry from one of the giggling girls with whom I had shared breakfast at the temple in my first days in Kyoto, asking me whether I thought the Japanese were superficial.

Next day, I awoke at first light and buried myself again in Ryōkan, reserving his words for moments when the morning was new and the early light gilded the houses of my lane, painting gold stripes across the corrugated iron. Later, after the day was smudged, and encumbered with emotion, it was never quite so easy to retreat into his silent hut within the woods. Now, on a cloudless, high, and Zen-blue morning, I drank strong tea and read through the old monk's verses, while Van Morrison sang 'She Gave Me Religion' in the Quaker's room next door.

That afternoon, as the New Year's holiday went on, I made my ritual visit to Sachiko's home in Peach Tree Mountain. She greeted me at the door in soft-lined winter kimono, orange with the delicate outline of plum blossoms, a red ribbon wound around her tied-up hair, and snow-white, split-toed socks around her feet. Motioning me to her couch, she served New Year's cakes, made in the temple by her children, then drew out an antique koto from its cover and played a winter melody. I watched her in the quiet afternoon – surrounded by two VCRs, a laser-disc player, a tape deck, a TV, two speakers, and a framed portrait of her children with the abbot of Tōfukuji – bent over her ancient instrument, the winter sun streaming through the wavering curtains at her back.

A little later, Yuki and Hiroshi clambered in to show me their first paintings of the year, and then, taking themselves quietly into a corner, began playing the traditional New Year's game of *Hyakunin-Isshū*, a version of Snap that used one hundred classic poems instead of cards. Already, I noticed, they were absorbing, from their mother, the whole standard repertory of Japanese gestures and emotions, the way children in America might be taught the reflexes of 'Please' and 'Thank you'. Yuki in particular, was already as demure as a courtier, handing me gifts with exactly the right intonation of *Hai dōzo!* (the equivalent of *Bitte!*), singing back *Arigatō!* to every greeting, sitting entirely upright, and silent, on the train. Already too, I noticed, the children were naming all their animals after TV characters, where we, perhaps, would be likelier to give them names of our own devising (Japanese training in received dreams began early). Then, after handing me New Year's gifts of origami raccoons, the children padded off to bed, and Sachiko shuffled round to serve apple tea, a tiny, antique figure in her small-stepping socks and kimono.

Yawning a little as she pulled out her guitar, I mentioned that it was still 4 a.m. for me, California time, and she, duly solemn, replied, 'Only monk awake time. You California monk, maybe?'

'Maybe,' I replied, thinking how appropriate it sounded: a Californian monk, lay acolyte of indiscipline.

Then, with the air of reverence that attended so many of her movements, she handed over a photo album, a fluffy Pekingese on its cover, a red rose on its head, and the printed message 'URBAN DREAM. Everyone has a precious memory with one's heart. Whether it is a small memory, for you it must be a world of wonderful dream. Place your dream in "Urban Dream".' Inside, mementos of the winter: temples under snow, canals all white, a new world covered and uncovered.

Seeing her at home again, I noticed how much younger she was in English, freed from Japanese assumptions, and able therefore to claim another self, for which her mother tongue seemed to have no terms. 'Why is Mummy waving her hands?' Yuki had cried over dinner. In Japanese, I gathered, Sachiko never spoke with her hands.

Three

Winter made everyone a kind of monk in Japan, bringing out a streak of worldly asceticism that was never far from the surface in this land of spartan epicures. It was not so much that the weather was punishing; indeed, it was cold only indoors. Yet even the affluent here, in the world's most advanced society, lived often, it seemed, in conditions that we would regard as neoprimitive, in miniature, half-furnished houses, with outdoor toilets, and flimsy walls, and an absence of all central heating. Their homes, very often, seemed as scaled down as their hopes.

Again, this suggested to me how public dress here was almost a form of public address. In public, people presented themselves in highly expensive clothes and shiny, late-model, lily-white cars; behind closed doors, they lived like paupers almost. The whole society, it sometimes seemed, schooled its people in denial even as it indulged them – as any parent might – allowing them to believe that they could find any kind of cake or good or service, at any time of day, yet reminding them that they could not hope to gain a more intangible kind of license. And winter seemed to enforce the lesson, bringing a penitential strain to the rites of self-negation.

Even the Emperor, as a boy, had been made to stand out under an ice-cold waterfall, in dead of winter, for fifteen minutes each day, without complaining or even permitting himself a grimace. And even Sachiko, jeans-wearing, Tom Cruise-loving Sachiko, observed her own monastic rites: each day, she told me, in winter or summer, come rain or shine, she got up at dawn and took a shower in freezing-cold water, crying out chants to the gods to ensure good health and fortune for her family.

The more time I spent with Sachiko, as the winter went on, the more ease and lightness we found together. I knew by now the mischievous glint in her eye whenever I teased her about pachinko parlors, and the speeding grace with which she flung her clothes into drawers as rapidly as she tossed her words into English sentences. I knew by heart now her bright smile and her photogenic grin; the way she'd let out a child's cry of delight – *Haitta!* – every time she sank a ball at pool, and the way she'd whisper, a co-conspirator, as she bent down to stroke the cats we met in the temple. I knew by now the way that, after a single glass of cider, she would careen down the street, arms extended like a plane. When I grew sleepy on a train, she sang me traditional Japanese lullabies, and whenever I thanked her, she'd flash back, with a lilting laugh, 'You're welcome!' She made my name new with the inexplicable high softness that she gave to it.

Through Sachiko, I was coming to see more clearly the Japanese way of glee, less famous than their gift for grieving. When I told her one day, after she had been talking and talking, '*Sumimasen. Kekkō desu*' (Thank you very much, I think I've had enough), she burst into peals of such wild laughter at my overformal Japanese that I began laughing too, in embarrassed perplexity. And often, she was so happy that she began, quite literally, to bounce on the soles of her feet. As soon as I began to anatomize her charms, I realized I was falling deeper than I knew.

Usually, though, her main gift was surprise, and

when she visited my room one day in early winter, she
flung open her bag and brought out one wonder after
another: an indigo pot of yellow flowers, wrapped in a
bright yellow ribbon; a guitar that she asked me to
keep and that, unasked, she began to strum, hair
streaming down one side of her face as she belted out
the sad folk songs she'd sung to her dying grandmother; and, finally, a brand-new Walkman. Silently,
as if performing some ceremony, she handed over to
me a second pair of earphones, and once she'd pressed
a pink button, I found myself listening to the gruff,
romantic tones of Georges Moustaki, crooning, '*Ah, je
ne suis jamais seul, avec ma solitude . . .*'

The irony of listening with her to this classic psalm
to solitude was almost too much for me. Sachiko,
though, responded less to its meaning than to its gauzy
atmosphere.

As soon as the song was over, she solemnly took off
the earphones. 'When I little high school size, this song
my favorite.'

'You mean you liked George Moustaki when you
were sixteen?' With Sachiko, I often sounded foolishly
incredulous.

'I like,' she nodded smilingly.

'But he's really obscure. The only people I know
who listen to him are lovesick seventeen-year-old
European girls and English schoolgirls just back from
their first romantic summer on the Continent.'

'Me too. I listen this song, then much, much dream.
When I little high school size, I also many dream. I
dream movie star.' She enunciated the syllables of a
name I could not follow, then burst into a Hindi
melody.

'No! Surely you weren't listening to this stuff too?'

'I listen,' she insisted, adamant. 'True! I many many
picture in my room. Indian movie on TV, one week,

one time! I meet Indian person in my parents' cigarette shop – they come here, Fushimi Inari Shrine. When I junior high school size, I play princess. *Ali Baba and the Forty Thieves!'*

Good Lord, I thought: this girl was more cosmopolitan than Isabelle Adjani. The next thing I knew, her eye had fallen on my copy of *Antony and Cleopatra*, which I was rereading as a handbook to the East, and its ambiguous charms.

'Ah, very beautiful story!'

'You know it?'

'I see movie! Four times! You know Jack Wild?'

'Jack Wild?' I hadn't heard that name in more than a decade. 'You mean the teenage boy who played the Artful Dodger in *Oliver!*?'

'Ping-pong,' she sang back in the happy affirmative of a TV quiz show ('yes' seemed a word of acquiescence more than of affirmation for the Japanese). 'And *Melody* too.' I thought back to a film I had seen when I was fifteen, at the same time I was reading *Narziss and Goldmund*, being serenaded by Georges Moustaki, and losing my heart to Olivia Hussey's Juliet. Somehow, I seemed to have more in common with this Kyoto lady, enjoying the same things at the same time, than with most of my contemporaries in England or California.

'Do many Japanese people like Jack Wild?'

'Many, many like,' she replied. 'I before, Jack Wild Fan Club. I see this man one time in Heian Shrine!'

Egad, I thought, almost ready for anything now, and she bubbled on to express her devotion to Alain Delon and Catherine Deneuve, and her love for Baudelaire. When I asked after Marcello Mastroianni, she nodded with delight.

'What does this mean?' I said, pointing to the red stone in the middle of her comb, with dancing figures all around it.

She sang back the melody of 'Over the Rainbow'. So then we were off on that subject too, exchanging reminiscences of ancient movies, and she was telling me, excitedly, 'When I little children size, only two times my father take me movie. *Hundred One Dog* and *War and Peace*. I much love Audrey Hepburn!' (Everyone in Japan seemed to love Audrey Hepburn, for her Japanese demureness and air of gamine innocence.) In some respects, indeed, Sachiko's tastes were strictly programmed by her culture (nearly all Japanese seemed to have cosmopolitan tastes, but nearly always they were the same tastes: Chopin, Baroque music, the Impressionists; Somerset Maugham, O. Henry, and the Beatles. In that sense, they were all somewhat received tastes, as ours are, no doubt, for Mishima or Itami). But Sachiko, as we kept on talking, often broke the rules: she liked Monet, she said, but preferred Millais; she liked Maugham, but got more out of de Maupassant. She even hotly expressed her love for Hemingway, and Steinbeck's '*Angry Grapes*', as well as his '*Red and Green*' (I could hardly carp, I thought, if she really had read Stendhal). When it came to names at least, and surface responses, there seemed no limit to her range. Trying to find some weakness in her repertoire, I chided her about her indifference to baseball; she promptly assured me that she did indeed like Sadaharu Oh, the foremost star of the Yomiuri Giants, but was not so fond of his celebrated teammate.

'Nagashima very good player,' she pronounced judiciously. 'But I think not so good man. He has child's heart. Little same Mozart!'

'Mozart!' For a moment, I was taken aback by a comparison that seemed to owe more to *Amadeus* than to the shadowed Requiem. Then I recovered. 'But Mozart's childishness was essential to his art; if he hadn't had that kind of heart, he couldn't have produced such sunny music.'

Silently, she accepted this. 'He have many dream. And very beautiful life. You know Jung? This man Jung say dream come true. Then I very happy.'

I clumsily replied that so far as I knew, Jung was addressing the mysteries of the subconscious more than the whimsical daydream of rock fans. And Sachiko, listening to her newly pedantic friend, took it all in philosophically. But still I could feel something in me breaking, and it was the sound of certain illusions about Japan.

When next I met Sachiko, outside a temple one frosty morning, the city all tingling and refreshed, I was terribly worn out; I had hardly slept all night for dreams, the worst of them featuring her (transfigured, by strange dream logic, into a beautiful nineteen-year-old cousin of mine in Delhi) arriving at my room one day to find three half-wanted friends there, all of whom refused to leave. After I recounted the dream to Sachiko, who took such portents seriously – Kyoto women, after all, were famous for listening to their dreams ever since the Heian period, and besides, Sachiko's brother had introduced her to the work of various Jungians – she nodded gravely. 'I much worry this dream,' she said.

Nonetheless, we walked together through lanes bulging with china raccoons, one of them, with impish eyes, dressed in the habit of a nun, and back in my room, I set about helping her through a passage of English, trying to teach her the meanings of 'mischievous' and 'brave' and 'clumsy'.

'I not so good study,' she said, after stumbling repeatedly over 'clumsy'. 'You think my grammar very bad?'

'Not at all.'

'My friend say, she talking phone, foreigner person, her grammar very bad. He not see her, then he think maybe she little black. If I bad grammar, other person think I black?'

'No, no, don't worry,' I reassured her.

Sachiko still looked glum, however, her attitude to English summarized in her furrowed brow.

'I not so like study. I little guilt feeling.'

I looked up, startled.

'Please don't worry,' she said appeasingly. 'Other person teach me this word, "guilt".' She tried it on again for size.

Just then there came a furious knocking at my door. Who on earth could it be, I thought, visiting me at breakfast time on a freezing winter morning? As soon as I opened up, a familiar figure extended a huge smile and a hand. 'Oh, hallo! Awfully good to see you again. Hope I'm not disturbing you. Very good to meet, actually. Very good indeed!' In the last ten years I had seen Matthew only once, and never even heard from him. But now he bundled in as naturally as if he were living down the street.

'Very good timing, actually; awfully nice to see you! Oh, terribly sorry to interrupt,' he said, smiling over at Sachiko, and talking in the speeded-up regimental voice that I remembered so well. 'Had some friends in Italy, actually, kept telling me about this place Kyoto. Then, few days ago, got your Christmas card. Thought it was a sign, perhaps, a karmic hint. Thought maybe I should come over here and try some high seriousness; austerity and all that. Rio, Bangkok, Italy – all terribly fun, of course, but really what's the point? Thought I might come over here, get some Buddhism. Get back on the spiritual track.' He flashed another reassuring smile at Sachiko, and she smiled dumbly back. For as long as I had known him, Matthew had been wandering the globe in search of the perfect place, or the perfect girl, and if ever he found one, he decided he ought to have been looking for the other.

'Very nice city, actually, awfully charming!' he went on, throwing a sheaf of tourist pamphlets on to the tatami and flopping down, with a thump, on a cushion. 'Really think this might be the right place for me. Looking for a place to stay, actually, just for a month or two.'

'But how long have you been here?'

'Let's see.' He looked at his watch. 'Ten o'clock now. Got into the Miyako at about eleven, then went round the entertainment quarter, got some bumf from the Tourist Information Center. Not quite myself yet, I suppose.' He certainly did seem even more revved up than usual. 'Twenty-eight-hour flight, actually, Milano to Zurich. Then Paris. Then Anchorage, and Tokyo. Then Osaka. Took a taxi over here.' It sounded like a précis of his life.

'Awfully sorry. Won't be a moment.' He smiled warmly over at Sachiko again. 'Wonder if I could just ask you a couple of questions?' He scattered the brochures around some more and started frowning over them. Sachiko, meanwhile, looked simply thunderstruck. Then, suddenly remembering his social obligations, he looked up again and began firing questions over at her, causing her to blink furiously and look plaintively over to me for help. Thus the three of us embarked on an utterly unnecessary conversation in which I deftly translated from English into English and then back again.

'Are your parents alive?' he began abruptly.

Sachiko looked over at me, frowning.

'Your parents are in Kyoto?' I tried.

'In Kyoto!' she said, looking over at him with a delighted smile. 'Please you meet!'

'Oh yes, yes, love to,' laughed Matthew in embarrassment, and then there came another yawning silence.

Now Sachiko attacked the issue at hand. 'What country you living?'

'Italy, actually,' said Matthew in his telegraphic way. 'Living in a hill town – very charming, actually – just north of Milano.'

Sachiko looked terrified. 'Hill?'

'Yes, yes.' Matthew gave her an encouraging smile.

'You live in hill?'

'Not quite. You see . . .'

'But my friend say, Italian man very dangerous. She standing street, man come here. He say, "Please you come together me, hotel."'

Matthew looked at me, perplexed.

'She means that her friend got propositioned by a man in Italy.'

'Oh yes, yes, quite.' Matthew beamed back. 'Awfully embarrassing. Must be terribly careful. Very roguish types all round. Can't trust them at all.'

Sachiko smiled in incomprehension.

'You very good smell,' she assured him. Taken aback, Matthew began sniffing around at his clothes.

'No, no. She means you have a good smile.'

'Oh yes, yes, of course,' he said, showing off his 'smell'.

Then, as abruptly as he had appeared, he bounced up and began clambering down the stairs again and wriggling and wiggling his way into his shoes.

At this, Sachiko tried to put the whole uncanny encounter into words. 'You little bad people,' she suddenly offered. 'I think you little bad!'

'Oh, really? Very true, very true,' he said, smiling with his lawyer's politesse and looking at me as if all his worst fears had been confirmed.

'She means that you are the thing with feathers, always flying from one place to the next.'

'Oh yes, a bird, quite so! Absolutely right! Couldn't think of a better way of putting it,' he burbled, waving cheerfully and bumping into the door as he walked, half backward, down the lane, in search of a place to stay.

Sachiko looked back at me, shaken. 'Your dream true!'

Though Matthew still seemed about as steady as a pendulum, there was never any doubting his charm, or the worthiness of his intentions: the only trouble was that his intentions were so varied and so versatile that he never knew which one he was pursuing. His genius for confusion had only been compounded by the fortune he had inherited, tying him up in golden knots. Still I was delighted to see him again, and by the time we met up two days later, he seemed already to have taken the measure of his new home.

'Went to the Philosopher's Path yesterday,' he shot out at 78 rpm as we walked, in thick coats, through the coldest Sunday of the year. 'Little quaint, don't you think? All these dainty tea shops and pink boutiques? Rather surprised, actually, to see a place called the English House on the road of contemplation!'

'A little twee, perhaps?'

'Exactly! Absolutely! So glad there's someone here who knows exactly what I mean! Rather like some kind of retirement home back in England.'

'Well, that's probably a good description of many things here. It's like a retirement home for everyone. Everything's as cozy and comforting as possible, designed to soothe and coddle. That's partly why the Japanese are so thrown off by foreigners: they don't know how to make us happy.'

'My inn, actually, feels rather like a hospital.'

'Well, everything's got to be streamlined here, and sterilized,' I went on, sententious, after three months here a self-professed Japan hand. 'And a customer is always treated to the same rather overpolite solicitude usually accorded a terminal patient.'

This did little to raise Matthew's spirits, and as we wandered through the temples along the eastern hills, I watched him get his first taste of what it was like to be a mascot and a superstar: a foreigner in Japan. As we strolled up to the main hall of the head temple of Jōdo Buddhism, an old man bustled up to us and, without introduction, declared haltingly, 'I was once in America. Two month,' then padded away. ('Funny,' said Matthew, 'he didn't look very American.') A little farther in, a gaggle of kimonoed girls, hiding their mouths with their hands, asked if they could have their pictures taken with this exotic creature with blue eyes and brown hair, in an expensive Italian coat. When Matthew, ever gallant, extended his hand towards one, four photographers crowded round to record the immortal moment. In Shōren-in, a whole traveling company of middle-aged sightseers hailed us beside a carp pond and had us stand poker-faced with them in a team photo, as proud as if they'd captured a koala and a hippo in the same frame. We played our part in the pantomime with silent acquiescence.

A little later, walking through the temple garden, Matthew suddenly looked up, bewildered. 'Is this supposed to be tranquil, or is it meaningful?'

'Well,' I said, accustomed to these abrupt gunshots of sincerity, 'I think the two are meant to be the same. The only meaning is the quiet you find within.'

'Oh yes, yes, of course,' he said, correcting himself quickly. 'No either/or in Zen.'

Four

One of the most famous of all Zen stories, sometimes ascribed to Hakuin, tells of the lovely young girl, unmarried though pregnant, who is asked by an angry community to identify the father of her child. Spitefully, she points her finger at an old Zen monk long renowned for his purity. When confronted with the charge, the old monk simply replies, 'Is that so?' and accepts responsibility for the child.

Many years pass, and the old monk diligently raises the child as if it were his own. His name is discredited now, his person derided. Then, abruptly, the girl confesses to her parents that she'd lied before – the monk had had nothing to do with her. Mortified, the family rushes to the monk to make amends, and tell him of the terrible error. In response, the monk simply replies, 'Is that so?'

As winter deepened, and I continued reading, the theme of the lady and the monk continued to pursue me everywhere, and everywhere I turned, I found new variations on the theme. It was there in Kabuki, in the celebrated legend of Kiyohime, a typical Japanese demon-woman who grows so obsessed with a monk that finally, in her fervor, she turns into a serpent and scourges him. It was there in Nō, in the classic work *Izutsu*, about a monk meeting a woman at a well and the two of them transporting themselves back into the love story that had once unfolded there. It was there in fiction, in Naka Kansuke's novel *Inu*, about a monk renowned for his unbending purity who grows so infatuated with a woman that he becomes demented, turning her into a dog, and himself too; and, again and again, it was there in folklore, as in Lafcadio Hearn's shocking 'Force of Karma', about a handsome monk so unsettled by temptation that he throws himself before a train.

That monks could be licentious – a satire on themselves – was hardly surprising or unique; Chaucer had written the book on that for us. And it seemed only natural that the Japanese boulevardiers of the eighteenth century should sing the virtues of tarts in the form reserved for Buddhist parables: prostitutes, after all, were called 'singing nuns', and the term *saihō jorō*, or 'Shimabara tart', slipped nicely into its complementary opposite, *saihō jōdo*, or Buddhist Pure Land of the West. Sukenobu's *ukiyo-e* picture book *Steeped in the Indigo River* could also be translated as *Sex at the First Encounter*. And a monk's solitary musings on the impermanence of life could easily merge into a woman's lonely complaints about the impermanence of love. If Saikaku's definitive courtesan, the Woman Who Lived for Love, retired into a convent (ambiguously known as the Hermitage of Voluptuousness), and Genji found his ten-year-old playmate in a religious retreat in the mountains, monks were meanwhile scurrying in the opposite direction. As the old slur had it, 'Never offer a night's lodging to a holy man unless you want your daughter raped.'

What was more surprising, though, was that sometimes the woman's virtue could be stronger than the monk's, that, in a sense, the woman could become an agent of belief and a gateway to a heaven not only seen in earthly terms. In the story of Gyoren Kwannon, a lovely girl, by virtue of her loveliness, entices people to the sutras; and Kawabata's *House of the Sleeping Beauties* was only the most famous example of a story in which girls of easy virtue were taken to be emblems of a higher purity. 'Religion is not to go to God by forsaking the world,' the monk Sōen Shaku had written, 'but by finding him in it.'

Mostly, then, the two impulses lay tangled together as a passionate couple, as troublingly intertwined as in the lyrics of Emily Dickinson or Madonna.

> *I fell in love with the Lord Buddha*
> *when I kiss his chill lips sacrilegiously*
> *my heart swoons.*

Belief itself, as in Graham Greene, could be the highest version of romance.

The next time I ran into a gathering of monks was when I went one night into Mark's house, to find Mark himself seated in a corner, deep inside his painting, while the one-pointed Joe was sitting at the wooden table, drinking beer and listening to a tape of a mandolin player from the streets of San Francisco. The screens were all pulled in tight in the early-winter dark, to give a sense of warmth and close enfoldedness (with their sliding screens and panels, Japanese rooms were as malleable as their selves). A kettle was steaming and puffing atop the kerosene heater.

The minute I pulled back the front screen behind me, Joe fixed me with a penetrating stare.

'You know Ted Williams the ballplayer?'

'Sure.'

'I read someplace where the reason he could hit so well was he could slow the ball down. His fuckin' concentration, man, it was so good, he could make the ball come slowly. That's what I do when I'm playin' the piano. It goes slow, man, real slow.'

'Or chess?'

'Sure. It's like goin' into a trance, man. Only thing is, you gotta do it alone. All movements, man – fuckin' Moonies. I remember this one time, these guys from the temple were doin' *takahatsu* – daily beggin', y'know – outside my window, doing that weird kind of chanting of theirs. It was like seven in the morning, man – on a Sunday! – and I was tryin' to get some sleep. And I was in this tiny old room, with a leak in the ceiling, and I had this bucket of water by my bed. So I picked it up, and I opened the window and . . .'

Joe began chuckling, and I braced myself for another strong dose of unorthodoxy. 'Those monks, man, they can really put the sake away. Only people drink more than they do are the geisha. On New Year's Eve, man, you just see these senior guys grabbin' some monk and pourin' sake into him till he's spewin' the stuff up. Other times, man, they go, like once a month, on their day off, down to Tōji – you know, the strip joint south of Kyoto Station – and all these girls, they come up to the front of the stage and say, *"Hai dōzo."* Come and get it.'

Again I was taken aback, and again I realized that Joe was dispensing Zen wisdom in a purer form than any textbook: the need to slow things down, to speak your mind, to shake up lazy assumptions. Going to the famous Kyoto strip joint was still, after all, known as 'going to see Kannon' (the Goddess of Mercy); and Mishima's *Temple of the Golden Pavilion* had largely dealt with Kyoto monks' visits to the red-light district. I was just about to ask Joe something about whiskey priests when Rick, the onetime monk, came in, just returned from San Francisco. Today, for the first time in seven years, he had seen his wife again, his teacher, and his daughter. Now, on his way back from the encounter, he looked overwhelmed, as if the occasion had taken him so deep he could not easily bob back to the surface.

'How was your daughter?'

'Great, just great,' he said, a long way off now from *The Tao of Sex*. 'She's really pretty.' His eyes were shy now, self-denying. 'Not, like, model pretty, but she's beautiful to me.' He told us how he had talked to her about 'Für Elise' and how the two of them had just sat there alone, for the first time in their lives. Later, he said, someone or other had come in and taken a picture of them – 'some monk, or the abbot's wife, or someone, I don't know. I was just so moved, I couldn't focus on a thing.'

Then, unable to put words to his feelings, Rick picked up his bamboo flute, made for him by his teacher, and played along with the Billie Holliday melodies seeping through the room, summoning all the feelings that he could not voice.

'The only thing you need, man,' Joe piped up, as soon as he was finished, no more respectful of his friend's sentiments than of any other doctrine, 'is more rests. Like Mozart, man. That guy, man, was a genius, a fuckin' genius. All the music he made was in the pauses. Everything in the symphonies depends on rests. A fuckin' genius, man, and at thirty-six he died, and they put him into the ground and covered him with lime. Death, man, it's a bummer.' He looked around at us and chuckled, and, as ever, I felt that what he was getting at was a little less obvious than it seemed. 'That's why you gotta have a baby in the house. Baby's a real good thing to have in the house. Like right now, Sammy's nine months old. He's gonna be grown up. So we've got to get a baby in the house.' This was the way he operated: to start with some truism and then, like a jazz musician, to work improvisations around it, turning it round and round like a stone, till it began to throw off unexpected lights. 'Man, you gotta have a baby in the house. Like my wife –if she wants to go out and hustle all day in the rat race, she can have it! She's welcome to it. I can just stay home and watch my children grow. Makin' money's the least interesting part of life; I'd rather be at home, man, playin' with my kids. You know why? Because a baby, man, he's just seen the light! He's just sittin' there, and he's light! I pat him on the head, and I'm touchin' light. You know *The Tibetan Book of the Dead*? It's all in there. Why babies are light.'

'That's also why Shelley used to accost babies in the street,' I broke in, 'and cross-question them about life in the hereafter. He wanted to get a first-person account of what it was like in heaven.'

'Jesus fuck,' said Joe, shaking his head and grinning broadly to himself. 'I wish I believed that, I really do. I really wish I believed that was true.'

And I remembered how the demon Mara, when he was trying to tempt the Buddha, having failed to bring him down with discontent or desire, unleashed his strongest weapon: love.

Whenever I wandered the winter streets alone, though, Kyoto still aroused in me a surge of unaccountable elation: even in winter, the skies were unreasonably blue, and the days had a bright, invigorating chill that seemed to admit of no despair. In Japan, there was truly a sense of a culture calmly on the rise, in possession of itself and buoyant, and the mild air itself felt cleansed of cynicism and decay. Nothing was left to age here (much as the conservation-minded foreigner might have wished there to be); everything felt newly minted as a nickel. Other countries – my trip had reminded me – might seduce or assault or implicate one with the challenge of an outstretched hand; the influence of Japan, by contrast, was soft as a sheet drawn over one's body.

I knew, of course, that it was dangerously easy for a foreigner, who enjoyed a kind of *carte blanche* in living outside the system, to endorse a world in which men dragged themselves off from 6 a.m. to 11 p.m. six days a week, while women were condemned to a kind of emotional exile. I knew, too, that the lightness of being here could be unbearable – an evasion or a denial – and that Japan's optimism was willed, sometimes, or no deeper than its sugar-coated surfaces, its pink-ribboned girls quite literally trying to make their eyes as wide as possible. (When she asked her students to find three adjectives to describe themselves, a longtime foreign teacher told me, she had had to ban the use of 'cheerful', or else every girl in class would use it.)

Yet still, I thought, it took a certain courage to be positive, and it was always easier to negate than to affirm. The fact that they had been trained always to see the good, and to expect the same in others, might make the Japanese vulnerable abroad, but at home it worked as a kind of self-fulfilling prophecy. And the smiles might be all artifice, but better false smiles, I thought, on the level of daily routine, than honest rudeness. Within its strict limits, and on paper at least, the Japanese seemed to have created a kind of child's utopia of clean surfaces and safe pleasures. One reason Kyoto took me back to England was that it took me back to childhood, and to its sense of protected calm.

My one problem, in fact, with Japan was that it sometimes seemed so free of problems. That was one reason, I often thought, why these people, so famously considerate in the domestic realm, appeared so notoriously indifferent to refugees, or war victims, or to the demands of the world at large. In its way, Japan had constructed such an orderly, friction-free society that its young, at least, free of the Occupation, could not easily grasp the details of a world of pain and privation – the real world, in short. Human rights and suffering made little sense in this shiny, wound-up society where both were either taken for granted or denied (even the beggars here seemed mannerly and sane, while cripples were ritually shipped off, in many cases, to the Philippines). This removal from all pain gave Japan at times the air of a wealthy, well-intentioned dowager, alone in the comfort of her home, and responding, without malice, to stories of need elsewhere with an airy 'Let them eat cake!'

Besides, pretense could have its virtues. I thought back to the line in the Singer story 'A Piece of Advice' I had read a few months before: 'If you are not happy, act the happy man. Happiness will come later. If you are in despair, act as though you believe. Faith will come afterwards.' Certainly, belief in the virtue of Japan could be as self-validating as any other leap of faith; egotism itself almost seemed collective here. And only a little later, when I returned to Kenkō, the fourteenth-century monk who wrote with a duchess's fastidiousness, I found again the perfect defense of pretense. 'If you run through the streets saying you imitate a lunatic,' wrote the monk, 'you are in fact a lunatic. If you kill a man saying you imitate a criminal, you are a criminal yourself. By the same token, a horse that imitates a champion thoroughbred may be classed as a thoroughbred, and the man who imitates Shun belongs to Shun's company. A man who studies wisdom, even insincerely, should be called wise.' And, I thought, a society that keeps telling itself it's unified is on the way at least to being what it says.

Five

One day a little later, the phone in my guesthouse trilled, and I happened to be the one to pick it up. *'Moshi-moshi.'* *'Moshi-moshi?'* *'Hai! Moshi-moshi.'* Through the inevitable tangle of *Moshi-moshis* that followed, I could make out a flustered middle-aged female voice. *'Moshi-moshi?'* *'Hai, hai, moshi-moshi,'* I replied, and then she started up again, in English. 'My name is Tsukimoto. I want foreigner person for job . . .'

'No,' I replied with careful patience, accustomed by now to such requests. 'I do not want to teach English. But there may be other people in this house who do.'

'No, no,' she said. 'Movie. We need character in movie. We need foreigner character. Why *you* not come along? We give you three thousand yen, interview fee.'

Twenty-five dollars, I thought: that would be the first yen I ever earned. 'What kind of movie?'

'GI. Occupation movie. Why you not come? Three thousand yen for one hour.'

Two days later, I arrived, as arranged, as the Takashimaya department store downtown. Tsukimoto's face, when she saw me, was not a picture of joy: apparently the *gaijin* who sounded so English on the phone was in fact a small and scrawny Indian. Loss of face seemed imminent.

Nonetheless, she took me in with harried stoicism and, gathering together a circle of twelve specimens of foreign manhood, bustled us all into a fleet of waiting taxis. Twenty minutes later, our convoy pulled into Eigamura – Movie Village – the Universal Studios of Japan. A little man hurried up to us and led our ragtag group into a dingy little room, Tsukimoto bustling along behind. In her wake came a clutch of harassed-looking teenage assistants and the director, a smoothly grinning dandy in bomber jacket, muffler, and Yves Saint Laurent glasses.

The picture of worldly urbanity, thick gray hair flopping over designer glasses, he let a few words escape through his ingratiating smile. There was silence. Tsukimoto stared at him in terror. There was more silence.

'He said the movie's name is *Nikutai-no Mon*,' a shy sociology student from New Zealand finally piped up. 'That means "Gate of Flesh".'

The director purred a little more.

Looking around at the blank faces, the New Zealander gamely took the bit between his teeth. 'Apparently, the film is about the Americans in Japan after World War II,' he continued, mumbling under his spectacles, locks of brown hair falling across his face. 'It features GIs, prostitutes, *yakuza*.' The director fired out a few more mellifluous sentences. The New Zealander, looking down at the table, condemned now to translate, gamely soldiered on. 'Some of it is very brutal. It will require people to get hit very hard.' The director, smiling all round, rattled off some more. 'Also, it does not portray Americans in a very favorable light. If that bothers you, please say so. And' – the poor shy fellow was now muttering through his hair in embarrassment – 'there will be some carnal scenes.'

There were titters all round.

This was too much for Tsukimoto. Firmly stepping forward, she handed out a few sheets of paper to a handful of foreign men – the largest in the room – and asked them each to read out the first sentence. One after another, the foreigners intoned the opening line: 'From border to border, from coast to coast, here comes the Happy Cowboy!'

'Wait a minute,' someone cried. 'Japan has no borders!'

'Maybe "From island to island, from coast to coast," would be better?'

'No. The thing doesn't make sense anyway. Who in hell's the Happy Cowboy when he's at home?'

At this point, Tsukimoto quickly interceded once again.

'Please stand up!' she barked, sensing that things were not going well. 'You must be seventy inches high!'

All of us got up, and I cast an eye over my rivals: an aging Brit, who had recently starred in another sex-ploitation movie, thanks to an earlier Tsukimoto casting call; a phlegmatic, *tanuki*-bellied Israeli with a walrus mustache and a look of deepest sorrow; a sour, balding American in a green down jacket, who looked like a graduate student on his way to the stacks; an improbably beautiful blond German in a leather jacket, who resembled a West Hollywood waiter; and a six-foot-four-inch Larry Bird look-alike from Lafayette, Indiana, whose main qualification for becoming an English teacher in Japan had been selling Dove Bars outside Trump Tower. There were short *gaijin*, fat *gaijin*, tall *gaijin*; thin *gaijin*, dark *gaijin*, squat *gaijin*. Every kind of *gaijin*, in fact, except the type likely to belong to the Eighty-second Airborne.

As Tsukimoto anxiously surveyed the talent before her, questions began to fly.

'What kind of picture is this?' 'What sort of person do you need?' 'What scenes will we get to do?'

'Well,' said the New Zealander – now, unwittingly,

the official spokesman for the film-makers – 'he did say it was pretty brutal!'

'Yes, yes,' said Tsukimoto excitedly. 'We need man for lape.'

There was a startled silence.

'Yes, yes, we need lape scene. Very important lape.'

Several comments, few of them pious, escaped from the thirteen assembled males.

'We don't know how to rape – Japanese girls are so willing,' smirked a handsome Austrian in a brown leather jacket. 'If you want a rapist, look no further,' cooed a South American. 'How are you going to measure us up?' 'Don't worry about that! You're not going to get to do the rape. You're going to get to *be* raped!'

Again the flustered Tsukimoto burst in.

'You have experience?' she said, earnestly turning on a small, round New Yorker well known in Kyoto as a serious student of *kyōgen* drama. 'You have done before?'

'Experience as a rapist?'

'Yes, yes. Lape scene need lape experience. Very important.'

At that, the director clearly tired of the whole song-and-dance routine and pointed a brisk finger at the five men in the room with beards and three others who were plump. The lucky eight were led off to a separate room to demonstrate their skills as rapists, and the rest of us were left, as it were, on the cutting-room floor.

Tsukimoto, however, was eager to give solace. 'They have bad-side atmosphere,' she told us kindly. 'Very bad-side. They look like lape men.'

This was not altogether reassuring. I was sorely tempted to confess to Tsukimoto that I did in fact have just the kind of experience she wanted: my only other major motion picture role had featured an unhappy impersonation of a Mexican military cadet in a tragically overlooked horror movie, *Evilspeak,* about a trio of wild boars that attack naked girls in the shower while the former child star of *Gentle Ben* networks with the devil on his computer. My auditioners then had been a pair of bikinied Californians whom memory conveniently recalled as Cindy and Candy, and who stretched themselves out on poolside deck chairs and languorously fingered anyone willing to get a military-length haircut.

Before I could make this known to my employer, however, the would-be rapists were led back in again, the Pyrrhic winner the paunchy *kyōgen* actor, now looking more than a little molested himself. 'I guess I just looked the scuzziest,' he averred modestly as the runners-up barreled in, slapping him on the shoulder like Miss Universe contestants in reverse. 'I don't know how my wife and her family are going to take this!'

Tsukimoto, however, was in no mood for small talk. 'This lape we need very badly,' she assured us once more. 'Lape very important with this movie.'

A little later, in the taxis heading home, as people began to discuss the hazards of trying to simulate rape, even for $250 a day, the New Zealander turned his sociologist's eye on the experience. 'That's the way it is with movies here,' he began, earnest as a lecturer already. 'All their B movies are set in the Occupation, and they always have the GIs as these hulking murderers and rapists. That's the way it always is.' (Just as American movies filmed in Japan, I thought, always involve the *yakuza*.) 'But I suppose it does make a certain kind of sense. A lot of the foreigners here, they aren't here to do any teaching. They just like to fool around.' He was hitting his stride now. 'Like I know this one guy who rides every day on this special train full of college girls waiting to be picked up. And this other one who goes to discos all the time and kept up four girls at a time – until he got the clap. And I heard about this one bloke from Zaire – you know, black, really scary and fascinating to these people – who had them lined up outside his door and took care of six of them a day. At first when you come here, your ego gets a real massage. Then you realize that they're just saying the same thing to everyone. It's a dangerous psychology.'

Certainly, I could see by now how the Land of the Rising Sun could be the ruin of many a poor boy – not least because being taken as an exotic, or a demigod, was one of the hardest states to abandon.

The movie call, however, had a particular aptness for me. For often, with Sachiko, I felt as if I were responding to a similar kind of summons, auditioning to play the part of a freewheeling foreigner in the long-running romantic picture she'd been screening in her mind. Often, in fact, I got the sense that she was trying to squeeze out of our times together every last pretty or haunting image she'd ever taken in from movies or songs or ballets, as if this were her first, and perhaps last, chance to experience all the sensations that she'd always heard about. Marriage she clearly regarded as a businesslike proposition – a matter of domestic deals and daily accounts in which emotions were as irrelevant as love songs in a résumé; now, though, suddenly, she had a chance to walk across a bridge of dreams, as the Heian courtiers had it, and find all the sensations she kept so neatly in her head, of 'First Love' and 'True Love' and even 'Lost Love'. Sachiko, like many Japanese perhaps, was an uppercase Romantic, with an innocence that idealized experience and turned it into a reflection of itself.

No less than her words, then, her gestures summoned

all the props of high and courtly romance: the hankie smothered with perfume that she gave me to keep in my pocket, the love songs with which she serenaded me, her constant plea to make contact with her by looking at the moon. And already, I could tell, she was developing her inner photographs, turning our times together into pretty, plaintive images – *memento amori* – that she could look back on as a trip to a foreign country. Sometimes she seemed almost to be inspecting her feelings like an enraptured tourist, never troubled by a sense that 'perfect' and 'true' need be incompatible.

Thus every aspect of our friendship was efficiently made to correspond to something from her pool of dream images, rather like the New Year's game in which people matched the opening of ancient poems with the close. One weekend she went with her family to Nagasaki, and came back excitedly telling me how she had seen there Rembrandt's 'Face of Christ'. 'This picture little same you eye!' she announced. I had hardly had time to savor this rare compliment, however, before she was also telling me that the raccoons in the zoo had my eye too (and, presumably, that of Christ). My voice, she said, was 'little same Michael Jackson', and my spirit, 'little Baryshnikov feeling'. Whatever face I presented she managed to match with some counterpart in her anthology of ready-made images – mysterious Indian, history-steeped Brit, fun-loving Californian, romantic loner, wandering writer, sometime monk. Partly, I could see, this was just a way of crossing the language, and the culture, gap, finding a common frame of reference, and partly, too, a reflection of the fact that we were obliged to speak in metaphors and images (and she variously represented me as a penguin, a bear, an owl, a raccoon, and a mole – she, too, it seemed, knew more animal words than adjectives). Partly, perhaps, she could only apprehend a foreigner – and romance – through the imported images she'd consumed, just as I could see her only through the keyhole of ancient Japanese love poems. But partly, too, I could see, with a pang, how keen she was to remove our lives from the everyday world, to lift them to some timeless, fairy-tale realm, immutable, imperishable, and immune from unhappy realities. Realism was reserved for what she did at home (where she wore different clothes, spoke a different language, and used a different voice); our time was 'dream time'.

Thus boundaries began to blur, and the fact that our friendship was described in terms of movies led her more and more to see movies as a reflection of our friendship. The first time I took her to the cinema, to see the Ken Russell extravaganza *Mahler,* she filed out of the auditorium in tears. 'This movie little same you-me feeling,' she said, too deeply affected, almost, to speak. Insofar as Mahler had, as I had seen it, been portrayed as a cruel and egotistical tyrant given only to abuse of his women, this was not, I thought, a happy parallel. But Sachiko, true to her vision, had somehow succeeded in screening out all the negativity and taking away nothing but reassurances. 'First time, I many, many movie understand,' she whispered, awestruck.

And sure enough, when she saw *Out of Africa*, she found it so close a reflection of our relationship that she was moved to tears too. *9½ Weeks* made her think of our 'cherry blossom love'. Even *Fright Night* left her stunned. 'I little see this movie,' she whispered to me, breathless, 'I think of you.' I began to hope she'd never see *In the Realm of the Senses*.

Songs, too, were a receptacle for all the powerful emotions she had never had the chance to experience in real life, and after every other one, I found her in tears. When I played her Springsteen's 'Independence

Day', I was touched and pleased to see that she was all choked up when it finished, a reflection, I thought, of how closely she identified with its character's yearning for freedom, and an escape from the cycles in which his parents were trapped; my pleasure was dimmed a little, however, when I saw that Aerosmith also moved her to tears, and Michael Jackson's synthetic version of 'I Can't Stop Loving You'. Her feelings were so strong, and her opportunities for releasing them so limited, that they came out in torrents, poured into the unlikeliest of vessels. One of them was me.

In the midst of winter, I accompanied her one chilly night to Osaka to see Bryan Adams in concert. The minute he came out on stage, Sachiko began dancing, and so she continued, eyes flashing, smile unfailing, through song after song after hard-driving song, her energy never flagging. When Adams took a brief break, she turned to me and suddenly recited an unearthly poem from the *Manyōshū*, the famous eighth-century anthology of lyrics; eyes shining, with a lingering intensity whose depth I could not fathom, she told me that she now knew all the delicate sadness of a lovesick maiden at her window. Then, when the concert ended, and we streamed out amidst packs of cheerful teenage girls, she suddenly, in a rush of exhilaration, burst into the choral section of Beethoven's Ninth Symphony, in Japanese, as we headed off for dinner at the nearest Dunkin' Donuts.

Occasionally, I could see, the transposition of the movie world and reality played havoc with her mind. When, a little later, she saw *Another Country* on TV (a great favorite in Japan, thanks to its endless shots of pretty young English boys swapping daisies and sonnets against a backdrop of quaint historical buildings), she rang me up in a frenzy of confusion.

221

'This your high school?'

'Yes,' I said.

'Then you little spy man? My mother say maybe you spy.'

'No, no, Sachiko, I'm not a spy.'

'And you not gay?'

'Gay?'

'Then why you go this gay school? Why you not same *Stand by Me*?'

I'm sorry, I felt like saying; not all of us can come to maturity in Steven Spielberg's imagination.

Usually, though, her wish for seeing our lives as gauzy art, a permanent monument to evanescence, made for scenes as artfully composed as postcards, and dreamy, gentle Sachiko was as expert at spinning dream images as at producing gift-wrapped memories: she, looking over the Kamo River, eyes shining in the dark; she, in plum kimono, plucking the koto in front of billowing curtains; she, holding her breath and closing her eyes tight as she stood before the Buddha. Coming to Japan in search of romance, I found myself now a protagonist in someone else's dream, and found, too, that the favor was returned.

'This dream?' she often said, and the only answer I could find was yes.

Six

One day, thrilled to learn that the fabled Shigeyamas, the first family of *kyōgen* comedy, were bringing a whole program based upon raccoons to town, I bought two tickets and dragged poor Matthew off to inspect this curious spectacle. Ready to try anything in his quest for he did not know what, Matthew had already started attending aerobics classes with Sachiko, flopping up and down amidst rows of grinning, fiendishly energetic housewives; accepted an offer from the matronly owner of his inn to accompany her on a pilgrimage to Tokyo Disneyland; and sat through an eight-hour session of Sumō.

None of this, though, has prepared him for a raccoon theatrical festival. Soon after we take our seats, I, in the spirit of a West End theatergoer, bundle off to purchase a bag of Green Tea candy. Inside is a sachet full of blue and white micromarbles, designed to keep the candy fresh. Matthew, however, is not accustomed to such tricks of Japanese ingenuity. He peers down dubiously at the bag. 'Sugar, do you think, perhaps?' he begins, breaking open the bag and shaking a few of the baubles into his hand. 'Some kind of exotic confectionery?' he goes on, tossing them all into his mouth and beginning to crunch appreciatively. 'Very strange, actually,' comes his first report. 'No taste at all. Really rather strange. Can't taste a thing!' He tries to bite into one. 'Awfully strange! Must be glass!'

In a flourish of fellow feeling, I, too, pop a few of the

marbles into my mouth. Matthew is right: there is no taste. They are, in fact, without a shadow of a doubt, glass. I spit them out. Matthew, however, continues chewing, as serene as a cow in pasture.

On stage, a curtain is rising on a striking blue-and-golden lacquer set, five musicians sitting stock-still, in indigo and gray. One of them begins a piercing, dissonant melody on a flute. The others pound drums. An old man walks on to the stage and goes through a strange, slow dance, flinging his sleeved arms out like wings and emitting occasional strangled grunts. We sit back in gloom: the whole thing, clearly – and understandably – is to be in Japanese.

Next to us, two schoolchildren crane forward with the attentiveness of critics, recording the pathos on a Sony. The unearthly sounds continue, redolent, to our philistine ears, of nothing but John Cleese.

Then, like an Indian raga, the invocation suddenly gains momentum, picks up speed, gathers an almost mesmerizing intensity – and is over. We sit back exhausted, and to celebrate our release, purchase two ice creams from an aisle-patrolling lady while Matthew looks about.

He is still muttering something earnest about George Romero's *Night of the Living Dead* when the curtain ascends once more, and, the lights still on, we watch a raccoon masquerade as a teakettle.

'Very primitive,' Matthew shoots out in a staccato whisper, settling back in his seat with a copy of *What's on in Kyoto.* 'Very strange.'

Then, of a sudden, he sits up sharply. 'Think it is glass, actually! Can feel it in my throat! Rather bizarre, actually!' The comedy on stage has nothing on this.

Meanwhile, the audience breaks into uncontrollable hysteria as a servant is surprised by the kettle-impersonating raccoon. Matthew is looking less and less enraptured. Then 'The Miraculous Teakettle' gives way to 'The *Tanuki*'s Belly Drum' and a classic fairy tale of a raccoon dressed as a nun trying to outfox a hunter by delivering a sermon on the iniquity of taking the life of any sentient being. Matthew looks positively sick by now. Then at last the *tanuki* passes round a bottle of sake and brings all the loose ends together in a cheerful, transformative dance.

Matthew looks over unhappily. 'Childlike, don't you think? Terribly immature, really.'

'Maybe. But just imagine a typical Japanese businessman going to the theater in London and ending up at *No Sex Please We're British* or a Christmas pantomime – especially if he can't speak English. Not really very different.' As the instigator of this expedition, perhaps, I have good reason to defend what really feels like a reproach to dilettantishness and a reminder of just how culture-bound we are.

Afterwards, less than satisfied by the entertainment so far, Matthew expresses his keenness to sample Kyoto's nightlife. I, having always assumed this to be a closed shop, know nowhere to go except the prescribed foreigner's haunts. At a noisy dive called the Earth Bar, we munch on cucumbers in plum sauce, cold Korean tofu, and white mushrooms cooked in butter, while drunken laughter and reggae music rise up from along the crowded wooden benches on which sit jostling multicultural couples. On a blackboard, obscene graffiti has been scrawled – to import an air of foreign aggressiveness, perhaps – demeaning Jesus with various four-letter words and culminating in the unexpected declaration: 'Get your shit together: everybody must get stoned.' In a culture where exactly 6.1 ounces of cocaine was confiscated in all of 1988 and swear words are famously nonexistent, this strikes me as a curious motto.

Matthew looks up and down the smoke-filled room mournfully, then tells me what is bothering him.

'It's not that one has to understand other people,' he begins plaintively, 'but one does want to be understood. I'm fascinated by the Japanese. But I have the feeling they're not at all fascinated by me.'

'I think they're just shy, or afraid, or too embarrassed to express themselves in a language whose codes they haven't mastered,' I opine. 'It's just as if you were to run into Bruce Springsteen or Robert De Niro in a restaurant; you might be too shy to go up to them. And even if you did, you might not know what to say. They seem to belong to another realm.'

'Yes, yes,' he says impatiently. 'But where are all the girls who idolize Sting and ought to see that I'm the closest they'll ever get to him?'

'All around. You just don't recognize them because you're looking too hard.'

'But somehow the charm doesn't work here. In Brazil, in Italy, in Thailand, I never had any trouble meeting people. But this place is like another planet. I mean, people stare at me in the street as if I were a kind of animal.' He looks puzzled, and my heart goes out to him. 'Actually, I suppose it's all rather good. Awfully good, actually. Terribly liberating.' He doesn't sound convinced.

'But why should they want to be friends, Matthew? Why should they make the effort to cross the culture gap? It's not as if we have that much to offer them, scarcely speaking their language and ignorant of their culture. When I'm at home, I certainly don't go out of my way to befriend the Hmong, say, or the Japanese, especially if they can't even speak my language.'

'Yes, yes, suppose you're right,' he says, gloomier than ever.

'Remember, too,' I go on remorselessly, 'that we're

seeing them in the one context – speaking English – where they're liable to seem most ungraceful and ill at ease. And yet we bridle when they mock – or even when they compliment – our Japanese. Complaining that Japan is closed seems as beside the point as a Japanese complaining that America is open.'

'I know,' he continues sadly. 'But I still feel like the man who fell to earth.'

Outside again, we thread our way across quiet canals in the dark, the winter silence broken only by the cracked importunities of husky streetwalkers with the voices of old men. Around us, amidst the reeling neon, hostesses in tight makeup and cocktail dresses are wriggling out of the entrances of clubs, bowing their customers into taxis, arranged like nodding dolls on the sidewalk. Weaving through the water-world, Matthew suddenly looms up before a gaggle of startled-faced girls. 'Hallo! Any of you interested in a Merchant Taylors' man?' Often, I think, it is his genuine charm that makes his unacknowledged sadness all the deeper.

In Pub Africa, a kind of social club for the foreign dispossessed, five or six lonely *gaijin* men are seated around a semicircular table in front of a giant video screen, munching tiny pizzas. In booths around the darkened room, clutches of Japanese girls, maybe three or four in every giggling party, nervously look around them, drinking in the air of foreign danger and looking up occasionally to where Suzanne Vega is sitting on a video-jukebox stoop, singing about child abuse. Unable to catch the Japanese, I hear only the usual litanies of *gaijin* talk. 'The Japanese are really obsessed with keeping themselves apart! Hypocritical bastards!' 'My students are really a pain! They're just too damned shy to speak English!' 'I can't believe how narrow these people are, how superficial!' On and on go the conversations – condolences in disguise – delivered I think, with something of the overwrought intensity of a teenager spurned, trying and trying to understand why the object of his affection won't return it and replaying all their arguments in his head ('She said I didn't talk. But I did talk. Look at her! And why all the time . . .'). 'You know the Japanese word for "different" is the same as their word for "wrong"?' I hear someone say. Does that mean that the Japanese are wrong? I wonder. Just because they're different? Sometimes the fabled ethnocentrism of Japan seems more than matched by that of many foreigners in Japan.

As we stuff coins into the jukebox, pressing numbers so haphazardly that, suddenly, a Japanese teen idol appears on the screen before us, Parker, a friendly Southern boy from my guesthouse, appears at our side. 'I need a girlfriend,' he begins, after shaking hands with Matthew. 'I just broke off. I had a Japanese girlfriend for two months, then I found out that she'd had a boyfriend all the time.' Determined to find a partner in Japan, Parker has effectively ensured that he can never find one; his insistent trying seems only to confound itself, and the girls he does meet see only a man in search of girls. Thus he ends up like a kitten with a ball of string; the more he tries to untangle himself, the more tied up he becomes.

As Parker heads off into the night, an Australian hippie, shaking his long, heavy-metal hair out of his granny-glassed eyes, leans back in his chair and extends a hand to Matthew. 'Scuse me, mate. I'm Brad. Just got here, and I'm lost. All my ideas of the place were erased as soon as I got off the airplane.' 'If you look for anything here,' declares Matthew, wise now after a couple of weeks, 'you won't find it. But if you don't look for it, you'll find it. Somewhat paradoxical, I suppose.'

With that, we dutifully proceed on our hegira, passing strip clubs, sake bars, and weeping willows, peering in on a 'live house' (with a 'Snobbery Connection' badge on its window), where four boys in pink tuxedoes and black bow ties are singing 'La Bamba' in the original. The main other spot on the *gaijin* map – the only other night stop more or less colonized by aliens – is Rub-a-Dub, a wall-to-wall reggae joint that encourages cross-cultural communication by squeezing people into so small a space that they are obliged to sit in one another's laps. This is too much for Matthew, though, who now feels let down by both traditional Japanese culture and the foreign imports. By now, he's getting desperate.

Finally, we find ourselves in front of a glittering eight-story building along the canal, as slim and elegant as a giant Parker pen in the Kyoto night. Lights wink and glitter up and down the spine of the Imagium, a pleasure dome situated somewhere east of *Blade Runner* in the year 2040. Outside the glowing block is a board of shiny panels advertising the names of the boîtes inside this sybarite's Tomorrowland.

'Which shall we try?' asks Matthew, determined to break through Kyoto's panels of glass screens.

'Well, I don't think one can really go to any,' I offer timidly. 'It's not like Thailand here.' Above us, the building towers, enigmatic and reproachful as the mysterious block in *2001*. 'Most of these places are Members Clubs, and the ones that aren't are by invitation only. They're virtually closed to foreigners.'

'Oh no, not at all,' he says, and off we go. Up and up and up the silent elevator glides, through the winter night, up to the very peak of the thin wall of lights, and then it begins to come down, one floor at a time. At each stop we peer out into some postmodernist dream

229

chamber: Hip to Be True, Nostalgia Space Was, the Pleaisure Dome. Finally, at a 'café club' called Is It a Crime?, we step out into a dark chamber done up in soft indigo and sapphire neon. Inside, in the funeral hush of some rich gangster's nightspot, an unnaturally pretty girl in a slim white dress to offset her long black hair leads us, bowing, into the club. Within, four waitresses, all in black or white, are arranged next to pillars like counters in Go. One of them steps forward and leads us to a small round table, black-and-white chopsticks placed atop a black marble surface. Behind the bar, three more color-coordinated girls, long black tresses against sheer white dresses, strike fashion-model poses, showing off their profiles. One of them shakes up a drink, white arms flashing teasingly above the sleek black counter. A girl in black stands against a pillar, ramrod straight and motionless; across from her, another unmoving girl, all in white. Men in expensive dark suits sit beside the cash register, whispering.

Matthew turns his Milano eyes around the darkened room, one silent capsule of blinding white and black. 'No good at all,' he pronounces. 'It'd look terrible in the daytime. All *maya*, really, all an illusion. Just animated mannequins.'

'Animated?'

'Yes! Like in a cartoon! All here to impress. No heart. Just for show! What time is it?'

I look at my watch and realize that here, on my first night inside the circles of the pleasure quarter, I have swallowed a kind of lethe; the night feels as weightless as some Armani ad. The Japanese seem to use their dreams less as stimulants than tranquilizers; like the death chambers in *Soylent Green*, almost – convenient, soundproofed ways to ease oneself away from time and space.

The girls in black and white rearrange themselves, their dresses knotted loosely in the back.

'Do you think we should get the bill?' Matthew says at last, another vision closed to him. A girl delicately lays the paper on the table, and he consults it with horror: two glasses of iced oolong tea – more ice than tea – cost thirty-five dollars. 'Is it a crime?' he huffs. 'Yes!' The beautiful hostess in white bows winningly and presses the elevator button for us. Then, as the door closes, she bows again, very deeply, and the hushed style sample disappears from view.

Seven

One day I got a call from Sachiko, even more
breathless than usual.

'You know passport?' she gasped at the other end.

'Yes.'

'I have!' she exclaimed. 'I get. Husband not know.'

'Your first time?'

'First time passport!' she announced. 'I little go
office, Osaka. Then many many question answer. Now
I have! Please I show you!'

'Yes, please. *Demo ima tottemo isogashii desu.*'

'*Ima* now? You little busy?'

'*Hai!* Yes! Why? Are you free now?'

'*Tabun* maybe.'

'*Demo* today is very beautiful day.'

'*Tabun* maybe.' Our conversations, as ever, were
strange affairs, shards of different languages flung
across distances we couldn't gauge.

A few hours later, though, with a speed and
efficiency I was coming to see as characteristic,
Sachiko arrived at my room, proudly bearing her new
possession, very likely the first Japanese passport she'd
ever seen, let alone owned. And already – for between
the intention and the action there fell no shadow here –
she was working on a larger plan.

'I much reading newspaper. Then maybe I little try
tour-conductor course, Osaka! I not so strong, maybe
little difficult. But I want try. I want little wing.'

'You'll go to Osaka every day?'

'One week, two times! Maybe I go five o'clock, come back ten o'clock.'

'And what about your children?'

'I find baby-sitter. Many, many baby-sitter. I not want mother know. If know, biggg problem!'

Before, when she had said, 'I little jealous, you job,' I had thought, in my vanity, that she resented my work for keeping me away from her; only now did I realize that what she had really meant was that she, too, wanted a job, and a self of her own. Looking over at her bright-eyed resolve, I could not help but wish to cheer her on.

'Usual Japanese person believe, *akirameru* life better,' she went on. 'You know this word?'

I flipped through my tiny dictionary and found it: 'resignation'.

'But I not so want this life. I want dream! My mother all life very lonely,' she went on. 'My father very good man, but not so good husband. Always tired. Sometimes little angry. They not so close feeling. I not want this same, my mother's life.' Her mother, I inferred, had been obliged to fill up her emotional life with poems and temples and flowers, and it was precisely the absence of any real companionship that had made her so close to her daughter and, in a sense, so dependent on her. Now, I imagined, it would not be easy for her to watch her daughter seeking out the freedom that she herself had always lacked – and, in the process, depriving her of her only confidante.

'But, Sachiko, this will be very difficult.'

'I know.' She smiled back with determination. 'But I little thinking *Gone With the Wind.* You know last scene? Tomorrow bring new world. I little hoping my life same.'

That afternoon, she asked me to go with her to Osaka

to visit the office where she would be taking her classes. As we chugged along through mile after mile of factories and featureless suburban housing, she gradually turned more philosophical.

'All life,' she began, looking out the window at the offices, 'I think, woman very weak.'

'But in Japan, don't you think that the women are often stronger than the men?'

She nodded gravely. 'They must! If not so strong, then little big problem! But woman try man's life, very difficult. Woman very lonely life – only thinking – very difficult. Woman need Nature!'

As usual, I had no idea whether she meant this in some spiritual or elemental sense – that women were in constant touch with moon and tides and cycles of the earth – or whether it was a more social meaning she intended (that in this perfectly organized society of distribution of labor, their job was to raise children and nurture the men who were money-earning boys). Yet still I could catch her mood, even when the meaning vanished.

Then, ruminative once more, she went on, 'Man world, woman world, very different. Woman live in feeling world, man in reason world.' This was standard enough. 'Man do baby-making ceremony, body only, very easy. Woman have two part: body and heart.' All this, I thought, was not so unusual. But then, as ever, she took me by surprise. 'Man go away, woman heart very easy. But body much much miss him.'

'Wait,' I said. 'You mean the other way round? Body, adjusts, but heart misses him?'

She shook her head firmly. 'Heart no problem! Heart have many memory. But body much need him.'

This in itself I had not expected, though the notion that memory could appease the mind was familiar to me from every classic Japanese love poem I had ever

234

read. Then she extended her metaphor to Japan. 'I think all Japan two side: one very strong side, man side. Like Emperor. Many thing happen, he do nothing. You know *Bushidō*? Little *samurai* feeling! Other part, woman heart, see many thing, but little fragile. Not so strong. Very sad.' Stoicism and sensitivity, I thought; self-discipline and self-pity. That might almost be the warp and woof of this practical, lyrical land of down-to-earth aesthetes and self-denying pleasure-lovers.

Arriving in Osaka, we walked among the early plum blossoms and, in the brooding shadow of Osaka Castle, wandered through a long avenue of pink and white flowering trees, chilled by the stiff February breeze. She stood stock-still and closed her eyes, imprinting the memory on her mind. By now, I was coming to know the alphabet of Sachiko's smallest gestures: the way she'd whisper, as if in church, 'Thank you very much, give me dream'; the way she'd turn down her eyes at moments that moved her, demure as a medieval maiden; the air of transported breathlessness that made her greet each moment like an explorer coming for the first time on the Taj Mahal.

'Japanese person say, *hidamari*,' she explained, pointing to a small patch of sunlight along the otherwise cold stone of a nearby shrine. In the dark of the Kyoto winter, Sachiko was my *hidamari*.

One cold, bright Sunday in early February, I awoke in the chill blue dawn, flakes of snow swirling across the sky in drifts, and, breath condensing, hurried across town to the chilly silence of Tōfukuji. Sachiko had offered to take me to one of the *rōshi*'s early-morning *zazen* sessions for the public – the Buddhist equivalent of a Sunday service – and by seven o'clock on this freezing morning, I found myself in a large, spotless hall, with perhaps fifty other people, all but Sachiko and myself elderly patrons of the temple. Four monks, baleful in black robes, stood silent sentry at the far end of the room, holding wooden sticks upright above their shoulders. All of us were instructed to take off our watches. Then there was absolute silence. Nothing but the early singing of the birds.

For a while, as the *zazen* began, I entered the darkness and felt cleansed. Time and space and self were lost. Then, inevitably, the monkey mind began to frolic. Eyes still shut, I heard the almost silent padding of the monks, as they trod on patrol, step by step, down the line. Occasionally, the silence was cracked by the sound of a stick thwacking some sluggard – two sharp, swift blows on one side, two more on the other. Soon, the sound of hits took on a regular beat. I held my breath as if to disappear when I heard the footsteps approach; then, as they receded, I relaxed again, my mind still full of unsolicited distractions.

Half opening my eye – a child playing hooky – I saw old people in their seventies bowing before the policing monks, asking to be cudgeled. The monk stepped before them with his stave. Then the miscreant laid his head on the ground, right hand clutching his chest to prevent his shoulder from being separated. The stick rang down on him. Then, changing hands, the meditator exposed the other shoulder and was whacked again. He bowed his gratitude, and the monk moved on, feet lobster red in the February cold.

As the minutes seeped on, meandering and ponderous, I felt my sense of stillness intensifying, as if I were gaining weight and depth; but then again my mind began to buzz like a cicada-crowded glade, with thoughts, recollections, plans, worries about punishment, anxieties over the form, questions about the purpose of the exercise. My legs began to ache, and I grew desperate to stir – to move my legs, to go to the bathroom, to steal a glimpse of Sachiko beside me, to do anything at all. The whole exercise began to seem like just another Japanese hardening of the will, an act of mindless discipline. How did everyone else know the proper way to bow? What if I, the only foreigner and the only newcomer here, inadvertently violated some sacrament? Where were these people going in the dark?

Finally, the darkness lifted, as looked-for as the dawn on a night when one cannot sleep. The parishioners lined up in rows before the feet of the *rōshi*, and the *rōshi* delivered a ninety-minute *teishō*, or talk, on the Five Buddhist Precepts – a shorter and simpler version, as it happened, of the Ten Commandments. 'Do not kill. Do not steal. Do not lie. Do not commit adultery. Do not drink.' When he was finished, the four lieutenant monks served tea and cakes, and questions were asked. Then we issued forth, out into the tingling air.

One reason, I began to realize as the winter deepened, why I was following Matthew's progress with something more than mere sympathy and amusement was that he seemed to me the perfect advertisement for Zen; with his lawyer's determination to do anything but follow his instincts, and the congenital self-contradiction that resulted, he was himself like the sound of one hand clapping. Yet the very equivocation and restlessness that made it so important for him to come to Zen was precisely what made it impossible for him to get to Zen. As Mark once put it, citing the old Zen parable, 'He's searching for the ox while riding on the ox.'

One blue late afternoon, drifts of snow coming languidly down along the narrow streets, leaves blowing over the slow-moving canal, we met up in the Afternoon Tea coffee shop downtown. Pink Floyd was seeping out of the sound system, and Matthew, when I arrived, was deep in a book on Zen – in part, it seemed, in the hope that it might attract some stranger into conversation. Many a foreigner came here ostensibly to study Buddhism but in fact to find a partner; if he failed to find a girl, he'd leave, complaining about the lack of Buddhism.

By the time we wandered out, night had already fallen. Tiny lanterns had come on along the doorways of the ancient teahouses lining the narrow canal, and above them, their upper rooms glowed quietly, as quaint, in the falling snow, as in some child's paperweight. Down and down came the flakes, all about us, silent and mild, 'with the stately solemnity', in Mishima's phrase, 'of an ordered ritual', and as we crunched along the newly fallen white, we could see diners in rows along the upper windows and red lanterns reflected in the water, a winter scene of old stone bridges and weeping willows, silent as a photograph.

More and more convinced – and alarmed – that he was being locked out of the real Japan and that his time was running out, Matthew was determined now to break through Kyoto's walls at any cost. In the slimwaisted street of Pontochō, in the geisha quarter, he knocked on one locked door after another and finally, finding one open, jumped breezily into the entrance hall, calling, 'Hallo? Hallo? Anybody home?' A frightened grandmother appeared before us, bowing.

'Oh, hallo,' he greeted her with all his London suavity. 'Awfully nice to meet you. Do hope we're not intruding. Could we come in, please, take a look?' He pointed into the inner sanctum. This, however, was too much for the lady. Violently shaking her head no, she made a cross with her arms and brandished it in front of us as she might with a vampire. We headed back out into the gently falling snow.

Matthew, however, was in no mood to be thwarted. Every time we passed an open alcove, he charged in, greeting the blinking proprietress with reckless good cheer and shooting out such a flood of accelerating pleasantries that even I could scarcely follow. At last, we passed the Pinky Pinkum, as private and barred a place as all the rest. Without a moment's hesitation, Matthew led me in, and together we began hopping around, stork-legged, in the entrance hall, removing our thick shoes.

There were only six seats in the Pinky Pinkum, and four of them were occupied – three by besuited businessmen and the fourth by a professional-looking lady in her early forties. One of the men was squeezing a microphone between his fingers, singing some ineffably sorrowful old ballad while video images of white-maned horses galloped, in slow motion, across the wall. A young girl slithered around gracefully from behind the bar, got down on her knees, and, bowing at our feet, welcomed us in. Then she showed us to the bar, barely two feet away, where a pretty young boy stood at attention.

Matthew was exultant. 'Yes, yes,' he cried excitedly. 'This is it! Absolutely the same as the Japanese bars in Thailand! Video, singing, the whole thing! Quite charming, actually!' Newly invigorated, he ordered a whiskey, and a Coke for me. Meanwhile, the microphone was slowly passed along, precious as an Olympic torch, from one person to the next. Song followed heartrending song. Before long, the microphone had arrived at Matthew's neighbor. He crooned a dirge.

'Very good indeed! Awfully good, actually! Better than La Scala,' cried Matthew, beaming over at him, ever friendly. 'Excellent! Really excellent!' The man stared back at him, perplexed, and then, very slowly, realizing that the praise was genuine, beamed back. The next thing we knew, the microphone was suddenly passing into Matthew's hands, and the businessmen were bustling about to find a list of English songs: 'Yesterday', 'Take Me Home, Country Roads', 'Green Green Grass of Home', 'Love Me Tender'.

'Oh no, no, couldn't, I really couldn't,' he smiled back at them, unaware, as yet, that in this country foreigners, like performing seals, were often expected to sing, quite literally, for their supper. 'Awfully nice of you, very kind, actually,' he went on, 'but really I can't.' The microphone passed down in the opposite direction.

The first businessman received it and started unburdening his sorrow in a deep bass again, and then his neighbor, and then the woman, and soon the place was rocking. All of us were clapping along, the businessmen were delivering wrenching threnodies, and Matthew was slapping his neighbor on the back and smiling at him with an almost hysterical infectiousness. Just at this tender moment of cross-cultural communication, the bartenderess suddenly took up the mike and broke into sweet song. Matthew gazed up at her adoringly. 'Will you marry me?' he asked, as she belted out some plangent ballad about a young girl's errant marriage.

'Absolutely wonderful,' he confided under his breath. 'The real Japan! Maybe we should go before the moment fades. How much do you think it'll be?'

'Thirty-five dollars, maybe,' I answered, trying to soften the blow.

'Oh, very good. Awfully good value, actually. Very good deal: native culture and all that.'

Then the pretty hostess – his fiancée manqué –

handed us the bill: sixty dollars for a whiskey and a Coke. Matthew stared at it unhappily.

I refrained from reminding him that we had, in a sense, gotten off lightly: the traditional teahouses of Gion were famous for their expensiveness – that was one of their traditions, in fact, and that was part of the attraction for the Japanese, who came here exclusively to pay $330 for a single drink, with a bowl of special nuts. Matthew, though, was in no mood for consolation. Jet-propelled, he charged out of the place and started marching through the falling snow. 'Noodle shop, noodle shop,' he shouted mirthlessly as we walked down the canal, past the soundless, lit-up teahouses. 'Noodles! That's what the evening calls for!'

Finally, we retreated to the relative safety of a Mexican restaurant, and over enchiladas, Matthew started discussing the competing merits of the high life and the higher life.

9:00 p.m.: 'Really think I ought to make a go of it here.'

9:15 p.m.: 'Actually, if it doesn't feel right, why force it?'

9:30 p.m.: 'But if I leave now, I'll feel I've failed.'

9.45 p.m.: 'Really, though, Thailand's so much more pleasant. If you're not comfortable, how can you grow?'

And on and on, et cetera, et cetera, *und so weiter*, for two hours or more: Thailand was seductive, so he ought to go there; Thailand was seductive, and therefore to be avoided. Japan was hard, so it was eminently good for him; Japan was hard, so it was not for him at all. He really wanted to try to find a home; he really ought to let a home find him. Unable to accept anything less than everything, he ended up with nothing, reminding me, often, of a man who has waited for so long to take a plunge into cold water that his legs at last have gone dead on him.

'Thing is, I've got all the time and money, really want to be of service. Really ought to find how I can be of use. Could be a lawyer, I suppose, but that's so corrupt. Should become a monk, maybe, but really takes a lot of discipline. Suppose I could go back to college, but then I'm not doing anyone any good at all. Could become a teacher here, but it doesn't feel quite right.'

Finally, I could take no more. 'Look,' I said. 'The more time you spend wondering what you're going to do for others, the less time you spend doing anything at all. And the more you keep looking for a perfect answer, the less likely you are to find one. Stop second-guessing your own emotions, and do something.'

Captive to my own mind now, I started babbling on, determined to try to shake him out of subjunctives and optatives, into simple declaratives.

'But what about understanding?' asked Matthew, a little plaintively. 'Isn't that any good?'

'What good has understanding ever done you? When has understanding ever brought you happiness or goodness or peace? It's useless, it's got nothing to do with anything! The mind's an obstacle; it teaches you only what you never need to know. Just be decisive, single-pointed. Make a choice – any choice at all – and you'll be happier.'

Matthew nodded gloomily, as startled as I was to hear this sudden burst of bromides. He didn't know, I suspected, that one reason for the vehemence was that I was talking to myself. One reason I got so impatient with Matthew was that I saw so much of him in me.

Sachiko, meanwhile, still and always had an unrivaled capacity for touching me, her gestures were so thoughtful. For my birthday, she asked if she could take me out to dinner. When I arrived at City Hall, at the time we'd arranged to meet, I found her standing there, waiting patiently in the cold, in a red and golden sari – as she had promised several months before; with it, under kohl-rimmed eyes, a thick mink stole and black high heels. She looked like a Rajput princess. Handing me a rose of the most delicate lavender, she began clopping along the street, not with her usual easy fluency but with precise, clear-stepping elegance.

'Please,' she said. 'I want give you present. We go Osaka?'

Together, we rode the train through the winter afternoon. She opened up her Paddington datebook (which came here with a space for listing one's 'Tax Accountant's Number') and pointed at the paw mark on the day, symbol of a national holiday: my birthday, she reminded me, was the same as that of the Japanese Empire. I explained to her about Tibet, and the Tibetan New Year that I was going off to celebrate the next day, and she, nodding solemnly, said, 'All life there, very severe! All life, I think, little *sesshin*.'

Later, when we got to Umeda Station, she led me through the crowds to the Hilton Hotel, and up, up, up in the elevator to the sixth-floor Photo Studio. Around us, clutches of apprehensive wedding parties stood around gravely, waiting to have their moment immortalized. I looked on in surprise as Sachiko fell into animated chatter with the startled-looking lady at the desk (not accustomed, I suspected, to seeing a Japanese girl in a sari asking for a wedding picture alone). Then, eyes alight, she handed over $160 for two formal portraits of herself.

'But, Sachiko,' I protested, bursting in. 'That's enough to buy an air ticket to Thailand! Surely you can use this money better!'

'Please,' she said, putting a finger to her lips. 'Please

don't worry, Pico! I want give you something you always keep together. Photo never change; you take many place, always happy memory. Later, you old man, maybe you little look this photo, time stop; you always remember this time. In photo, I always very young, maybe little beautiful.'

'But, Sachiko, it's so expensive. You don't have that much money!'

'Please stop. This very cheap price, I give you all-life present. I not so rich, not so special. I cannot give you many thing. Then I want give you dream!'

I didn't know what to say.

Later, on a night of pale light and water and mist, I told her, with regret, that I had never seen Kyoto in its full winter dress, steeples blanketed with snow, temples covered in white. The next morning, when I awoke, the flakes were coming down in long silent flurries, falling soundlessly upon gray roofs and canals, falling down upon dark temples and back streets, leaving scant trace of the buildings, making no sound as it made the city new.

With that, another cycle seemed to end, the drifts smoothing out all imperfections and presenting me with a world reborn. I looked around at the other presents I had received: the photo from Sachiko, together with an elegant, high-tech case of writing implements and a temple charm; a merry Falstaffian *tanuki* from the Brooklyn lawyer Shelley, wrapped in paper scattered with red and green cherries and inscribed with cheery cherry quatrains: 'To make you happy, my pretty many cherries / I wrote you a netter my dear cheery / We play on the garden our hand are touch / We take each other and run away.'

And, from Mark, a beautiful *sumi-e* drawing of a Buddha, still and depthless, found in meditation.

Spring

Spring rain
In our sedan chair
Your soft whisper.

—THE ZEN POET BUSON

One

On the night I returned from my trip to see the Dalai Lama, only hours after I stepped off the plane, I got a call from Sachiko, more softly urgent than ever, begging me, through snuffled tears, to meet her now, please, anywhere, even though it was almost midnight. I hurried over to the coffee shop she mentioned, and felt a pang of fondness as I saw her standing there, her small figure patient in the dark. Smiling bravely through her tears, she led me inside, still sniffling, and ordered 'milk tea' for us both, then flung herself sobbing into my lap.

'Sachiko, Sachiko, what's wrong?'

She sat up, brushing the tears from her face. 'I little see movie, *Mannequin*.' This in itself did not seem cause for sorrow. 'No, no,' she went on. 'You not understand! I plan go together Sandy, Canadian man. But Sandy, many plan change, all cancel! Then I go together Canadian man! Very good movie, I very fun. But then he attack me!'

'What do you mean?'

She shook her head, inarticulate with grief.

'What exactly did he do, Sachiko?' I persisted, typically crass. 'I don't understand.'

'He try kiss me,' she finally got out. 'First time, my life! Japanese man very gentle, very kind. But foreigner man so different. I very shock.' She gulped down sniffles and sobs. 'Foreigner person very dangerous!' In all her life, she had told me in the autumn – and it

247

was easy to believe her – she had only ever kissed her husband. And in a life so empty of event, even the smallest upset could seem like devastation.

'Don't worry, Sachiko,' I reassured her with spurious fluency. 'Not all foreign men are terrible. Two kinds come to Japan: some wanting much money, many girls; some who truly want to understand the Japanese heart.' She looked at me solemnly, swallowing back her tears, attentive as a chastened child, but I could tell that theories wouldn't help, and I could tell that she was already beginning to feel the terrors of straying far from native ground.

Back in Kyoto now, I settled back into myself as into a hot *sentō* bath, feeling invigorated by the city, and cleaned out. Sitting at my sun-washed desk in the quiet days, I returned to familiar observances: the punctual singing cry, each morning, of the little girl calling to her mother; the midmorning walk of the hobbled old lady with hair the color of smokers' teeth to the coin laundry down the street; the afternoon tinkle of trilling piano melodies; the lonely, melancholy sound of country ballads from the Chinese laundry shop drifting through the narrow lanes at night.

In the weeks I had been away, my neighborhood had, on its surface, transformed itself: a two-story concrete block with the look of an ice cream sandwich towered now above the grandma-and-pa grocery stores, and in the next alley down, a gleaming new health food store was trying to attract new customers. A card dealer from Reno – and, before that, Santa Barbara – had moved into my guesthouse, as well as a tall, brittle businessman from Harvard, who stalked up and down the corridors, in two-tone shirts and three-piece suits, howling, 'Blow, winds, blow.'

The coordinates of my own Kyoto, however,

remained unchanged. When I went to the copy shop, the cackling, clown-faced proprietor was so delighted to see me – her most faithful, and I sometimes suspected her only, customer – that she even effected an introduction to her growling familiar, a lumpy, sad-eyed dog called Goro, thirteen years old now and half blind. The matron at the photo shop demurely murmured 'Pico-san,' as soon as I walked in, and chuckled happily as she tried once more to turn my name into phonetic Japanese characters. And the three girls at the post office, though looking up in alarm from their abacuses when they saw me enter, were sufficiently worldly now to deal with a letter to Brunei Daressalam, to know that American Samoa (despite its zip code) had little to do with America, and to handle a parcel to a person whose surname I didn't know. When I rang up the Tourist Information Center to ask who had won Miss Universe, the girls who worked there not only surprised me with the answer but, after a giggling conference, asked if I approved.

So much of my Kyoto life caught up now in these unprepossessing associations, and, by now, so much of myself. Giving up the world, I thought, was easy; renouncing the Rolls-Royce or Rolex I had never wanted in the first place was no harder than going on the wagon for a teetotaler. But giving up my world – the specific feelings and mementos that seemed the fabric of my being – was altogether different. On that form of attachment, though, as on every other, Zen was singularly uncompromising: memories could be as possessive, and as wasting, as sapphires, or lusts, or hopes.

Though I had been four months in Japan now, it still seemed, often, as if I had landed, with an unseemly bump, on some unworldly star. Whenever I walked down the street to my local convenience store, the Familiar, I felt as if I were walking into a surrealist's collage. On the wall of my lane, a sign informed me, pleasantly:

This is my STYLE
The city is a 24-hour stage where we act out a life that is lively, free, and convenient. Be it day or night, we go out at any time to wherever we like, looking for something new. This scooter is just right for a life-style.

—CITY MOTORBIKE

Around me were fresh-faced, bespectacled boys in warm-up jackets that said 'Neo-Blood', shy teenage girls whose coats said 'Dental Democracy'.

Inside the store itself, where a Japanese Springsteen was delivering a Muzak version of the Boss's 'Brilliant Disguise', I bought some Chips Company pototo chips, their box announcing, disarmingly, 'We are the nicest friends in all the world.' As a happy-voiced announcer on the PA system advised us all to enjoy our stay in the store, I went over to buy a Clean Life Please dust-cloth. 'FACILE for your clean life,' this helpful rag declared. 'You grow to be beautiful in a pleasant and unforgettable mood.' Nearby, goods were clamoring to reassure me: My Green Life utensils, Enjoy and Laundry cloths, hand soaps for 'creating your dreamy life'. Sometimes the objects here seemed almost more animated than the people.

As I headed home, newly befriended and more beautiful, in a pleasant and unforgettable mood, past the machine that offered Drink Paradise and Your Joyful Drink, I glimpsed a pink cushion embroidered with renditions of a cartoon cat. On it, entitled Fleçon Chat, was an atmosphere scene:

There's a tranquil mood all over Montparnasse in the afternoon. The only sound is the gay chattering of Lyceenne and her mates. A persian cat with a beautifully silky hair hunches down gracefully near the window. She looks a little like a lady putting on airs. Her fascinating blue eyes! What a brilliant, happy afternoon, as if we're in the world of Baudelaire's poetry.

These sunny, baffling sentiments were everywhere in Japan – on T-shirts, carrier bags, and photo albums – rhyming, in their way, with the relentlessly chirpy voices that serenaded one on elevators, buses, and trains; it did not take a Roland Barthes to identify Japan as an Empire of Signs. These snippets of nonsense poetry were also, of course, the first and easiest target of most foreigners in Japan, since they were often almost the only signs in English, and absurd: creamers called Creep, Noise snacks that came in different colors, pet cases known as Effem (whether in honor of the fairer sex or high-frequency radio, it was hard to tell). Every newly arrived foreigner could become an instant sociologist when faced with this cascade of automatic writing, not stopping to think, perhaps, how often we may spray paint our T-shirts with elegant-looking Japanese characters that mean nothing to us, or something worse.

Nonetheless, it was hard not to notice how often certain words recurred in these slogans and contrived to create a certain atmosphere. Multimillion-dollar ad campaigns were no more random here than in America, and it was clearly no coincidence that they chose again and again to return to 'dreams' and 'feelings', to metaphors of community and gentleness, to imported notions of freedom and society. ('Coke is it', the slogan nearly everywhere else in the world, became, in Japan, the moodier, and more involving, 'I feel Coke'.) So too, it was hard to overlook how many of the T-shirts spoke of 'clubs' and 'tribes' and 'circles', and how often kiosks or clubs or signs invoked the first person plural (Let's Archery or the Let's grocery store). Even packs of cigarettes announced themselves as 'An Encounter with Tenderness', and Toyota and Honda gave their domestically sold models unusually soft and feminine names. Sometimes, in fact, the Dada fragments seemed almost to be inventories of cherished values, as in the Roget's exuberance of the ad for Nescafè's Excellent Coffee:

It's happiness people loving casual time caring friendly tasty everyday relaxing cosiness fun intimate heart open likeable and togetherness. It's warmth heart embracing pure gentle comradeship you us family sharing sociable aroma liveliness tenderness smiling easy and yours.

Occasionally, too, they let out the other side of Japan: a group of S & M kiddies on motorbikes, fierce-eyed and demented, with hostile scowls, under the legend: 'Though They're Hot-Blooded, Hard-Nosed and Crazy, Really They Act According to Their Principles. It's a Purple Story at Midnight.' Rebellion made user-friendly; just another fashion statement.

Most often, though, the Japanese brought their poetic touch to English and created out of the imported sounds a haunting kind of synesthetic beauty, with an air of lulling, melancholy mystery; often, the buzz-words came together to create a kind of Pop Art haiku, rainswept and misty as a video.

SMOKE ON THE PURPLE TOWN

When time is softly

Veiled in a flower of black
tea, what dreams are your dreams?

ran an ad under a picture of a Picasso-like fellow enshrouded in fog on a Dantean New York street, under the warning: 'All worldly things are transitory.'

In the same magazine, another set of images again turned rough surfaces into poems:

BEYOND THE MEMORY OF MAN

my sepia memory
blurred with tears. I long
for it so much now.

These dreamy flights of inspired lyricism could work on one strangely, composed as they were not of words but associations: syllables used as moods, as ideograms. I came in time to find my imagination expanded by my Clean Mail writing paper, subtitled 'Sounds of Waves', or the monochrome photo album entitled *Les Étoiles Brillantes* (its subtitle sketching a Japanese ideal: 'The wind whispers softly, the sun shines brightly all around, the flowers radiate joyfulness. Here the animals live cheerfully in peaceful co-operation'). Even the paper on my individually wrapped Fine Raisin Cookies declared, 'Beautiful things are beyond time. Woman's history never ceases to yearn for beauty.'

This poppy poetry was, in spite of itself, Japanese, I thought: in some sense, it meant nothing, and yet – in the Japanese way – it substituted atmosphere for meaning and so caught the aroma of a feeling. Meaning or its absence hardly mattered; there was no more point in belaboring a meaning here than in trying to pin one down in a photo or a *tanka*. Instead of analysis, one should simply surrender; surrender to the lovely, strange *trompe l'oeil*:

> *City streets at dawn*
> *A soft mist*
> *Fire on the mountainside.*

Downtown Kyoto was strange to me in different ways, for as I came to know the central covered mall, I registered a curious discrepancy. There were two parallel aisles in the arcade, both of them typical strips of buzzing lights, cartoon faces, fast-food joints, and the occasional porno store. One, though, was always in the usual Japanese state of perpetual quiet rush hour, crammed with uniformed schoolgirls, sleek ladies of the water trade, and beribboned office ladies; the other was as lonely as a ghost town.

One day, as we wandered through the mall together, I asked Mark about this. Well, he said, one of the streets, Teramachi, or the Street of Temples, had long been a place of religious sites and graveyards, razed now by the mallifying city. But Kyotoites still tended to shun it as much as they did the areas of the untouchables, or any haunted house: they did not relish the sensation of walking on the bones of their ancestors. So the whole strip was generally empty, save for its Buddhist shops.

Certainly, the longer I stayed in Kyoto, the more I discovered how many spirits still lingered in its byways and back alleyways, and how much, even now, an animistic strain still haunted this sleek and secular society. For all the futuristic finish of the city's ways and surfaces, it had never fully relinquished its wilder pagan past. The Japanese still slept in certain directions that they deemed auspicious, and left food out on their doorsteps to appease the fox spirits; in the countryside, where houses lacked air-conditioning, people still told one another ghost stories to keep each other cool in summer. Sea spray was said to be the heads of shipwrecked ghosts, and a winter exorcism was still conducted near my home. One foreigner I knew lived rent-free in a huge old house that no Japanese would enter because it was said to be haunted; even a seven-hundred-dollar Shinto priest had failed to clean it out.

I noted too, as time went on, how often Sachiko referred to God, and how much he resembled the stern Calvinist dispenser of the West. If clouds began to gather on a day we met, she'd grow quiet, very often, and say, a little ruminatively, 'God little give this day. Maybe he want punish me.' When I told her that I had had a chilling dream of her turning hard and brittle, she startled me by explaining, 'You me very close. Then maybe God little jealous.' Most often, though, she would interpret – or describe, at least – every happy development in her life as a gift from heaven. 'I get very good Benny Goodman ticket,' she said once. 'Maybe God give me!' 'I don't think so,' I replied, a little churlishly. 'I think God has bigger things to think about.'

I knew, though, that I was being less than fair or understanding. For God was clearly one of the terms that got most thoroughly misplaced in translation (with singular and plural fatally blurred, and Sachiko, perhaps, translating her beliefs into words I'd understand), and however much she seemed to be conflating Christian images with Shinto superstitions in the rites she performed in Buddhist temples, she was clearly committing herself to something more than form or ritual. Whenever we passed a Buddha, she would stop and close her eyes, her palms pressed tightly together. And whatever the communication taking place, it clearly involved some exchange of feelings so intense that I stood back so as not to trespass on it. It reminded me at times of Niels Bohr's answer to the people who said that he could not truly believe in the lucky charm he kept on his wall. Of course not, he said, but it was said that it brought you luck even if you did not believe in it.

When harassed, Sachiko still took herself to the daphne-scented quiet of the temples. And when she had done *kendō* fencing at dawn, she said, or when she listened to the *rōshi* speak, or when she went alone to Eikandō, she fell into a place so still, it sounded like a higher self. It was not so much, perhaps, that her feeling for Zen betrayed a Zen spirit as that both her feeling and Zen betrayed a common source still deeper in the Japanese heart, a natural sympathy for purity and peace.

At the same time, in Sachiko, I was beginning to see a plaintive sense of guilt that made again a mockery of the sociologists' explanations of how the cultures of the East have a sense of 'shame' and not of 'guilt'. Again and again, when we were together, she said darkly, 'I very bad daughter. I very bad mother. I bad wife,' and though some of this may only have been a ritual disclaimer, some, I could sense, really did prey on her. For a while, I had wondered whether perhaps she had a secret life that was the subtext of these self-reproaches. But in time, I realized that she didn't, and that her sense of insufficiency stemmed only from the fact that she longed now and then to be away from her children, chose on occasion to go out without telling her mother, craved sometimes a little time for herself. In Japan, of course, that was tantamount to heresy – if everyone started indulging herself in this way, the whole system would collapse. Self-interest must be communal.

Sachiko, then, was tyrannized by the cult of perfection here. But more than that, I could see that she was haunted by the fear of failing other expectations, which were something more than social: she felt discomfort at her knowledge that her mother's death might be a source of relief as well as sorrow; guilt at the fact that she could not wholeheartedly embrace the notion of unquestioning self-sacrifice; unease at her sense that her dreams – or, more exactly, her wish to realize them – were a violation of the code in which she had been trained. She sensed that she was a traitor to Japan's values, and she knew that excommunication here was, quite literally, a fate worse than death (since death at least involved the preservation of honor).

Yet all these feelings had another, surprising twist, to me at least: for insofar as she felt any unease about our being together, it was clearly because she saw it as a betrayal, not of her husband but of her mother. Her husband, she often implied, was no more affected by her doings than a big boss might be; her emotional life had little to do with the practical setup of her marriage, and he, in any case, had little interest in her life. But her mother was the one she saw as conscience, confidante, and caretaker of her better self. It was her mother who checked in on her daily, closely assessed her performance as a mother, and told her often – this highly capable and efficient thirty-year-old mother of two – that she should not go out in the rain or venture outside after dark. It was her mother who exerted the gentlest kind of emotional blackmail, in large part because it was her mother who had always been her one and closest friend. And so her mother had become, in a sense, an instrument for her sense of religion, until her religion itself came to seem a reflection of her mother: both were symbols of a higher law that held her to moral standards.

Thus the qualities she responded to in the Buddha, she said, were his calm smile and 'sweet eyes' – like those of a mother; and the reason she listened to the *rōshi* was that he tended to his followers as a mother to her flock; and her favorite statue in Kyoto was the Buddha at Eikandō looking over his shoulder to check on his disciple, an emblem of maternal solicitude and love. Motherhood was, of course, her constant frame of reference – her job, in a sense – and therefore the keyhole through which she saw the world; yet it was also something more, as if the mother were as integral to her notion of religion as a father is to ours. 'Please you show me picture your mother?' she often asked, with even more urgency than the people from whom I had heard the same request in such matriarchies as Cuba and the Philippines.

It was, I supposed, only natural, in strictly partitioned Japan, where mothers have complete control of home and family, and fathers take all responsibility for work, that images of compassion and conscience be invariably associated with the mother. Doi Takeo's claim that *amae*, or the feeling of indulged passivity a baby feels at its mother's breast, was a sensation peculiarly important to Japan – the emotional heart of Japan, in fact – was all but a cliché now. Yet it also confirmed my sense of how closely the sense of motherland here reflected – and paralleled – the sense of motherhood. When she had got married, Sachiko told me, it had been as fearful an act to her as exile; and her mother, really, was her clearest embodiment of Japan, with her reverence for the Emperor, her love of ancient poems, her fidelity to all the antique customs. Conversely, of course, society itself here smothered its children like an overprotective mother, winding them up in a net of social securities that was all but impossible to escape. And when venturing out

of their motherland and into the world at large, the
Japanese really did seem often like chicks jumping out
of their nests into a *terra* that was all *incognita*. Japan
was a mother, mother was Japan: the two great
nurturing deities converged.

Even Ryōkan, I recalled, the high priest of unorthodox self-sufficiency, had returned, in his mind, to the
two still points of worship:

> *The island of Sado,*
> *Morning and evening I often see it in my dreams,*
> *Together with the gentle face of my mother.*

Two

One day, before the cherries came to town, I jumped into a bullet train – the perfect emblem of Japan, all noiseless speed and purpose, the world flashing by in a series of well-framed tableaux, all comforts brought to one in an air-conditioned space – and went to Nagasaki. All day I walked along its gently sloping hills, down an avenue of temples fringed by palm trees and cactus, through quiet streets lit up by kindergarten cries. Whether as cause, or effect, of its historical position as the one Japanese port mostly open to the world, the city had a looseness, and an ease, I hadn't found in Kyoto, a freedom from care that let dogs run around unleashed and taxi drivers go ungloved.

In the evening, I found a room in a tiny traditional inn, which doubled as a shell museum, and drew myself a deep hot bath. Just as I was settling into it, however, there came a frantic knocking at my door; it was one of the matrons of the inn, desperately summoning me downstairs. There, she pointed to the phone, dangling off its hook, and as I picked it up, stared at by the matron and a goggle-eyed accomplice, all of us surrounded by tanks of tropical fish, I heard a fact-checker in New York asking me whether the Thai name of Bangkok could be translated as 'village of wild olive groves'.

Since the answer (it could) had to be faxed off immediately to New York, I took the two ladies out of their misery by taking myself out of their hostel and setting off down the silent, empty streets. Then, after giving my fax to the largest hotel in town, I slipped into the nearest restaurant I could find: a basement dive called Caveau. Inside, amidst the clinking of glasses and the makeshift incense of smoke rings, I saw, to my surprise, one whole table of jolly young Japanese toasting two foreigners: a bearded, ruddy engineer, from Boston, I learned from eavesdropping, and a bewildered, fresh-faced Englishman. Every time either of them spoke, there rose up a great roar of approval, as the other diners clinked glasses and doubled over in loud mirth. I, taken aback, took a small booth in the corner and ordered pizza.

Before long, however, and inevitably, a couple of the *gaijin* groupies leaned over and invited me to join the party. I soon found myself in what seemed a kind of heretic clan, a secret society gathered in this underground haunt to imbibe and celebrate the values of abroad. All five Japanese at the table had the lit-up, fervent look of eager revolutionaries. One of them, a thirty-eight-year-old businessman, in pressed white shirt and black tie, a graduate in economics from Nagasaki University, leaned over woozily, extended a hand, and said, 'Bullshit. I am happy to meet you.' Another, a stocky young character, flop-topped and flip-tongued, announced over the general roar, 'My name is Shinji. You can call me Jason.

'Very strange Japanese guy, hey,' he went on, surveying the scene around us. 'Wild and crazy guy!'

'Are you a student?'

'Naw. I was in Waseda University, one year. Then I drop out. This stuff is bullshit! One hundred forty thousand dollars for one year doctor's school!'

Shinji presented himself, in fact, as a perfect inversion of the Japanese ideal. Instead of defining himself by his professional affiliation, he refused to admit to any job; instead of observing the same routine every day, he claimed that he spent most of his time just zigzagging around the country; and instead of pledging his life to family, community, and Japan, he seemed to dream only of escape. I could not tell whether he was ashamed of his job (as a glorified delivery boy, perhaps) or proud of it (as a smuggler of sorts?), but I could see that his main interest was to observe Japan through foreign eyes.

Later, as the party began to disperse in a cloud of happy *Fuck you*s and bleary toasts, Shinji showed again how eager he was to be an American by inviting me to hit the town with him the following night, the first such invitation I had ever received from a Japanese male (most of whom, in any case, had no nights at their disposal). The next day, he called me in the shell museum to assure me he was coming – even the rebels in Japan seemed inalienably Japanese – and then, on the stroke of seven, appeared on my doorstep. Diligent as a tour guide, he began driving me through the winding hills of Nagasaki, until we reached a lookout point, a classic lovers' view of the muzzy lights of the city, as romantic from here as Loti's city, with the great liners out at sea transporting their cargo of lights. A view of possibility, a vision of flight.

As we wound our way back down again, Shinji started to cross-question me.

'Who is your favorite musician?'

'Do you know Jackson Browne?'

His eyes widened. 'My favorite!' he exclaimed in astonishment.

Somewhat taken aback, I wrung his hand in delight.

'Actually, I also like Bruce Springsteen.'

His eyes brightened. 'My favorite!'

Remarkable, I thought: we seemed to have exactly the same tastes.

262

'You like Dire Straits?'

'Very much.'

'My favorite!' he exclaimed, in mock astonishment.

Clearly, 'favorite' was as elastic a term here as 'best friend'; and however much 'Jason' was keen to leave Japan, the Japanese wish to harmonize had clearly not left him.

'What about David Lindley?' I asked, trying to make my choices a little more obscure.

'Sure! My favorite!'

Then, just as credibility was beginning to snap, he added, 'I have a tape, very special tape, David Lindley live, together Clarence Clemons!'

Swinging into a parking place, Shinji announced, with his chuckling air of boyish bonhomie, 'Now I introduce you Nagasaki restaurant.'

'Excellent.'

We made our way through a generic mall, all dizzy lights and giggly girls, and into a McDonald's.

'Cheeseburger, cheeseburger!' he cried, doubling over in laughter.

Together we trooped upstairs and found a table under a cartoon landscape. Later, as we munched our fries, Shinji outlined his worldview.

'All Japanese like blond hair, blue eye, green eye, pale skin. To us is very beautiful. I don't like.' Around him, McDonald's was a clatter of trays and conveyor-belt fun. 'Japanese people do not know other country. Not interesting. Japanese people think all Americans open, friendly. "Hi." Some are. Some not so friendly. Many Americans do not like *Saturday Night Live* because it makes many jokes about the Jews, many jokes about the Irish. The Jews are not like other Americans. They have a too strange mind. Too strange!'

He let out a raucous whoop. They're not the only ones, I thought.

'I meet an American Jew one time – too strange! The Koreans here are the same as the Jews in America. The Japanese are very unfair to Koreans. Why? You know that eighty percent of pachinko parlor owners are Korean? Pachinko parlor owners very rich! Japanese people know about England and America. But they know nothing about Asia. But we are part of Asia!'

He was sounding more and more like a Kyoto *gaijin*.

'English people, too much snob – their nose in air! I have friend, his father friend Attenborough. But English people, French people, very gentle.' He meant, I saw, as Sachiko did, 'gentle' as in *gentil*, the back-derivation of 'gentleman'. 'Canadian man too.

'Which movie you like? My favorite John Belushi. And Jack Nicholson! Cheeseburger, cheeseburger!'

Then, with typical abruptness, Shinji lowered his voice and spread a softer kind of subversion. He was reading now a 'secret history' of the war – precisely the kind of book, I realized, that foreigners loved to read here. It explained how FDR was aware of Pearl Harbor in advance, and went on to outline all Japan's atrocities and cover-ups. 'Same *Last Emperor* movie,' he whispered, brandishing his heresy. 'You like Miami Dolphins?'

'Sure.'

'My favorite!'

Then, as we got ready to go, Shinji cast his eye over all the bright Formica tables, where chic college girls were sitting primly over Happy Meals and Corn Potage Soups. 'All of them,' he intoned, making his face cartoonish, 'pay much high money for clothes. But here' – he pointed to his head – 'empty!'

The next thing I knew, he was whizzing me back through the mall, and occasionally dancing up to groups of female passersby, like De Niro in *New York, New York*.

'You want to see my home?'

'OK,' I said, and again we were driving through quiet streets into a silent neighborhood.

'Why you so kind?' asked Shinji, not for the first time. My kindness, I knew, had extended so far to nothing more than accepting his hospitality, but I heard the same question from Sachiko too, and knew that it reflected not just empty pleasantry or routine inquiry: the Japanese really were anxious to know what was expected of them in return, and what kind of emotional debt they were running up.

Credit ratings uncertain, we parked along a canal and, slipping between wooden homes, stole into a house, and up a staircase, past his sleeping father. Shinji's room, not unexpectedly, was a perfect replica of Western undergraduate chaos, one skewed pile of tangled sheets and tapes and books and empty cartons of Kentucky Fried Chicken. Above the bed smiled a semi-life-size Shiseido girl.

'My parents are divorced,' Shinji announced, as if to certify his status as a crazy, messed-up Western kid.

In one respect, though, his room was typically Japanese. For the main item that commanded attention here was the high-tech HQ, one long black switch-board console of CD, VCR, TV, stereo system, and Bose speakers, lined up on a shelf as carefully as a shrine might be in an Indian household. And Shinji's record collection was like nothing I had ever seen before, big enough to stock a record store: hundreds upon hundreds upon hundreds of albums, all kept in clean, transparent sleeves, arranged by genre and alphabet, across shelf after shelf – soul, jazz, country, female vocalist, psychedelic, British Invasion, punk, L.A. session band, art rock, soft rock, surf rock.

'Cheeseburger, cheeseburger!' he cried again.

I looked up from all the albums, dazed.

'You know cheeseburger?'

'Sure! I eat them all the time!'

'Cheeseburger very funny,' Shinji pronounced. The Japanese word for 'funny' had the same double meaning as our own, I recalled. Then he flipped on a tape of Bill Murray and Chevy Chase doing some 'cheeseburger' routine on an old segment of *Saturday Night Live*: *samurai* humor took on new meaning here.

'You like all these kinds of music?' I went on.

'Right now, my favorite the Mersey Sound,' he said, shutting off the 'cheeseburger' routine. 'Gerry and the Pacemakers! Herman's Hermits! The Dave Clark Five! You know Manfred Mann?' I nodded. 'My favorite!'

'Do your friends like this too?'

'Naw.' He mimicked disgust. 'Japanese like only two kind music: Japanese pop and top hits, MTV style. They do not know Dave Clark Five, Sam Cooke.'

'You have Sam Cooke?' I said, perking up.

'Only six,' he apologized, pulling them out from the S section of Soul, rarities unavailable in the U.S. for years, complete with paisley-tone liner notes by 'Hugo and Luigi' and cover versions of classics like 'Blowin' in the Wind'.

'Kinks?'

'Only three.'

'Dead?'

He looked back, stunned. 'My favorite! "Playing in the Band". I am sixties person. Hippie. But Japanese people only like eighties.'

'You should come to Kyoto.'

And so the interrogation went on, through Elvis Costello, and King Crimson albums I hadn't seen since my teens, and even such arcana as Pete Sinfield. More surprising to me, Shinji wasn't just a collector; he actually knew the records well and had all the right rock-critic views on them. 'Carly Simon has same face Mick Jagger! New Springsteen record mā-mā [so-so]. Some of it, like "Nebraska", some very big sound. I think Mark Knopfler's teacher, Ry Cooder. My favorite Ry Cooder song is Hawaii one. He great! But not like money. Many star, too much money! Too much rich! MTV, videos, producer. Much money spoil people. Look Jackson Browne: first three albums very good, then too much money! Diane Lane same. She has old woman's face. And Daryl Hannah – she baka [stupid]! Nothing in her head.' Such was the predicament of a Japanese dissident, I thought: little to rebel against save MTV and Daryl Hannah.

Then he flipped open a box of tapes and pulled out a rare David Lindley bootleg.

'This is for me?'

'Sure,' he said.

As I looked it over, Shinji strolled over to the chest of drawers, reached for a bottle, and slapped on some aftershave. I stared with new intensity at his albums, eager not to know what was going on; Shinji began cleaning his teeth. I looked around for reassurances, and steadied myself with two framed photos of his girlfriend. Then, just as I was excavating some prehistoric Neil Young, Shinji started running his electric Norelco over his face. Now, I thought, I knew how a girl felt when her host started prettying himself up.

Suddenly, just as I was sinking into the Dead's 'Mama Tried', he jumped up and said, 'Let's go.' I looked at my watch and realized that it was eleven-twenty; to cover my options, I had told him that I had to be back at the shell museum by eleven-thirty.

Driving back through hushed and rainswept streets, he suddenly asked, 'Yesterday, what will you do?'

Another piece of surrealism, I thought, till I remembered Sachiko's similar confusion.

'Tomorrow, do you mean?'

'Sure.'

'I think I'll leave,' I said, to be on the safe side. 'Do you like Richard Thompson?'

'Sure! My favorite! Fairport Convention!'

'With Sandy Denny.'

'Hey, you like folk? Pentangle, Steeleye Span, Lindesfarne. You know "Led Zeppelin IV"?'

'Led Zeppelin?'

'Sure. Sandy Denny make guest appearance. Now dead.'

Then, his slaphappy exuberance not subsiding for a moment, he continued, 'What kind of dream you have tonight? Wet dream?'

'No. Very dry.'

'About exams?'

'Maybe. And the Emperor.'

That, I thought, should keep him quiet. But only briefly. 'How about I share your bed?'

This, it seemed, was taking his love of the foreign a little far. 'No, thank you.'

'Why?'

'I'd rather be alone, thank you. Good night.'

'Good night,' he said, politely dropping me off at the entrance to the inn and waving a cheerful textbook goodbye.

Three

Back home in Kyoto, the late-March days eased by in
one seamless flow of blue epiphanies: the first touch of
spring was bringing a refreshed brilliance to the
heavens, and mild afternoons of loosened shirts and
hopes. I drank tea with a slice of orange and ate melon
sorbet in a coffee shop whose window announced,
unexpectedly, 'I'd like to eat with you and gaze into
your eyes while we talk of UFOs', and I went to a
university rock concert where a couple of blue- and
pink-suited emcees exchanged TV patter while mop-
haired singers in dark glasses leaped up and down on
stage in a frenzy of punk nihilism, jerking themselves
around with borrowed fury while a guitarist played
solos with his teeth: I read articles about this year's
Miss Universe contestant from Japan ('Michiko Saka-
guia enjoys flower arrangement, playing the electronic
organ, and golf') and translated Latin tags from Iris
Murdoch – it was always Iris Murdoch here, among
the matrons and the *literati* – for an overzealous
professor of English literature who felt he could not
understand her without knowing the meaning of these
phrases. I caught a glimpse of the Grammy Awards on
Mark's TV and felt as if I'd stumbled on to hidden
treasure.

In Kyoto indeed, as anywhere abroad, I was recover-
ing a kind of innocence, as time slowed down, and
space opened up, and everything seemed new, even –
especially – the things I knew from home. Going to the

movies only once every two months, I found myself curiously spellbound: I went to *Fatal Attraction* (equipped here with a happy – or, at least, less savage – ending) and gasped at its most standard of manipulations; I saw *Benji: The Hunted* in a darkened cinema and was intensely moved by the otherworldly self-sacrifice of its eponymous hero – a kind of four-legged Bodhisattva – until I noticed that the only other person in the theater, a frazzled-looking salaryman, was slumped over in his seat and breathing very deeply.

Being abroad, in a place still strange to me, senses sharpened, and ready to be transformed, was like being a child again – or being in love. I found myself speaking more slowly, more deliberately, here, as I delivered simple sentences in Japanese, or in an English that a Japanese might understand. Instead of trying to make phrases, or impressive sentences, I was concerned only with making sense. In speaking around a foreign language, indeed, I was forced to rethink myself, to gather my thoughts in a state of preparedness and then translate them into clarity; to speak, in fact, with a little of the lucency of Zen.

The elegant Etsuko, meanwhile, was diligently trying to give me a taste of the other side of Japan, the fine-tuned, closed-door world of the upper-class matron. One day she invited me to a meeting of a special cultural group that she had formed to bring Japanese people (mostly women) together with foreigners, the better to get to know one another, and Japan.

When I arrived, in a smart modern salon in the fashionable area of Shimogamo, I found myself in a room bright with the chatter of dapper ladies in their early forties, trendily turned out in leather skirts and cashmere sweaters. This, it seemed, must be the Kyoto equivalent of what Embassy wives do at the club, except that here one found an air of sophistication more rarefied than even the dinner party rites of English country houses. As soon as I entered, a group of ladies descended on me, all smiles and English phrases extended as daintily as *hors d'oeuvres*, and I was divested of a small donation, ticked off a list, given a name tag, and handed a program. A Mr Ono, it seemed, a local graduate student, had planned the day's activities in an exhortatory spirit: 'Let's get on this special train leading to a galaxy of cosmic symphony.'

Looking around anxiously, I saw that I was the youngest person here by a decade or two, the only vagrant and the only male, save for an extremely rumpled old German professor in a dark-gray suit and an air of Schopenhauer gloom, his mood apparently not improved by being identified on his name tag as 'Rols' (his wife, more cryptically still, was labeled 'Bal'). Depositing myself down next to Rols and Bal, I was well embarked on lugubrious chitchat when suddenly Mr Ono called the meeting to order. His subject, he said, was play, and its meaning. His particular expertise was in the giant swing to be found in downtown Bangkok, and his belief that play admitted us to the same sense of liberating ecstasy as religion. Rols slumped back in his chair, the chirpy bird ladies craned forward, lipsticked faces alert, pretty skirts tidy against bended knees.

Then, leaping up, Mr Ono started playing *Jonkenpun* (or paper/scissors/stone) with himself and scribbled some marks up on an impromptu screen. The Embassy wives murmured a collective 'ooh', heads delicately balanced on fists. Rols, however, looked a long way from catharsis. Then, unexpectedly, Mr Ono darted around the room, handing out pieces of string. Please could we make cat's cradles? he urged. Doing so, we felt, in some cases, little of the liberating ecstasy of religion.

Then we adjourned for lunch, an exquisite affair of persimmons, strawberries, kiwifruit, salad, and pizza. Daintily, the Embassy wives picked at their pizza with chopsticks. I, circulating inwards more than out, ambushed a couple of them and made a bid for cultural understanding. One of them professed a breathless concern for the stories of Somerset Maugham, the other was reading *Les Misérables* in the original.

Then Mr Ono, a serious-looking fellow with spectacles above his broad young face, and a jacket and tie, strode back into the room with a cello, accompanied by another student, carrying a flute. A sweet-looking girl in black velvet dress and sheer white stockings — recently escaped, it seemed, from some heart-shaped Victorian locket — sat down at the piano and, pedaling with stockinged feet, unraveled a rippling melody. Mr Ono, closing his eyes with feeling, started bowing his cello in a series of plaintive duets by Elgar, Saint-Saëns, and one 'T. Ono'. Then, half collapsing from his exertions, the versatile hero sank into a chair, and we were treated to lilting piano and flute duets.

Then, just as all seemed lost, suddenly a revived Mr Ono burst into song, a ditty written by himself, no less, ineffably plaintive in its commemoration of lonely bicycles and vanished youth. Finally, the tireless trio tore into a sonata by Handel and, in response to cries of 'Encore!' from the enraptured women, yet another Handel trio.

Sitting in the sunlit room on this bright afternoon, a spotless tatami chamber beside me, and perky doctors' wives, conversant to a woman with Paris and New York, while a Masterpiece Theatre heroine played the piano in an Emily Brontë dress, I felt I had landed in a salon fashioned only from the imagination. And at the end, two pretty sprites, maybe nine years old each and fresh from *The Faerie Queene*, padded in, and shyly presented roses to each of the performers. Then – of course – it was photo time again (turning life into memorial art), and a departure from this Sei Shōnagon circle, back into the world.

As winter began to lift, Sachiko began to find new ways for us to spend time together. One day, as we were walking through a temple, she asked me, as if casually, 'You eat every day in restaurant?' And then, a little later, 'Where you wash clothes?' I answered her directly, and only later saw her drift. 'Why you not come here my house, eat dinner? Why you not give me dirty clothes? I have machine; no problem.' That was how the system worked: when her friend Hideko's six-month-old baby was in hospital, Sachiko visited him every day. The next week, she announced with delight, Hideko was obliged to baby-sit for her. One could no more say that this was 'calculating' or 'guileless' than one could say that turquoise was either green or blue; Sachiko's instincts were so shaded, I could not put a name to them.

One day, while I was writing, the phone in my guesthouse kept ringing and ringing. Picking it up at last, I heard Sachiko's soft excitedness. 'I'm so sorry call you house! I know you working! But before you say you much like orange cake. I find! Now I very close your house. Please I come here your room, give cake?'

I could hardly say no, and when she arrived, she quickly preempted all protests. 'I'm so sorry,' she began. 'I very bad, I know. You need work. But I much want give you this cake. Maybe you eat, then work very easy.' A few days later, it was some chocolate she had bought, and then a button she was eager to sew on,

273

and then the tatami that she wished to clean. And though I could tell she was holding me hostage with kindness, I could also tell that she truly did do her thinking with her heart, and that it was as natural for her to seek out opportunities for kindness as to exercise a kind of emotional usury. Every time she visited, by now, she brought some flowers, to match the day and mood, and then, unable to wait, started fishing out other offerings from her bag. 'I little give you present, are you OK?' she usually began, phrasing her question with such mischievous charm that it was all but rhetorical. 'You not guilty? Is OK?' And then she pulled out a pillow, or a washcloth, or a sea otter key ring. 'You hear this, you little think I here,' she said beautifully, hanging a dangle of wind chimes outside my room one day. But that night, they tinkled all night long, and their lovely silver music kept me up till dawn.

Before very long, as I looked around my room, I realized that Sachiko was colonizing me more subtly than Japan had ever done Taiwan; and the bare room that I had set up as my secular monk's cell now had more and more of a domestic aspect. Her claims on me were everywhere: in the long-birded 'Wonder Worker' mugs she'd given me (no random gift, of course – she saw me as a bird, and a long-beaked one at that); in the guitar she'd propped against the wall, a constant reminder of her presence; in the spray of flowers on my desk and the 'Bear' blanket on my floor. Taking me over with her gifts, she was remaking my room, and me, and each time she said, 'Please you take,' she managed to take over a little more ground.

Sashiko was also, almost unnoticed, installing herself in my life and putting her fingerprints even on the parts she couldn't see. She was courting my mother now with birthday cards, the more engaging because they were so transparently sincere, and when I mentioned, in passing, a seven-year-old boy I greatly admired, in California, she instantly came back with 'Yuki send this boy little letter, are you OK? He little new friend, no problem?' The next thing I knew, I was ferrying drawings and photos between this infant Pyramus and Thisbe, and Sachiko, pointing out all they had in common – Montessori schooling, a love of ships, and 'Sesame Street' – had acquired a new contact abroad, and a new claim on my California life.

Yet all this she achieved without ever making a demand on me or ever abandoning her natural grace; she had surrounded me with her presence, while scarcely seeming to move. And I could hardly blame her for wanting to stake a claim on her elusive new friend and seeking some guarantees in return for all her risks. 'You little same cherry blossom,' she said one day. 'Long time I waiting. Then you come back, I very happy. My life very beautiful. Then you must go again.' It was true, I knew, and there was nothing I could say.

It was also natural, I thought, that she try to lure out of hiding a foreigner who was almost Japanese in his evasiveness and self-containment. 'Strong heart,' she was finding, could be an antonym to 'soft' as well as 'weak'. Soon she was beginning to tell me, pointedly, of the new dress she had bought for going out, of how her husband was taking her to a piano bar, or of how the American monk at Tōfukuji could speak to her in fluent Japanese.

'One man,' she said one day, 'Canadian man, very warm, very kind, he say he give me English lesson. Very cheap. No problem.'

'Look,' I said, rising to the bait. 'I'll give you English lessons free, OK?'

'Really?' she said, delightedly, drawing out her

275

datebook to fix a time. 'Two times, one week, we meet, no problem?'

One night, not long thereafter, she suddenly called my house, her voice strangely coiled, and when I called her back from the street – not wanting to tie up the guesthouse phone – and cheerily sang out, *'O-genki desu ka?'* (Are you well?), she said, 'I'm fine. Not so fine.' A long pause. 'Not fine.'

'Sick?'

'Maybe. Little problem in heart.'

I didn't know exactly what this meant.

'I ask you many questions, are you OK?'

'OK,' I said, though the night was dark and cold, and faces kept appearing at the phone booth, looking in.

'Why you no angry if I have other foreigner friend?'

'Anger no good. I cannot control your heart.'

'Whyyy?'

'It is your heart, your choice. Anger doesn't help.'

'But you sad?'

'Maybe.' I was certainly turning Japanese. 'But I think it's fair: if I do bad thing, then bad things happen to me.'

'Please we meet,' she said urgently, more or less telling me that I had failed.

Twenty minutes later, on an unseasonably chilly night, we met outside the hooded gate of Chion-in, ghostly now in the late-winter dark, and walked amidst the stone carcasses of temples, cold and silent in the night, returned now to all their grave antiquity.

Shivering in the chill, her voice choked up, she began to talk. 'Today my heart little *muzukashii* feeling. I feel little dynamite in heart.' She laughed gaily at the new word she'd learned, but I knew it was her social laugh.

'I'm sorry if I helped you put it there,' I said.

276

'No, no,' she said, as she always did when I apologized (the Japanese seemed to use 'no' mostly to shrug off apologies or thanks, almost never to contradict or repudiate). Her voice then took on an unaccustomed hardness, a steeliness I had heard only when she was speaking Japanese. Her words came out with the condensation of her breath.

'If my marriage broken, what you think?'

'I'd be sad.'

'Why sad?'

'Because I think your husband is a very good man.' Anything I could say now would only incriminate me. 'He takes good care of you and your children.'

'Why you not happy?'

'Well, for example, if your brother goes away, you cannot stop him. But still you feel very close to him.' Everything I said was only digging me in deeper.

'But what you do if I say *sayōnara*? If I find other foreigner friend, what you say?'

Blowing out cold air as we walked side by side along the deserted temples, the street all hushed around us, I got every answer wrong. 'I would be disappointed,' I said, 'but I would accept that you had good reasons for it, or that larger forces were at work. I would be sad, but I would accept that I could not change your heart, or life.'

'I think maybe I wait long time for you,' she said.

She was correct, I knew, though I did not know what was the right thing to do.

Then, suddenly, eyes flashing in the dark, she said, in an eerie and unearthly tone, 'I'm very bad. I little devil. I fox-woman.' Her face in the dark was distant and haunted. 'I little ghost. Old Japanese story: ghost visit man many many times, many very happy time together. But man's friends much worry. His face more weak, more pale. Ghost eating his heart.'

She could hardly have given more eloquent expression to all my unspoken fears. I knew all too much about the Japanese fox-woman, who was said to possess innocent ladies and make them wild. I had seen the Lady Macbeth figure in Kurosawa movies, I had read about the avenging fury of Lady Rokujō in *Genji*. It hardly mattered that 'fox possession' now was said to have been taken over by 'TV possession'; ghosts in Japan were nearly always said to be jealous women driven by unburied grievances.

The next thing I knew, though, all the force had gone out of her, and she was crumpling down, sobbing (or laughing) as she said, through sniffles, 'I'm so sorry. I'm very bad. I'm very sorry! Japanese woman very difficult. Face very soft, but inside very hard. I little fox feeling, I'm so sorry!'

'Maybe you are an Inari fox,' I said to comfort her, reminding her that her hometown was the center of Japan's most famous fox shrine.

'I have two face,' she went on. 'Two side me.'

And then she broke into tears, the condensation coming out of her mouth in gasps, on the silent, deserted avenue of stone temples.

278

Four

When the cherry blossoms came to town, it was a punctual miracle, as well rehearsed and perfect as all the other events on the city's calendar. For weeks now, the preparations had continued: paper blossoms had been fluttering off the lampposts of the major downtown stores, and newspapers had run elaborate charts giving notice of the cherries' busy schedule. Mild Seven cigarettes had brought out their latest seasonal packs – all cherry trees and geisha – and *depāto* shopgirls had changed into their vernal clothes. Everything had re-dressed itself to show the blossoms off to advantage. And the trees themselves stood perfectly placed, as efficiently blocked out as seasoned actresses, arranged in such a way and so strictly trained that they were guaranteed to ravish.

So when the blossoms came at last, they mocked all jadedness with their otherworldly beauty, as stunning as a stage set by a heavenly designer. A blaze of lustrous pink above the city's canals, more dizzy and intense than any words could find, a shock of fluffy, fluttery pink frothing above the city roads. Pink-framed branches outlined against the faultless blue, branches drooping prettily above the pink-reflecting water.

All the people of Kyoto were well trained too, in amending themselves to the whims of the seasons, and so they streamed out on boundless Sunday afternoons and arranged themselves in well-framed pictures with the blossoms: old couples standing under sure-shot branches, young girls clad in the colors of spring, in peach skirts or apricot kimono, delicately fading into the retiring pinks, men in dark suits, stiffening their shoulders; the colors framing all of them as sharp as any dream. The Philosopher's Path was one foaming avenue of pink now, and couples meandered through long trellised tunnels of the blossoms, sun-dappled in the blue; along the Kamo River, lovers sat silent under the blessing of weeping canopies of pink; and on Mount Hiei, a cable car ride up the sacred slope through a psychedelic tunnel of overhanging pinkness left me reeling with its Day-Glo brightness.

It was not long, however, before I found that I was, quite literally, allergic to the photogenic images of evanescence, and soon enough, my nose was stuffed and my nights stretched out through labyrinths of headached dreams. But where previously, in such fever states, I had found myself going round and around all night the Mondrian maze of the Paris metro, now, in my delirium, my mind shuffled and reshuffled the names of Japanese companies: Sony, Matsushita, Mitsubishi.

My conscious mind was turned round, too, by all the well-prepared grace of the season. Was beauty beauty if it could be mass-produced on cue? Why not, I thought: a ballet or an opera or a symphony was performed again and again, yet each time was transformed by the interpreter, and interpreted again in the mind of every listener. Could there be paint-by-number miracles? Did assembly-line epiphanies make sense? Sometimes, in Japan, the seasons were so formulaically displayed and so formulaically enjoyed that one was tempted to eliminate the active voice altogether: just to say that sake was drunk, blossoms were observed, and merriment was had.

And when the blossoms began to fall, breezed down through the sunlight by a passing gust of wind, or by a fleeting rain, there was a silent, rushing snowstorm of pink, fluent, soft, and noiseless, down upon the ground, the water, the pink-kimonoed ladies. After the rains, dead blossoms carpeted the earth and blanketed the rivers, leaving the trees half nude, their branches outlined black against the cloudless blue.

'Marriages are such an efficient system in Japan,' a friend of mine called Michiko explained to me one day. 'The woman makes up a résumé list – it usually consists of tea, flower arranging, and a couple of more up-to-date skills, like tennis or *chansons,* to show that she is a *mōga* (or modern girl). For the man, it's mostly a matter of what car he drives and how much money he earns. Then the marriage broker puts them together, and they're wed.' Supply matched to demand; a minimum of risks and a pooling of resources. It was no wonder that marriages here came almost supplied with money-back guarantees.

After the wedding, things were no less sensibly pragmatic – he devoted his time to making money, and she to disbursing it; he took care of practical support, and she emotional. Formally, the woman was treated as a mere dependent (and the -ko suffix used for most woman's names here literally meant 'child'); behind closed doors, however, the positions were tidily reversed: the woman treated her husband like a baby, putting him to bed each night, giving him his allowance once a week, and sending him off each morning with a box lunch. Thus each party was allowed to be active in some worlds, passive in others, parent and child at once. The only complication came when feelings jammed up the system. (Kawabata's Chieko, asked if she has feelings, calmly explains, 'It seems to cause trouble when one has too many.') It was no wonder that Japan enjoyed the highest marriage rate in the world (more than 98 percent of women found a mate).

'But I don't think Japanese women resent their marriages,' Michiko went on, 'however much they may regret them. They know how to make the most of them, and they know how to turn them to advantage. In some ways, I think, they're much freer than many American women.' Freer? 'At least they do not live vicariously through their husbands. They function pretty much independently of their husbands. If you go to a party here, you'll find that the women hardly ever talk about their husbands. They define themselves in different ways. In some ways, they're more able to lead a separate life. That's why they tend not to get divorces. In any case, even if they do seek divorces, they rarely get the children – or any alimony.' It was no wonder, then, that as recently as her parents' generation, exactly one Japanese marriage in every thousand ended in divorce.

Michiko herself, though, was far from free of the system. Now thirty-four, she had been brought up and educated in America and worked now for an American company, even though she was entirely Japanese. (Talking to me, she seemed a regally tall, highly sophisticated, poised international businesswoman; the minute she addressed a Japanese, though, she became the very picture of a demure, deferential Japanese girl, all yielding softness and ritual self-denial.) Her mother, she told me, kept asking her and asking her why she did not have a husband. Her father spent all his spare time looking around for a potential son-in-law. And though they had lived for most of their lives abroad, her parents still could not get over the fact that their daughter was working for a company

– and, worse still, a foreign company. By having a job, she was writing herself out of the collective script.

A little later, as the cherries began to fall, I decided to return for a while to the temple where I had first stayed, to see how much it had changed, and how much I had. On a fresh young morning, the narrow lanes of pilgrims' shops quiet save for strollers, the trees in gorgeous flower – all the city stirring now with the first tremors of rebirth – I went again to the ancient part of town, where the seasons were marked as a millennium before. April had brought a gentleness to the air, after the gray tumult and anxiety of March; there was a sense of healing in the mild, warm days, and of convalescence.

As soon as I entered the front courtyard, full of motorbikes, the albino monk hurried out to greet me and, his astonished face more astonished than ever, invited me in for some tea. Donning slippers, I padded after him to the tiny TV room, scarcely big enough for three, where the head monk was sitting, legs splayed out in front of him, clicking over channels with a remote-control device. The Nietzsche-loving gardener was summoned too, to greet the returning prodigal, and I, feeling obliged to respond somehow, settled down, cross-legged, at their small square table and began to talk of Sumō.

Apparently, however, some intonation was off a half note, for the head monk, nodding gravely at everything I said, responded with a vigorous lecture on male-female relations in India – he had been to the Taj Mahal, he reminded me – and, after every phrase, turned to me for confirmation of the marvels he described. I, by now accustomed to lusty participation in conversations I couldn't begin to follow, nodded too, and said, with conviction, 'That's really so!'

whenever I sensed he was asking a question, and 'Is that so?' whenever it seemed that he had made a statement.

The proprieties observed, the albino then led me back into the room I had occupied many lives ago, and through the long afternoon, I savored the temple's luxuries of silence and open space. In the night, the outlined figure of the shaven-headed older monk shuffling through the blackened antechamber and letting out a startled, high-pitched cry upon discovering me, alone in the dark, looking out on the distant pagoda. In the dawn, my small bare room slatted with light, and the song of birds. In the chill first light, when some places look exhausted, and others seem reborn, Kyoto seemed always a miracle of early-morning hopes.

As I wandered in the days through the neighboring streets, I could begin to see how Kyoto had lost by now a little of its imagined purity to me, the simple clarity of myth; had become, in fact, so much a part of me that I could see it no more clearly than the back on which my shirt was hanging. The shops along the lanes seemed a little gaudy now, and no longer so uplifting – a sign, perhaps, that I was spoiled more than they were – and now it was the brassy American songs on their sound systems I noticed and not the lovely geometry of their goods. Kyoto was no longer a magic lantern to me; more an album of photographs, thick with associations, particularized, and domesticated. A certain hazy preciousness had been lost, on both sides, and in both senses of the word.

Yet in return, a certain specificity had been gained, a sense of detail that gave flesh and fiber to the dream. And as I walked through the drowsy streets one late afternoon to Maruyama Park, lost in thought, I looked up idly and, suddenly, lost all breath; the huge central weeping cherry tree in the park, its richly flowering branches drooping almost to the ground, was spotlit now, a blaze of burning pink against the dark-blue sky. I had seen this shot a hundred times before, in pictures and posters and books, but now, coming upon it unexpectedly, a royal elegance of blue and pink, I felt as if transported from the world.

In the shadow of the famous tree, revelers were seated in rows on blankets, eating bean cakes in the shape of cherry blossoms, strumming guitars, and bawling drunkenly as the sky turned pink behind the mountains. Shutters snapped, men in expensive suits put on the smiles, drooping girls made peace signs for the camera. And then, as darkness fell, torches came on along the waterways, their golden lights flickering in the pond. Suddenly, now, the park was a blaze of colors: navy blue and gold, a flash of pink, the black hills darkening in the distance.

In that instant I knew that Kyoto had installed itself inside me much deeper than mere fancy. No other place I knew took me back so far or deep, to what seemed like a better time and self. And as I wandered back in the dying light, lit up with a sense of rapture and of calm, I remembered the line of the poet Shinsho: 'No matter what road I'm traveling, I'm going home.'

Five

As spring went on, Sachiko and I still found ourselves often trading metaphors over the phone, exchanging complex feelings in pieces small enough to throw, and catch, I at a little open booth, on an empty, narrow alleyway, in the dark, she in the small room that sometimes seemed an almost unbearably wistful compound of her dreams.

'I want only dream time together you. You are from other world. I want see and learn this other world. But I cannot join. My heart very tiny – little fragile, like grass on windy day.'

'But dream world only not so good,' I replied, reflecting her English back to her. 'If I were talking to Yuki, I could tell her stories, because she is a child. But you are not a child. I want to help you if you have problems. Dream time only not so good.' I realized that I must be sounding bizarrely like Richard Chamberlain addressing the aborigines in *The Last Wave*.

'Then your heart change?'

'Not change. But sometimes tired. I feel I am on a beach, waving, calling out, "Sachiko," but you are on a far boat and cannot hear me. I want to help, but if you cannot see or hear me, I cannot give you food or medicine.'

'I little moon feeling, then you cannot reach?'

'Yes. And I cannot give an answer to your problem. I can only give you a quiet time, a relaxed time, the chance to forget your problems so that you will be more strong to conquer them. It's like going from South Kyoto to North: you cannot run all the time – you must sometimes walk, sometimes stop in a coffee shop for food. The coffee shop does not get you closer to North Kyoto, but you need it to arrive there. You cannot always run.'

'You say true. But if I much cry, have much tear in eye, then I cannot see star, or beautiful thing. Only cloud.'

To that I could say nothing in return.

Towards the end of spring, I made my first official trip to the water world, the fabled entertainment quarter, of Kyoto. So segregated was the demimonde from the daylight world that walls had once been erected to separate it as firmly from the temples nearby as, in Japan, one self is shut off from another (if you are relaxing, relax without scruple, goes the logic, and if you are working, work without distraction). The area was also largely closed to nonmembers, as Matthew and I had discovered. Now, though, a local business-man was eager to take his son – on his way to Santa Barbara – out for a farewell night on the town, together with his son's English-language teacher. Eager to make a grand show of his hospitality, he begged the teacher to bring along some friends, and I found myself invited as an expert on Santa Barbara, together with the ubiquitous New Zealander, here, yet again, to translate risqué Japanese quips into proper English terms.

Our group met in the coffee shop of a large hotel – the two other foreigners, father and son, and two attendant girls, giggling and bebanged, and decorously attached to son and teacher.

'How much does a Corvette cost in California?' was the departing student's first question to me.

287

'Oh, I don't know,' I said, ready to aim high. 'Maybe forty thousand dollars.'

'Phew!' The boy whistled through his teeth. 'Incredible!'

'Expensive right?'

'Expensive? No. Very cheap! I can buy two!' The father beamed down his blessing on Junior's ambitions. Then we went out into the streets of Shimabara, the ancient pleasure quarters, built around a willow tree, symbol of transience for both monk and courtesan. Piling into taxis, we headed off to the father's regular bar, in Gion.

Inside, the decor was meant to reproduce a French salon – plush sofas and love seats, a big grand piano, tall, heavily made-up vamps in short dresses, slinking around with iron smiles of uninterest. Hard-faced, hard-mannered, and hard-boiled, they glided about like tropical fish, objects of brightly colored weirdness. One of them sat down and played 'As Time Goes By' on the piano, another placed herself beside a baby-faced guy in a perm and white shoes, and smiled at him through clenched teeth. ('Look,' muttered the New Zealander to me, through his own clenched teeth, 'if you utter the Japanese word for that guy, we're finished!') Elsewhere, at another table, a handsome man in an expensive gray suit sat back while another woman, tall and cool as the drink she served, languidly lit his cigarette.

Truly, I thought, this was a shadow world in the Japanese setting, inverting all the laws and expectations of the daytime world, with everything reversed as in a negative. No reticence here, but boldness; no giggles, but hard smiles; not men in control, but women. It was, again, a form of Japanese pragmatism at work: if one had to find some relief or release, then one went to a special pleasure world in which certain ease could be found without danger of explosion or confusion. Debauchery on cue, a licensed kind of licentiousness. Safe sex might almost be a redundancy here.

The only exception to this Mardi Gras reversal was a young girl who sat down at our table and, perky as a university student, told us that she was doing this only as *arubaito*, or part-time work; the other ladies at the table laughed encouragingly and stared at her with hatred. In fact, she went on with engaging guilelessness, she was still taking classes. Tonight, Cinderella-like, she had to be home by twelve. This, as it happened, she continued sweetly, was her nineteenth birthday. The other girls cackled some more, their laughs like broken glass. For all I knew, hers was a role too, perfectly designed to offset the others, on this, her hundredth nineteenth birthday of the year.

All around, the ladies kept on slinking in and out, clouds of costly French perfume receding and approaching, whiskey glasses filling up, plates of cheese appearing on the table, fed to customers by hand. The English teacher did a brief stint on the piano, and in the giddy applause that followed, the father began talking to him casually, offering jokes and, parenthetically, a job worth two thousand dollars a month. The giggles and the backchat continued, glasses were clinked, a melon was filled with brandy. The teenage girl opined, 'I want to learn English,' one of her colleagues adding, 'I want to visit other country.' Beady-eyed, the company man threw in a couple of extra clauses to his offer. Then the mama-san sidled up to join our table, a small, hard bird, dressed all in white, with a soft, sweet face and gambler's eyes.

The night eased on, whiskey and tinkling laughter, and tinny melodies on the piano, and soon – most eerily of all – I noticed that I could no longer tell the difference between the professional hostesses and the 'respectable' girls at our table: both giggled too much at every comment, were promiscuous with flatteries ('Oh, you're so clever! And your Japanese is so good!'), and picked their way through English with sweet determination, dishing out an impersonal sweetness. All Japan, it sometimes seemed, came on like a hostess – sleekly appareled, full of automatic charm, and dedicated exclusively to your happiness, as if her life – or livelihood – depended on it. Yet all Japan also seemed like a mother to its own. And with classic neatness, the Japanese had always kept its women and its feelings separate: one for heart and one for hearth, one to take care of the man in the world, one to take care of him at home. The divisions were airtight. Geisha traditionally were supposed to have no home, while wives were known as *okusan*, or 'persons of the interior'. Geisha traditionally were not allowed to carry money, while women were deputed to handle all household finances. Geisha were not supposed to marry, while wives were desexualized by the husbands who called them 'Mother'. The Japanese were accomplished technicians of the heart.

Through Sachiko, meanwhile, I was beginning to see a little more of the other side of the female equation here: the young mothers I had so admired on arrival. Her best friend, Keiko, was an acupuncturist (like her father) and, like her father, a Communist; but her main activity seemed to be romance. 'She little Meryl Streep feeling,' Sachiko had explained. 'Japanese man much love this style.' And certainly, with her short bangs and whitened face, Keiko was the kind of Kyoto beauty that Japanese men adored. Her main outlet now, though, I found, was American football: by attaching herself to the Kyoto University Gangsters – as team herbalist – she had stolen into a world where she was the only woman among fifty fresh-faced boys (and vulnerable boys at that: when I attended a game between the Gangsters and the Kansai University Fighters, the shaven-headed linemen, the occasional postinterception jigs, the squeaky pom-pom girls shouting 'Dee-fense!' 'First down!' and 'Go go' – all in English – could almost have belonged to a California high school; but after the game, when I visited the locker room, the defeated *samurai* fighters were slumped amidst their pads like exhausted warriors, red-eyed, or sniffling, so choked up that they could not even speak).

Now, I gathered, Keiko lived with the twenty-one-year-old manager, her four-year-old daughter, and her ball-playing husband, in an arrangement they chose to keep ambiguous.

Hideko, Sachiko's other closest companion, was the opposite extreme – less than ninety pounds, her eyes shy and wide with childlike wonder, she was the very picture of propriety. Smiling sweetly, nearly always silent, carrying herself like a porcelain vessel in her neat skirts and expensive shirts, she was the Platonic incarnation of what a Japanese wife should be, one of those gracefully demure types, as Matthew put it, 'who would in England be called a cardigan-and-pearls lady'.

At least on the face of it. 'She very small lady, very fragile – little flower feeling,' Sachiko had told me before introducing her. 'Other person think very shy, very quiet. But inside' – her eyes flashed with mischief – 'very different! She not have dream. She love money only!'

I took this at first to be an exaggeration, or, at least, one Japanese woman's somewhat cutting appraisal of another. But as I came to know Hideko, I found that

291

Sachiko had not overstated at all: Hideko's main interest really was in money. She had married a doctor – as prudent an investment in Japan as in America – and, by virtue of having no feelings for him, was able to play the perfect doctor's wife. With all the energies and feelings that were left over, she devoted herself to becoming the very model of a high-fashion sophisticate: she played tennis, she went on scuba trips to the Great Barrier Reef, she spent her days buying Italian handbags and French cakes. She memorized all the foreign names she could, and still often boasted, this extremely poised and intelligent young woman, that she had been the only student in her college with a Gucci bag.

When Sachiko told me that Hideko loved living near banks – their presence actually turned her on – I took it as a joke. 'Very different,' Sachiko told me, shaken. 'I thinking little joke, I little laughing. But she very, very serious. Her heart not so open. She not so close husband. Then I little sad.' Hideko referred to money by the affectionate diminutive that most people reserved for children or close friends; she even got a corgi (in emulation of Queen Elizabeth II) and gave it a name that was a rhyming-slang homonym for 'money'. Often, said Sachiko, Hideko told her friends how she was planning to spend her husband's money as soon as he was dead.

There must, of course, have been a deeper side to Hideko that she did not want to show the world, or even acknowledge to herself, but certainly she played the part of loving money with unfaltering consistency. And though she was much too decorous to speak an English that she had not entirely mastered, she could hardly conceal her excitement when she heard that a foreign millionaire had come to town. So Sachiko effected an introduction to Matthew, and all three of

292

them spent long afternoons together, sitting in coffee shops and watching videos, engaged in discussions I could scarcely begin to imagine. Sometimes, he told me, they would just be sitting in the Café Mozart, munching on Viennese pastries, when Hideko, overcome by the moment, would cry out, genuinely transported, 'I'm so happy!'

Sachiko, in turn, seemed equally shaken by Matthew: here was the classic, almost ideal Japanese image of a foreigner – footloose, charming, with homes around the world and debonair Italian clothes – and all she could see in him was his sadness. He was sad, I told her one day, because he did not have a girlfriend, and he could not find a girlfriend because he was sad. She nodded solemnly. 'This man only stay Japan very short time,' she said. 'He have very sad eye. Then I want give him warm heart.'

Watching the three of them together, I began to see why Sachiko so exulted in foreign company, almost regardless of the person. Once, at her birthday party, as she bubbled on merrily, tripping over her ungrammatical English with careless delight and laughing with Matthew, Mark, and Sandy, I caught a glimpse of Hideko, in the corner, her eyes very hard: she did everything so perfectly, she was clearly thinking, why could the foreigners whose admiration she so coveted not understand that she was much better than her rough-and-ready friend?

Six

One day, I decided to surprise Sachiko with a message. I knew that she always went to the kindergarten at twelve-fifteen to collect her daughter, so at twelve-ten I stood inconspicuously around the corner from the gate. The other mothers were milling about, stoical, propping their bicycles against trees, tiny babies on their backs, waiting around outside the barred gates. I leaned on a bicycle rack and watched them small-talking in their sensible clothes. Then, with a sudden instinct, I caught sight of her, on the far side of the busy street, her white comb in her hair above the broad expanse of her forehead, where it kept the hair from falling in her eyes. Her mouth was red with unfamiliar lipstick. And her face was a face I had never seen before, hard and clenched and closed. By her side strolled her husband in a sports coat, cheery in his stride, blithely indifferent to his partner, everyone's picture of an amiable paterfamilias.

Suddenly, I saw all the sorrow of her life, caught by surprise in the passing seconds: she so taut and coiled, waiting to release her warmth on anyone who'd take it; he so friendly and impervious, jaunting along merrily by her side. The sight of the two of them – not a couple really, just two people walking down the street together – so shocked me that I left my post and hurried away, catching her eye across four lanes of traffic and seeing the sudden gratitude of her smile as I hurried home, very fast, to await her call.

*　　*　　*

Although I knew very well that the Japanese made a business, and an art form, of keeping up appearances, reassuring one with smiles and never once letting the mask slip, I was still somewhat astonished at how faultlessly Sachiko could maintain the pose. Through six months together, often for hours at a time, in situations of such closeness that every vulnerability was released, she had never once lost her temper with me, or betrayed any tiredness, or even said anything unkind – except for her one flight of foxishness. It was a kind of training, I supposed – just as some people never drink, or never, however desperate the circumstances, swear – but nonetheless it was unsettling to me how well she could play her part. Her command of her role was so perfect, she knew her lines so fluently, that it sometimes felt as if playing the picture-perfect partner came as naturally to her as being herself.

I knew, of course, that she was being especially tough in her self-censorship so as not to lose her hold on me, and the freedoms I could offer; but this very sense of vulnerability, I thought, would make most people fragile, or edgy, or brittle. That, though, was not the Japanese way: she liked me, therefore she made herself likable to me; she ran her emotions as efficiently as an office manager. Japanese women knew that the best way of attaining their dreams was by becoming dream objects themselves; that was how, like the Canadian Mounties, they always got their man. They told themselves they could not, or should not, get sad or angry or tired, and they did not. One time, when I asked Sachiko why she never lost control, she sounded, this intense and impulsive woman, like logic itself. 'You come here Japan very short time. One year. This year very important time my life. Then I want make only happy time: many happy memory and dream.'

I knew, too, that in part this was because, from birth, she had been taught that satisfaction came in service; that happiness came from making other people happy. Sachiko was so well trained in pleasing that it came to seem almost a reflex in her: if ever I told her that I liked a dish, a shirt, or even a phrase in a letter, she filed the like away and served it up again and again; when I gushed over a sweater she once gave me, she promptly rushed out and bought another one, identical. Indeed, she stored away my preferences as diligently as a courtesan and did everything she could to procure and accommodate every one of them: one week, after I had given her a tape made up of poems by Keats, Yeats, Marvell, and Shakespeare, she came to my room hoisting a Japanese edition of *The History of English Literature* almost larger than herself. She had already been boning up on the poets I had read to her, she explained, and now was eager to ask about other figures she had run into before. What did I think of Arnold Bennett? She had read one of his books long ago. Did I enjoy Orwell? Which was my favorite work of Somerset Maugham?

In time, too, I noticed how determined she was that we should always be of one mind. Whenever we went to a restaurant, I began to notice, she always ordered what I ordered, even if it was something that almost made her sick. At first I thought this was because she was new to Indian food, or Thai, or Mexican. But in time I came to see that it was simply an unvarying pattern, part of her strenuous desire to please. Soon she was beginning to drink Earl Grey tea, very strong, with milk and sugar, and to school herself in Van Morrison. One of her favorite phrases in English, which she deployed as often as possible, was 'Me too!'

When I explained to her one day my boyhood

fondness for Paddington Bear – we were contemporaries and had grown up in the same cozy, protected, English middle-class world – she dutifully went off and opened an account with Mitsui Bank, because their mascot, represented on every book and desk, was Paddington, At every opportunity, in fact, she went out of her way to harmonize, to reflect my own tastes back to me. In Japan, I gathered, opposites detracted, and even on the personal level, unity had to be asserted at every step, in every detail – most graphically, to us, in the honeymoon couples who traipse around Waikiki or Surfers Paradise or Anaheim in identically colored shirts, slacks, bags, and even belts, perfectly color-coordinated twins for every day of their trip.

I could find explanations for all this, but still I felt unnerved by Sachiko's unslipping perfection; at times, I began to wonder whether she was not more honest in her words than in her actions. Part of it, I could tell, was her gift – her culture's gift – for always seeing the best in things and always putting the best face on them: not exactly distorting the truth so much as always accentuating the positive. Sachiko saw great beauty in Nature where I saw nothing; but she also saw great beauty in Rob Lowe movies, Steve Perry songs, and her Betty Boop pencil box. She took away from *Stand by Me* the golden vision of boys together, but recalled nothing of the extended mass-vomiting scene. When I told her of someone I knew who had destroyed his whole home by carrying on a twenty-five-year illicit affair, she gasped, enraptured, 'Very beautiful story. True love, I think.' In return, she implicitly asked me only to give her happy or reassuring news (certain topics were taboo, I could tell, and if ever I brought them up, she would say, 'I not so like this *thema*', and filter them out as efficiently as her culture had done with the Rape of Nanking).

It was not, really, that Sachiko was naive; rather that she had been trained to find reassurance everywhere. It always amused me when she extolled her friend Sandy because, she said, Sandy was always smiling, never raised her voice with her children, never let her sadness show; because, in short, Sandy embodied for her all the sweetness, cheerfulness, and self-control that we associate with Japanese women. To me, this was mostly a reflection of Sachiko's own innocence in reading foreign cultures and of her penchant for sifting out only the good and remaking the world in her own happy image. The first principle of Japanese Romanticism seemed to be the culture's Emersonian assumption that it could refashion the world as it chose, and might as well do so, therefore, in a bright and pleasant light.

Yet her unfailing self-command only aggravated the eternal game of she loves me, she loves me not. I often wondered: was I attracted to her because she was so like me, or was she so like me because I was attracted to her? In Japan, this was as vexing a riddle as the chicken and the egg: *dakara* all over again. When it came to shopkeepers, say, I could happily accept that all their kindness was feigned, or functional at least; but when it came to Sachiko, that was less easy to acknowledge.

And then, at last, one night, I got my answer. Just as I was getting ready for sleep, the phone rang in the corridor downstairs, and it was Sachiko, asking me to come across town to her house; when I arrived, I found her sobbing and sobbing, her lavish hair tied up in a scruffy ponytail, her unmade-up face puffy and smeared. As soon as she caught sight of me, she threw herself upon me and buried her head in my chest, her small body heaving, and sobbing, and sobbing, as if with no hope of respite. I could feel her convulsions around me, her fingers tightening round my waist so hard I shook. I leaned back to look at her, but she grabbed me again, digging her fingers into my back, and sobbing, and sobbing, and sobbing.

Finally, motioning me to a chair, she pointed, through tears, at her tiny, worn dictionary, opened up on her 'Bunny' tablecloth. I leaned over to where she put her finger under a word: 'sacrifice'.

'So,' I said, as gently as I could, 'you think that you must make all the "sacrifice", and I don't have to make any?'

Eyelids bruised and tired, she nodded.

'I know; maybe you're right. And you think my life is easy and free but yours is very hard. Because you must make plans, find baby-sitters, give excuses to your mother. While I am alone, and everything's easy. And you have to live with your husband and your children, while I have only myself.' A small nod, that of a little girl getting told off.

'I know, Sachiko. I know it's hard for you. Please cry if you like.' And she did, flinging herself round me once more. I held her, and looked round – at the otter smiling down at me from the ceiling, at the jigsaw puzzle on the table, at the winking red jewel in her Wizard of Oz comb.

'You can cry,' I went on. 'That's all right. Don't worry,' I mumbled into her hair, and she sobbed, and clung, and shook in my arms. 'That's all right. Please don't worry.' Her Swiss cuckoo clock struck ten, and at last she sat back and brushed away her tears.

Then, over the little table, in one steady, uninterrupted flow, she came out with the whole story of her life, and all the accumulated sadnesses that had brought her to this lonely, perky room. 'Before I always living parents' house, I little prison feeling,' she began. 'Mother many times sick, father always tired. Grandma die. Dog die. Brother go many place; but I must always help parent. Then first time I meet husband, little rescue feeling. I dream maybe little *Gone With the Wind*.

'But soon true marriage, very terrible feeling! Mother-in-law, father-in-law, more more prison feeling. Husband all day work, never together time. Then I have first child, I more more excited. But children not so help. Soon very tired. I have many dream. But I think I cannot find.'

Outside, a train whooshed past, drowning out her words.

'Husband many times promise we little visit my brother, America. But he never do. My husband very kind man but not so strong: usual Japanese situation. He want only usual life, very quiet life. He not have dream.'

That, I could see, was his main transgression: he was not, in her telling, a drunk or a tyrant or a philanderer or a crook; just a regular, fallible man captive to his received sense of duty and too small to accept the challenge of change. 'He very good man,' she went on. 'But he much afraid his mother and father. Last year I ask, which you prefer: me or mother? Please you choose. And he choose mother. Then I "all lost" feeling.'

My heart went out to her, and to him too, this fond and dutiful father and husband, clearly decent and agreeable, and confused now, surely, as he felt his pretty, vivacious wife slipping away from him, but not sure what he could do to reverse it or what he had done to deserve it. He was only guilty, in a sense, of innocence; but now, unable to get home before eleven-thirty six nights a week, and totally exhausted on the seventh – working all through the night, sometimes, at his parents' shop – he could not find the time to turn things around. He might wish that he had more time with his family, but that seemed as fruitless as wishing he had six legs.

And Sachiko, too, was clearly captive to nothing but her situation; captive to Japan, in fact. I could see why she wanted to escape and how difficult it must be to have that hope centered on another. And as she went on talking, all her heart came finally tumbling out: how her perfection had indeed been an act of will; how she had wanted to be flawless lest flaws drive me away; how she had tried to act out only the best parts of herself. I had upset her sometimes, and she had smiled; she had worried, and had laughed.

That night, Sachiko crossed a threshold of sorts, and ever after, I saw a more relaxed and shifting kind of person: a heart, in fact, not so different from the ones I knew at home – spontaneous, scared, willful, and warm. She allowed herself sometimes to get put out, or jealous, or depressed; she grew more direct in her requests; she even started ordering her own dishes. I came to know the feel of her warm tears on my cheek (though if ever there came a knock on the door, she composed herself instantly and put on a radiant smile). I came to see her emotional prudence, always watching the endings of movies first (in order to enjoy the pleasure of melancholy in advance). I came to recognize her favorite, self-delighted cry – 'I cannot stop. Cannot control. Cannot other! I so sorry!'

Yet even now, with so much to lose, she still responded to most disappointments more in sorrow than in anger; and I felt her occasional reproaches the more because they were unvoiced. If ever I did something to upset her, Sachiko's eyes would silently fill with tears, and I felt more strongly rebuked than by any rough obscenity; she was Japanese enough, I thought, to be truly gentle, and to use that gentleness to induce a sense of guilt as well as debt.

Mostly, though, I could never get over how happy she remained, even now. Ardent, dreamy, mischievous, and sweet, she giggled on cider and got up at dawn for *zazen*; practiced kung fu kicks in the temple and spun herself around in her joy. Here she was, I sometimes thought, loosed of all moorings, her parents antagonized, her family all but abandoned, and an unknown future in front of her, and yet, even now, she humbled me with her good nature.

Seven

One day, on a clear spring morning, I decided it was time at last to go and stay in a Japanese monastery – not a temple like the one where I had lived on first arriving, but a training center where I could briefly sample the rigors of the monastic life. The natural choice seemed Tōfukuji, where first I had tried *zazen* and where first I had met Sachiko. The largest Rinzai sect monastery in Japan, Tōfukuji was also well known for its cosmopolitan *rōshi*, one of the few Zen masters in Japan willing to take in Western students – even women – and concerned about the state of Zen around the world.

When I arrived at the temple gates, I was met by a young fifth-year monk from California. In the heavy silence of the entrance hall, a would-be monk was kneeling on the polished wooden stairs, head bowed in supplication, maintaining a motionless position that he would have to keep up for two days or more while his petition to enter the temple was ritually refused. Nearby, in a tiny antechamber, another aspirant – at the next stage of the process – was seated alone, in silence, in a position he would have to keep up for five more days before being admitted to the temple. Once inside, each of them would have to spend three years or more in a regimen unswerving as the temple's cedar pillars.

Greeting me in the silence with a bow, the monk led me along the narrow polished corridors of the monastery, a few busy figures robed in black gliding past us. As we went, he explained, in a whisper, all the disciplines that I would have to observe: how I must walk, hands folded across my chest, and how I must bow each time I entered and left the *zendō*; how I must step across the threshold with my left foot first, and how I must line up my sandals, in a perfect row, at the base of the meditation platform. How I must sit, how I must breathe: how I must learn to live deliberately.

He led me to a tiny guest room and asked me to take off my watch. Then, serving tea, he told me a little about his life. At times, when he talked of L.A. and his family, he sounded like a kid again, the twenty-two-year-old college boy he had left behind as soon as he entered the temple; at other times, when he talked of Zen, he acquired a sonorous *gravitas* that made him indisputably my elder. It was a little like being with Sachiko again: when the monk asked about where he could find the best pizza in town – on his one day off each month – he seemed a guileless teenager; when he told me how he wanted to live, I could see why he was the *rōshi's* prize student.

Then the training began in earnest. In silence we went into a simple medieval chamber, and in silence ate a dinner of vegetables served from wooden buckets. If I wanted more, my guide had explained, I would have to tap my bowl; and after I was finished, I would have to rinse out the bowl with my finger and hot tea, ensuring that not a speck of rice was left. Then I would have to wrap the bowl up, left over right over bottom, in the *furoshiki* that was almost the monk's only possession. They were allowed no books, no keepsakes, no reminders of their lives outside; nothing but their robes, their bowls, and the body-length mats on which they slept face-up.

Our dinner finished, we walked across, in the chill

304

of the darkening afternoon, to the wooden shack where the monks were allowed, once every five days, to take baths. The man preparing the bath today, a bespectacled man in his fifties with a look of frightened bewilderment, was rushing around in panic while the younger monks shouted orders at him. Only a week before, I learned, this man had been a regular salaryman, living with his family at home; then, however, he had learned that he would have to take over his family temple and been obliged to join a monastery. Now, as the junior monk in the place, he was the one the others were obliged to toughen up.

Scrubbed and rinsed clean in the scalding water of the tub, we proceeded to the ancient meditation hall. As the last light of day seeped in through the pulled-back screens, I sat with the monks, erect on the wooden platform, in silence. Occasionally, a monk, standing silent sentry by the door, strode forward and whacked, with his long wooden stick, anyone whose form was slipping – usually the terrified-looking newcomer in spectacles. The other seven sat in motionless *zazen*. Now and then, in the bird-scattered quiet of dusk, the mournful melody of a garbage collector's truck floated up from a nearby street. Occasionally, there was a swish of black robes, a flash of motion, as a monk headed away for *dokusan*, his daily private conference with the *rōshi*.

I too, once, at school, had gone off on evenings such as this for private meetings, and alone with my thoughts – too new to be above this – I thought back in the dark to school in England, so similar to this: the cold showers at dawn, the ascetic bare rooms, the beatings, the daily prayers in five-hundred-year-old chambers. The sense of hierarchy, the all-male rites, the chores, the fears, the longings – all seemed eerily the same. But that kind of school had been preparing its students to take over

305

the world, while this one taught them to renounce it; ruling ourselves, at school, we were made to feel we could rule everything; while here, ruling the self, one was trained to need nothing from the world.

My legs by now were aching, my body was stiff; I waited and waited for the session to end. Finally, with relief, I heard a monk stir, and draw back the screens against the night. In a flash, with movements as quick and precise as in some army drill, the monks whipped out their bedrolls and stood at attention; the poor businessman, wrestling unhappily with his lot and unable to get it all done in five seconds, earned more sharp shouts and rebukes. Then, single file, we walked off to the temple garden, silver in the moonlight.

Nine figures, eerie in black robes, shaven heads shining in the silent dark, sat perfectly erect in the cool night air. When at last I left to sleep, all eight were sitting there, ready to continue through the night.

By three o'clock the next morning, my guide was rustling me awake. Bare feet cold on the wooden planks, we shuffled back into the meditation hall. There, still groggy, I followed the monks to another room, where gongs sounded and sutras were chanted, broken by the silver ringing of a bell. Then we returned to the hall for more *zazen*, screen doors open to the chilling dark as, very slowly, the light began to seep in and the birds to sing.

Hours, many hours later, we took a brief breakfast of gruel and pickled plums. Then we went out into the golden light of morning and began sweeping leaves, the monks working rapidly, in silence, sweeping and sweeping till every last inch was spotless. Above us, the temple's cherry tree blazed against the dawning blue.

Then there was long scrubbing of floors, on all fours,

and chopping of wood, a quickly taken snack, and more hard physical labor (a form of moving meditation). In midmorning, the monks donned straw sandals and wicker hats and went into the neighborhood on their daily alms-collecting rounds. Then they returned for more work, more meditation, and, perhaps, at night, a few hours sleep on their mats. To an outsider, the Californian monk had told me, the temple seemed as calm and motionless as a river; inside, however, you got caught up in the rush and intensity of the surging currents. Every day was so full, he said, that there was never a moment of true rest. Did he ever miss the world? I asked. No, he said, touchingly. Nothing but his books.

Before I left the monastery, I went for an audience with the *rōshi*, whose presence I had felt all the time I was in Kyoto, as Mark's longtime friend and Sachiko's steady counselor. Seated in a thick leather chair, a tiny figure in huge orange robes, his windows thrown open to the green and golden quiet of the garden, he looked at me with warm and piercing eyes. He greatly feared for Zen in America, he told me over tea, because everyone there was after instant wisdom. Some people were so intent on *satori*, or instant revelation, that they actually bought books with answers to koan. The Americans did have one advantage over the Japanese, insofar as they were willing to take one day a week off. But as long as one reminded oneself constantly of how much fun one should be having on a holiday, it was not, in the true sense, a 'holy day'.

The 'pride' of Americans, he went on, and their openness to challenges were exemplary; but he worried about their ambition, their love of cerebration. By coming to Zen with their minds, they were all but ensuring their failure at a discipline whose aim, after all, was to short-circuit the mind. 'You should not think about the koan,' he said, as any Zen master must. 'You should become the koan.'

During his own training, he explained, his teacher, Shibayama-roshi, had shouted at him constantly, 'Be an idiot! Be a fool!' And in time, it had worked. At first, when he had begun, he had always been thinking of his girlfriend and his college pals. For five years, he had not been free of this. Intense meditation, after all, sharpened the very powers of memory that were the main block to meditation. But then, at last, he had learned to live in the moment.

The *rōshi* ended, in the classic Zen manner, with a story. Once upon a time, an old man was trying to explain to his grandson the belief of Jōdo Buddhism that the Pure Land lies in the West. Practical and alert as children are, the little boy had pointed out that if you go west, and farther west, you end up going around the world and back where you first started. Paradise, in short, was all around us, if only we would stop and look.

I, however, incorrigible foreigner, was still lost in books and hoping to bring Zen home to me by reading in Thoreau. For the rough earth of his prose was crisscrossed with the footsteps of Zen poets. Certainly, his ground seemed theirs – and his heaven too! – as if all of them were acolytes living in hermit huts scattered across the slopes of some sacred mountain. With his discursive essays on 'Moonlight' and 'Autumnal Hints', his retreat into the woods to 'transact some private business with the fewest obstacles', and his insistence on living in a society of one, Thoreau seemed to have worked out for himself what was sacred in Japan (where the very character for 'Nature' could be read as 'self-seeing'); and every Zen wanderer and poet and solitary seemed, in his way, another

308

sojourner in Walden, living off berries in the wood, sustaining himself on natural scriptures, devoting himself to slowness and to idling. Having given up everything, he had nothing to lose – and all the world to gain.

So when I read in Bashō, 'My solitude shall be my company, and my poverty my wealth', I felt I was reading again the anarchist of Walden, pursuing his nonviolent revolution of words, remaking the world by reversing its meanings. And when I read in Dōgen, 'Why leave behind the seat that exists in your own house and go aimlessly off to the dusty reaches of other lands?' I could almost hear his neighbor in New England declaring, 'It is not worth the while to go round the world to count the cats in Zanzibar.' And when I read Kamo no Chōmei's 'Account of My Hut', singing the praises of a simple life of solitude, I found Thoreau again in the recluse's famous claim that none can know the pleasures of loneliness who has not tasted them himself.

Soon, in fact, the parallels started doubling back on themselves, till the Buddhists almost seemed the Transcendentalists' disciples. When Emerson wrote that 'The great gifts are not got by analysis. Everything good is on the highway', he all but enunciated the guiding principle of the wandering Zen monk. And when he wrote, in a poem, 'Sleep is not, death is not, who seems to die, lives', he sounded almost like a Buddhist haiku master. Even the Buddha could sound at times like a follower of the Sage of Concord: 'Self is the lord of self, who else should be the lord?'

I got the strongest chill, though, when I read in Emerson: 'Women, more than all, are the element and kingdom of illusion.' What could be closer to the old Mahayana saying: 'Of all the forms of illusion, woman is the most important'?

*   *   *

Just as I was pursuing these connections, Mark, with his unerring gift for reading my thoughts the better to guide them, handed me a volume of Santōka, one of his favorite poets, a monk who was said to have walked 28,000 miles on his path, along the back roads of Japan, in a straw hat, retracing some of Bashō's steps. Though the natural descendant of Bashō and Ryōkan, this solitary figure was a citizen of our century, who sustained his 'walking meditation' through all the tumult of the early decades.

Santōka's free-style haiku were a model of the form, so cleansed of ornament and abstraction that they sometimes ended less than ten words after they began; his art seemed to come to him as naturally as breathing. Free of pretension, his poems were free of tension. And in accordance with that spirit, his life was also as clear and simple as running water. His great joy, he said, was 'one room, one person, one light, one desk, one bath, and a cup of sake'. The only journal he read was his own, and what little extra he had, he gave away. Even the constant sake drinking he did, he did, as he did everything, with all his being.

When I read of Santōka's defection from society and most civil of disobediences – refusing to participate in the preparations for war – I could hear his words echoing round the woods at Walden, and so too, when he wrote, with characteristically bracing simplicity, 'To do what I want, and not to do what I don't – this is why I entered such a life.' Yet the most striking thing about his wanderings was that they were always in pursuit of something more than self. 'My pilgrimage,' he wrote beautifully, 'is into the depths of the human heart.'

A little later, in the spring, Mark and his teacher put on an exhibition together of paintings based on Santōka's poems, Mark translating them into simple images, his *sensei* scrawling the poems, in vigorous calligraphy, round the edges of the shapes. And when I went to the gallery and spent an hour or two with the pictures, slowly, in the silence of the department store, I began to feel I could understand a little, for the first time ever, the power of blank space. How space can live, and draw one in, as silences can speak; and how the Japanese, more than anyone, could charge the emptiness. When Mark drew the lonely figure of Santōka, one felt the space around him, irradiated with his quiet, and when he drew a flower, he drew nothing but its shape. Autumn was merely the faintest outline of a falling leave. Attention had been brought to such a point that it turned into a kind of meditation.

At the exhibition, I realized, for the first time, why the Japanese were fascinated with *ma*, or space, and how they tried to sustain it inside their crowded homes and lives. They sought to approach life, in a sense, the way one spoke one's language to a foreigner, in a spirit of simplicity, sympathy, and clarity. In Santōka's poems, translated by the side of the paintings, nothing extraneous intrudes.

> *My begging bowl*
> *Accepts the falling leaves.*

Mark's painting of the poem was just a leaf in downward flight.

> *No more houses to beg from,*
> *Clouds on the mountains.*

Mark's painting showed just clouds.

> *All day I say nothing,*
> *The sound of waves.*

The painting caught sound, and nothing more.

The poems themselves, in their clarity and ease, began to open up a space within. One had to tread them slowly, as through snow; and step by patient step, one began to savor the crunch, the texture, the depth.

> *Brightness of the snow*
> *Fills the house with calm.*

Reading very slowly, I began to feel the calm of that, the soothing quiet of the falling snow, remaking the world without a sound. I began to see the warmth of the poem, too, and its freshness; how snow brought silence, and a spaciousness within. The gradual movements of its flight began to slow the mind down, as surely as the tolling of a bell.

> *No path but this one,*
> *Spring snow falling.*

As I wandered round the room, with Sachiko by my side, I began to think how much we need space in those we love, space enough to accommodate growth and possibility. Knowledge must leave room for mystery; intimacy, taken too far, was the death of imagination. Keeping some little distance from her was, I thought, a way of keeping an open space, a silence for the imagination to fill.

'At the same time that we are earnest to explore and learn all things,' Thoreau had written, 'we require that all things be mysterious and unexplainable.'

And as we walked around the paintings, Mark's teacher, eighty-six years old now, but alive with coiled energy, his shaggy gray hair falling bohemian across his face, came into the gallery. Full of energy, he began telling us about his coming trip to China, his various projects, the classes he gave, the books he was working on. Then he spoke warmly of the abbot of Tōfukuji, a friend of his for life.

'*Chotto kibishii*,' said Sachiko of the *rōshi*. 'A little strict.'

'*Demo yasashii*,' added the painter, smiling. 'But gentle too.' 'Strictness without gentleness is not so good,' he went on, 'and gentleness without strictness is not so good. Strictness and gentleness together are the best.'

Eight

Sachiko's goodbye, when it came, was as perfectly planned, as exquisitely decorated, as everything else in this land of ceremonies.

One day, towards the end of spring, she invited me and Matthew to join her and Hideko at a tea ceremony. She appeared in the hotel lobby in a radiant blue kimono, hair done up in the style of a Meiji maiden, her steps in pure-white socks and wooden sandals slow and reticent. We watched a woman in a white peacock kimono glide along against the paper screens, flooded now with early-morning sun, and we entered our names with thick brushes in a visitors' book. Then, with a bow, we were ushered into a room full of bowing matrons, all beady-eyed and kimonoed, as used to this as we might be to church. Seated cross-legged, we sipped at our tea, dutifully inspecting the lacquer tea box, inscribed with a scarcely visible tracery of cherry blossoms. 'Night cherry,' Sachiko whispered under her breath, and the matrons leaned a little closer. 'Little *monoganashii* feeling.' We inspected a scroll that told of a flower and a butterfly, and, eyes bright, she looked over at me meaningfully as the springtime message was translated.

Matthew, meanwhile, was his usual engaging self, and as the matrons looked at us in wonder, he started pulling at the legs crossed under him, forming a hideous frown and delivering, in loud stage whispers, a moving account of his torments. 'Can't understand it.

Terribly simple, actually. Legs quite dead. Can't move. Don't know if I'll ever recover!'

'Are you OK?' Sachiko asked anxiously, leaning over me towards him, to extend a hand.

'Oh yes,' he said, smiling tightly. 'Fine, fine. Just a little stiff. Can't move, you see. Awfully painful, actually. Quite extraordinary.'

The pantomime continued, I as ill at ease as Matthew, and the matrons staring over at us with quickened excitement, exchanging happy glances and then looking back at us, in awe; for them, I imagined hardened veterans of these rites, the presence of two galumphing foreign males, banging against walls, attacking their tea with chopsticks, and pulling at their limbs like pretzels, was doubtless a welcome gust of comic relief in what was otherwise dull routine. 'Terribly sorry, awfully embarrassing,' Matthew apologized, smiling unhappily back at them. 'Not sure, actually, whether I can move!'

'This was something Merchant Taylors' never prepared you for,' I whispered back.

'No, quite,' he answered, tight-lipped, then erupted into schoolboy chortles.

The tea bowl went round and round for our admiration, we munched at our sweets, scattering crumbs, which we proceeded to fold ineptly in the napkins Sachiko gave us. Then at last it was over. Matthew and I disentangled limbs and got up, legs so dead that I, standing up, reeled and staggered against the paper screen before bowing farewell to the delighted matrons and tiptoeing out to the lobby. Outside, in the soothing sun, Sachiko led our incongruous band to a coffee shop, and as the four of us settled round a circular table, Matthew filled us in on how a two-day trip to Tokyo Disneyland had somehow kept him away for a month. In Tokyo, he explained, he had found everything he wanted: high fashion, neon futurism, even an English-speaking girlfriend. After two weeks, however, of a consuming intensity that had almost frightened him, he had rung her up one day, to find that she had dropped him for a new foreigner.

'Ah, very beautiful story,' said Sachiko dreamily. 'Little cherry blossom feeling. One-night dream.'

'Yes, yes, precisely,' said Matthew agreeably, used by now to the Japanese habit of turning even pain into something lovely, and unaware, perhaps, that she was in effect referring to a one-night stand.

After our coffee was finished, Sachiko dispatched the other two into a taxi bound for a department store, and clomped along the wide boulevard by my side, in tiny footsteps. 'I come you room?' she asked. 'Are you OK? We little buy cake?' and, stopping at a bakery, we made our way through a riddle of sunny streets, back to my room. There, sitting down, she unclasped her earrings and, laying them tidily on my table, took me by surprise.

'Today,' she began, 'I wear kimono so you always keep very happy memory of me.' I could not fathom what she meant. 'You give me much dream, much imagination. I want you write many thing, very beautiful memory of Japan. We together time, very happy, many dream. But then, other life, very difficult. I much much thinking in my heart – then little stomach problem. My heart little sick.'

She stopped, and I, accustomed both to the solemnity of her feelings and to their sudden turns, held my breath.

'You have very beautiful bird life,' she went on. 'Very free, very easy. But my life very different. I tiny, I not have wing. I need more *akirameru*.' She stopped and, turning to her crumpled, leather-bound old dictionary, skimmed through the pages and stopped

316

on the word she wanted. 'Re-sig-na-tion. Here in Japan, this very important. All person must have this resig—'

'Resignation.'

'Re-sig-na-tion. If not have, many problem. Then maybe I must little say goodbye.'

Looking back at her, I fumbled for my words. Then, turning to the only piece of paper at hand – the happy orange-and-white bag of the bakery – I sketched a diagram of my heart, and she, a little sadly, nodded over her cake. I then drew another picture, of the three routes open to us.

'Maybe goodbye best,' she said. 'But please today, you come together my house, play together children?' There was nothing I wanted less to do right now, but I could see that she needed to recast the play, to establish herself again in the mother's role and me as the friend of the family. And so we went back out into the mild spring sun, and on the long train ride across town, I watched her rearrange her self, as I did too, putting on a bright smile and an air of cheerful competence.

Back at home, Yuki and Hiroshi raced out and bounced all over me, pulling me this way and that, and I began roaring at Hiroshi like a bear, and lifting Yuki high into the air while she screamed, and, when they were not looking, wheezing and whistling like an imagined raccoon. Then Yuki careened off to grab her moth-eaten, one-eyed orange raccoon. ('Lasker,' explained her mother. 'Lasker?' And she sang me the jingle of a TV cartoon, 'Rascal Raccoon.') Then the children, well trained already in how to entertain all visitors, changed into their best clothes – Yuki into a pretty frock, Hiroshi donning a red bow tie – and solemnly took turns playing the piano, feet dangling poignantly only halfway to the floor. Then all four of

317

us went back to the Nogi Shrine, in a light spring rain, and played hide-and-seek in the gathering dark, as we had done on the day we met.

In the dying light, Sachiko bought us all cans of milk tea, and while the children played with acorns, the two of us padded around the noiseless shrine, dedicated to the hero of the Russo-Japanese War, the man who had been the Emperor's headmaster and role model. The walkways were deserted now in the rain, the wet ground strewn with petals; the bare branches were black against graying skies.

'Yesterday,' she said dreamily, guiding me to her favorite tree, 'I lie down this bench, and look at sky. Sky very blue; cherry very pink. Spring wind come down, so soft. I look up, I dream I have little wing. Bird talking, leaves dancing in spring wind.'

She pointed out the different trees to me, told me the stories that she shared with them, explained which one was king and which his ladies-in-waiting. 'But today,' she went on ruminatively, 'all cherry fall. Little fox wedding day.'

'Half rain, half sun, you mean?'

She nodded, and I could see her in a fox wedding mood herself, caught between conflicting dreams.

In her flat, she cooked a quick dinner and packed the children off to bed. Then, seated at the small table that took up nearly all of the poster-filled room, she told me, eyes shining, about all the hopes she'd ever had, and how they'd disappeared. I looked around at the pictures of a-ha, the grinning sea otter on the ceiling, the framed photo of her children with the abbot of the temple: this was how the Japanese ended things, I thought, avoiding the embarrassment and mess of sudden death with the clean break of a kind of suicide. Everything brought to a ceremonial close, as shapely as a morning-after poem.

When it came time for me to leave, she brought out a scarf and tied it round my neck to keep me from the cold, and then walked, as usual, to the train station, as on the first day that I'd visited. As the train pulled away, I watched her standing alone on the platform, waving and waving till her small figure was finally out of my sight.

Summer

Surface is an illusion, but so is depth.

—DAVID HOCKNEY

One

Now that Matthew had finally exhausted Tokyo, there
was nothing left for him in Japan. Having found the
worldly life he'd always craved, he decided that he
should, in fact, be seeking out the spiritual life. He
doubted what he knew, and then revised his doubts.
And the very qualities that attracted many foreigners to
Japan – that it left one alone, and therefore free – were
for Matthew, I could tell, an ordeal; Japan offered him
everything except direction. He felt his own uncertainty mocked by the equable calm and self-
containment of Japan. Besides, Japan had little time for
agonized self-scrutiny or coffee-house ruminations;
speculation and introspection were regarded as
indulgences that took one away from the matter at
hand. So now, having stuck it out through the darkest
days of winter, just as the weather was beginning to
clear, he decided to leave.

I was sorry to see him go, my partner in bewilderment,
especially since he had no special place to go, and on
our last night on the town, I invited him to come along
with me to one of the year's last performances of the
Miyako Odori, the biannual geisha dance, which had
been, for more than a century, the only occasion when
the general public could see the most storied and
private of entertainers in action. Performed in spring
and autumn, when the blossoms were pink and the
maple leaves red, the all-woman show was a kind of
counter to the all-male performances of Kabuki. And

over the years, the show itself had generated almost as many legends as those it represented: most famously the tale of George Morgan, the American millionaire, who had grown so smitten with a young apprentice geisha, or *maiko*, whom he saw onstage that he had embarked on a love affair as famous as those of Mademoiselle Chrysanthème or Okichi-san. Nowadays, however, there was such a shortage of girls willing to enter the old profession that the producers had had to turn to local high school students, and the daughters of loyal patrons, to fill the twenty places.

Seated in the quiet auditorium, having missed the tea ceremony beforehand through our inability to read the tickets, Matthew and I watched scene after scene unfurl with the precise exquisiteness of watercolor prints, in richest indigo and whitest white. A chorus line of *maiko* came prancing, tiny-footed, on to the stage in tidy, decorous rows, bearing crimson leaves of maples or blossoms of the daintiest pink. The geisha, however, who lined the balconies, cradling samisen and letting out screeching cries, were the most terrifying hags I'd ever seen: craggy old harpies, dressed all in black, their unsmiling, berouged faces soured with the lines of scowls. Refugees from some country production of *Macbeth*, they gave new meaning to the notion of a dragon lady. They also put one Japanese romance firmly in its place.

The show, however, unfolded in one shimmering sequence of gossamer backdrops – love stories presented as immortal tableaux, emotions translated into standard, stunning gestures. Then we streamed out into the bright afternoon and began walking along Hanamikōji-dōri, or Flower-Viewing Street, the paper lanterns outside the ancient teahouses painted all with plovers in the dying afternoon. Suddenly, I heard a voice behind me.

'Excuse me, are you Pico?'

I looked around to see a young foreigner, with a bright-eyed woman I took to be his mother.

'Yes.'

'I'm John Horton. You may not remember me, but we were on a bus together in Tibet two years ago!'

'Of course,' I said, looking at him again. The last time I had seen John, he had indeed been in a rocking vehicle crowded with peasants, bouncing across Tibetan plateaus, while his brother has been stretched out on the back seat, moaning, the simultaneous victim of Chinese food, altitude sickness, Chinese airline service, and the bus itself. At the time, I remembered vividly, John had been on his way to Kobe; a quick-witted entrepreneur who'd been in business since his teens, he'd told me he had heard that Japan was good for quick kills and, better yet, that Japanese girls were mad for Western men.

'You're living here now?' I asked him.

'Right!'

'Doing business, I assume.'

'No, no. My only interest is in Buddhism.'

'But the last time we met . . .' and then, seeing his expression, I let the sentence trail.

'Yeah. My plan is to go to China, learn the language, and then go to this Vipassana meditation center in Bombay.' Japan had a wonderful knack, I noticed, of awakening foreigners' interest in every form of Buddhism except the Japanese. Still, John's conversion had at least been in a relatively positive direction; most people seemed to come to Japan for Buddhism, and end up after girls or cash.

'Good luck with your studies,' I said, as Matthew and I strolled away. It was apt, I thought, that Matthew see this before he left, and I, too, of course; the confusion of interests – of people coming here for good

325

deeds as well as good times – was everywhere.

The guesthouse in which I lived, in fact, might almost have been a sociologist's model designed to illustrate the varieties of romantic experience, made up, as it was, mostly of lonely foreign males and shady, water-world Japanese. The place's noises alone were a constant register of frustration and fulfillment. One Belgian girl loudly satisfied herself each day, while the room next to mine was a veritable laugh track of giggles and slaps and high-pitched squeals of 'Stop! Stop it! Please stop!' in Japanese.

One night, a man down the corridor began howling and howling, rending the night with obscenities. 'Oh god, oh fuck, oh jesus!' he cried. 'Oh god, please stop, I can't stand it.' Wrenched from my dreams, I lay there in the dark, listening to his terrible wails. 'Oh god, oh jesus, oh god, why did I do it?' The shrieks of the damned must sound like this, I thought. 'Oh jesus, oh fuck, oh god, how can you do this to me?'

Later, I learned that he had been in great physical pain; his main affliction, though, was loneliness.

Another night, at 3 a.m., I was woken by some banging and knocking on another neighbor's door. A few hours later, I was startled out of sleep again by a clamor of excited whispers in the corridor outside. Opening the door, I found three teenage Japanese girls, no older than fifteen, apparently camped out on the floor. The day went on, but they did not, and every time I came or went, I found them squatting on the floor, next to a pair of his-and-hers Snoopy slippers, laying sustained siege to the quiet, studious Swede who lived next door to me.

For three days, the unlikely pop trio remained there, as patient as a courtly lover outside his sweetheart's balcony, cleaning their teeth at the basin in the corridor, padding, in towels, to the shower, and occasionally finding other foreigners to take them in for the night. When finally Hans returned home from a trip one night, he surveyed the scene and shrugged his leather-jacketed shoulders. 'I only meet these girls one time,' he said helplessly, 'in Pub Africa. I do not understand.'

A couple of days later, when I went down to the guesthouse telephone to make a call, Parker, the gracious Southern boy, shyly opened his door and invited me in for a chat. By the time I arrived, he was deep in Hume's *Treatise Concerning Human Understanding*.

He put the book down. 'I need a girlfriend – and bad!' he began disconcertingly, this tall and scholarly lawyer's son whose dream was to go to divinity school. 'I haven't had a woman for so long that if I don't find one soon, I'm going to leave.' I looked around at his monastic cell: Heidegger, volume after volume of Kierkegaard, *The Principles of Buddhist Psychology*. 'Maybe summer will be better. Have you seen all the pregnant women around right now? I'm thinking, if they're pregnant now, summer must be the time when it's all happening.' He looked at me pleadingly, with an eager freshman's smile that bespoke the depths of his desperation. Around him were volumes of Rilke and Nietzsche and Zen.

'You like philosophy?'

'Yeah,' he says, a frat boy abashed. 'Didn't I tell you? I lived in Oxford last year, studying being. And I'm spending a year over here, doing nothingness.' There was no apparent irony in his voice. 'I really love books, Books and women. If I can't have one, I've got to have the other.'

Parker, I recalled, had managed in his nine months here to pick up precisely four words of Japanese – 'little', 'horny', 'sorry', and 'cockroach'. (I often wondered what kinds of sentences he fashioned with this small but pregnant repertoire – 'I'm a little horny cockroach', perhaps – and what effect they had on the girls he was trying to impress.)

'I wish one could be married and still be a monk,' he said.

'But that's exactly what they have over here! That's one of the principles of Buddhism in Japan.'

'Then why become a monk?'

I, thinking of Sachiko, and my plans of being alone, could give him no answer: all of us, it seemed, found only what we did not crave, and vice versa.

Two

On the night of the May moon, the famously hazy
spring moon beloved by monks and second in importance only to the harvest moon, I walked with Mark
through the local temples in the early warmth. The
moonlight magnetized my attention this night, glowing at the edges of my mind – it blazed – and Mark told
me the story of the Chinese poet who tried to grab the
moon's reflection in the water and drowned. For
the Buddhist, the moon was illusion, *maya*, all that
was chimerical; yet it was also the Tathagata, a symbol
of enlightenment, and of the operations of divinity in
the world. The Buddha's mind was said to be like the
reflection of moonlight in clear, deep water; and
the Buddha himself was said to be as constant as the
moon, though sometimes he looked full, sometimes
empty, sometimes half shrouded in clouds.

Meandering slowly past the silent, shadowed houses
– a woodblock of ancient stillness – I thought again of
how the lady and the monk interacted here, as did so
many of the riddles of Japan. Was the moon a symbol
of some higher beauty, or was it just a pretty earring in
the sky? Enlightenment, I recalled reading in Dōgen,
was 'like the moon reflected in the water. There is no
disturbance here, and all the moon is reflected in a
drop.' Sei Shōnagon, though, in certain moods, had
taken it for what it was, no more: 'At any time, and in
any place, I find moonlight very moving.'

Mark, then, went on to tell me of the Bashō poem of

the clouds that obscured the moon, and as so often with him, I could see how much he had picked up from being around Zen monks and teachers; how he, too, had the gift of keeping one true to oneself, yet always thinking the best of one: a rigorously monitored idealism. I mentioned this to him, and he grasped my meaning quickly.

'The whole idea of a teacher,' he said, blue hawk eyes flashing, 'is to present a reflective mirror. Not a blank surface, really, but a screen, on which you have to confront yourself. Like the moon on the water, in a way. When you confront a Zen master, what you're really seeing are not his limitations but yours.'

'So that if you think he's strict, it's because you're guilty? And if you find him silent, it's because you talk too much?'

'Yeah, I guess. There are many ways to do it. Sometimes they just let you talk yourself into trouble. Or they'll shock you out of your assumptions. Or they'll cut you down. Everything you think you're seeing in him is actually coming from yourself. A saint, I think, is someone who brings out the good in everyone he meets.'

'So it's almost as if he's your true nature, in a sense, the better part of you?'

Mark, schooled in silences, said nothing.

A little later, at the beginning of *tsuyu*, or the rainy season, I went to stay with Mark in a temple on Awajishima, the resort island not far from Osaka. The monk who came to greet me at the ferry landing, a puppyish and frisky rock-star fan, thirty years old but still living in the temple that his parents ran, ushered me eagerly into his Toyota Crown, buzzing with bright lights now, a full moon cradled in its skylight and soul music thumping out of its tape system, its dashboard fit for a 747. I pushed a button, and the back seat beneath me began to recline, till I was all but supine, looking out at midnight-blue neon and green, clean bright colors inscribed across the night. Through the sleek, rain-washed streets of the little town we drove, the lights out to sea like ornaments, the big hotels strung along the coast like candles on a birthday cake. Past floodlit courts of tennis, and eerily spotlit swimming pools.

The temple, when we arrived, was a sleeker and more high-tech contraption than any I had seen in Japan. Inside, red lights were humming in the darkness of the entranceway, a panel to control the other lights and the clean white lanterns set atop the bushes. I followed my guide through long brown corridors, shadowing the small, lush garden, and lit so quietly I felt I was trespassing upon a daydream. In a perfect, clean-swept room, we ate strange celery and a rainbow of pickles, followed by ice cream made of strawberry, carrot, and plum. Afterwards, the monk went upstairs and I wandered round this house of marvels. Using the toilet, I found myself in some electric wonder system, with different mechanisms to warm the seat, shoot up hot air, expel a spray of water, and flatter one's behind – do everything, in short, but flush. From upstairs, meanwhile, where the young master of the household was commanding a whole bank of videos, Betamaxes, laser discs, and Bose speakers, I heard the gunshots of a *Rambo* tape, some dialogue from *Flashdance*. Outside, I saw the temple's switchboard lights, as complex as a deejay's console; beyond, the neon of the city, as still as night lights on an airport runway. A silent summer night alive with lights, as if, as Pynchon had written of L.A., one had turned a transistor upside down and opened its back to see the tangle of wires, alive with humming energies.

                              *   *   *

In the morning, I walked with Mark through the quiet,
windless streets of what looked like an English country
town, the glowing, twenty-four-carat neon signs and
Members Clubs all vanished now in the shiny Sunday
calm. Girls in red shirts, pink ribbons in their hair,
stepped through polished arcades of smiling bunnies,
puzzled pandas, chuckling raccoons. A Wildean photo
album in a store said: 'TRUTH: Virtue is the beauty of the
mind'. Schoolgirls, tethering their bikes to trees,
whispered excitedly when they saw us, unaccustomed
to foreigners, and then, 'Brazil? Brazil?' In the local art
museum, where Mark was having an exhibition, a
grandma, given license to do anything by her age,
appeared before us, with an equally ancient friend, in
sunhat, giggling at her side. 'I am eighty-eight years
old,' the woman said. 'I dreamed of being a lawyer. But
when I was young, a woman was not allowed to have a
strong position. I pity myself. I am eighty-eight years
old now.' With that, she bowed and padded off.

   On the beach, in the afternoon, the waves were
deferential as a waiter, lapping quietly against the
shore, a shock of white sails behind them on the blue;
in front of me, eight matrons in a perfect row, lined up
like birds, surveying the sea, identical in their pretty
skirts and sweetly appreciative coos. In the twittering,
sultry afternoon, a hot siesta stillness fell upon the
town. The long thin lanes resembled alleyways in
some sunlit Sardinian town, sleepy in the steamy
afternoon. For once, all the country's energy was
motionless and mute.

'If you were to believe some of the things you read,'
Etsuko began, 'all of us Japanese are living in some
cobwebbed net of obligations, our hands tied by *giri*
and *on*. Of course, these elements are there. But to

concentrate entirely on them is to produce a kind of caricature, a comic version of us. It's like taking an X ray, which catches the outline of the skeleton but has nothing of the spirit, the humanity. Or' – she paused while a former *maiko* came to deposit a few more mysterious delicacies on the table before us – 'or like a bowl of seawater in which one has all the component parts, but they do not cohere to make a whole.'

'It's too disembodied, in other words?'

She nodded ruefully.

She had taken me, this rainy-season evening, to one of those celebrated hidden centuries-old Kyoto restaurants where there was no menu and no bill, and there were no customers who could walk in off the street. Few, perhaps, would be induced to do so, in any case, since the entrance was an unassuming one, just a single small banner above an aged wooden gate at the foot of the eastern hills, on one of those narrow-waisted Gion streets that were all white lanterns and stone passageways.

We had walked along a moss path, lanterns jutting this way and that through the garden, to an entrance, where the madam, with the painted face of an old courtesan, in electric-blue kimono, had come out and bowed profusely before us, her head almost reaching to the floor. Given special slippers, we followed a wooden corridor, past rooms full of parties and the phantom forms of young geisha, to a large, empty room, bare save for an alcove in which there was a scroll lit up by a flash of calligraphy and, under it, a slim vase cradling a violet tea flower. New screens and mats had recently been installed to register the summer – they were changed with every month, I gathered – and our own screens gave out on to a trim garden, vibrant green intensified in the early-evening gray. A single tiny hole had been made in the wall so that the

333

moon, coming through, would be shaped as a pretty crescent. The crockery was antique, chosen only for us; the small talk as delicate as china.

On Etsuko's pink kimono was a tracery of rain.

'Is that seasonal?' I asked redundantly.

'Yes, but just a tiny bit off, a few days early. Really, this should be worn in July, with the end of the rainy season. It's like these dishes.' She pointed out the pattern of a well, or a whirlpool, on the goodies before us. I recognized the way that every detail had been made to fit the moment, the room itself turned into a seasonal poem. 'These, too, should be eaten just a little later in the year, as you know.' I did? 'And of course, all these foods have water in them.' Of course. It was not the first time I realized that Japan was so strictly trained that it took a trained eye to appreciate it.

Etsuko watched approvingly the silent bustle of the woman bringing in more dishes. 'We Japanese ladies have a way of effacing ourselves without losing ourselves,' she explained. The woman, with a little bow, stole away from the lanterned room.

'Do you think Japanese women are the strength of Japan?'

'Yes. But we have to keep it a secret,' she giggled coyly. 'We know how to seem weak. You can see that in our women writers.'

'Are there women's presses in Japan?'

She looked surprised. 'You have them in America?'

'Oh yes.' I went on to explain their assumptions to her.

'But surely that is a poor reflection on women, to be published only in women's presses?' The quiet rebuke stung like a needle. 'If they are good, should they not be publishable anywhere?'

Having lived so long abroad, Etsuko regarded her country now, I sometimes felt, as a mother might an

334

errant daughter. And as she tried to bring each culture to a better understanding of the other, she fretted, I could tell, about all the same issues that routinely vexed every foreigner: was it better to leave the people here in their state of happy ignorance, like the dwellers of Plato's cave (surrounded, in this instance, by Platonic forms), or should they be schooled in the facts of life, in the ways of the world, in uncertainty?

In the midst of all this, though, Etsuko was still Japanese enough to dodge every question with a smile, to talk in enigmas, to keep herself mostly to herself. One day a little later, she called me up to tell me that she could not, alas, attend a meeting of her culture club; I was hardly surprised, I replied, since I knew her life was so full of obligations. We talked for a while of *ma*, the Japanese notion of 'betweenness', and the space between people, and the summer. Finally, after perhaps twenty minutes of chat, I asked after her father; when last we had met, she had told me, in passing, he was ill. 'He died early this morning,' she said calmly, 'Luckily, I was there at the time. But I have to return to Tokyo tonight for more arrangements and the service.' That was why, I realized, she could not come to the club meeting; but she would never have told me had I not brought it up.

I dream one night I am on the Big Sur coast. The fog is rolling in across the sea, and a strange aircraft above makes me feel as if all the world is moving. I am talking Ryōkan with a hippie there, and we walk across stepping-stones in a quiet lotus pond, where I find, somehow, that everyone is speaking Japanese. The man at the front office, recognizing me, says, 'Sachiko is going into fits. You probably don't remember her, but you knew her very well once. Now she doesn't know whether to ask you to dinner or not. I hope you don't mind my . . .' 'Of course not,' I say, startled to find that there is a Sachiko here. The coastline is magical today, high above the surf, and the cedar tubs take me back – far back – to Japan.

Three

The night I got home, after saying goodbye to Sachiko, I lay awake for most of the dark and silent hours. Outside, the rain was coming down so gently I could scarcely hear it, trickling down pipes, pattering into gutters, tapping as silently on my roof as a mother awakening her child. At times, when I could not sleep, I rose and penned mock-Japanese poems.

> *All night, the rain.*
> *I listen again in the dark*
> *To the sound of footsteps departing.*

And as the daylight came in, I felt that what I wanted most to express to her was admiration: out of habit, I clambered up to my desk and looked up the Japanese word for 'respect', though by then, perhaps, the chance to use it was gone, and I felt a little like someone who's holding a winning lottery ticket long after the deadline has passed.

Sachiko's goodbye marked, so it seemed, the ending of a cycle; from now on, I sensed, she would be charting a new life on her own. But as the days went on, I also came to see that she could not so easily hold to her resolve, if only because she needed some external impetus to help her to break free. By now, she was fully embarked on her tour-conductor course, attending classes in Osaka twice a week, committing to memory the niceties of foreign customs and places, taking tests in the logistics of a 'bird life'. And for the first time ever, I suspected, she had found a field wide enough for her to spread her wings, a forum large enough to accommodate all her diverse energies. Everywhere one looked in Japan, one saw an identical sorrow: so many women with so much to give, and so little occasion to use it. Nine in every ten women here had completed twelve years of schooling; yet in their brief stays in the office, they were rarely allowed to do anything more than look decorative and make tea. Put the character for 'woman' together with the character for 'woman' twice, and you got the character for 'trouble'.

This it was, I assumed, that produced the notorious super-moms, who trained all their formidable powers of will on Junior-chan's success, and this it was that began to explain that other infamous figure of urban folklore, the rapacious landlady, who threw herself on any foreigner with such naked intensity that he was left, very often, shaken, almost terrified, by the ve-hemence of her unspent passions. If the first cliché of being a foreign male in Japan was finding a faultless dream girl, the second was to find oneself almost consumed by the ravening ardor of these women, who could, if they chose, turn that same unearthly attention, in an instant, on someone else. Regardless of their object, they were as obsessive and Zen-pointed in love as in every other pursuit and brought the same degree of concentration, and full-bodied surrender, to their affections that they might elsewhere bring to their company, or their baseball team, or their religion.

Now, though, for the first time ever, Sachiko seemed to have moved beyond mere diversions – first Zen, then aerobics, then a-ha, then me – to some larger sense of destination. And as she did so, inevitably, she found her whole society arrayed in a vengeful chorus all around her. Her mother had told her that if she continued the course, she would never talk to her again. Her brother, recently returned from Switzerland, had warned her that she was 'little balloon. If not usual Japanese-style life, I cannot stay ground'. Her Japanese friends were either jealous or disapproving of her for seeking out the freedom they had so diligently denied themselves. And her husband was sorrowfully bewildered, gallantly giving her a tour-conductor record for her birthday, then silently going off to another woman. Only her father, the longtime adversary whom she affectionately thought of as a child, now became an unlikely ally, secretly urging her to see the world (and asking her if she'd take him with her).

Watching her swimming bravely against the current, I longed to do everything I could to help her. One day, therefore, in early summer, I invited her on a tour of Osaka Airport, only the third time in her thirty-one years she had ever visited this thoroughfare of dreams scarcely an hour from her home. In wonder, when we arrived, she gazed up at all the people moving off to other lands and lives, and tried out the new phrases she had learned. 'De-par-ture lounge,' she spelled out to herself. 'In-ter-national arr-i-val.' 'CIQ,' she proudly informed me (customs/immigration/quarantine). Together we stood before the departure board, and she recited to herself the destinations clicking over, a registry of hopes.

After that, still far from Japan, we traveled to Kobe, the city closest to a foreign place, and nibbled on tacos in a Mexican restaurant, complete with Mexican waitress, *piñatas*, and ponchos on the wall, then climbed up to a tiny second-story sari shop, with soft sitar music piped through elegant, silk-wrapped chambers, copies of *Vogue* lying beneath framed Kashmiri miniatures. On the way back into town, we stopped inside the English House and posed for photographs in Victorian gear (Japanese tourist sites always had these props on hand, so that one could actually occupy a foreign identity for a moment and have the moment commemorated). 'I little crazy?' she asked, more in hope than apprehension. Craziness, I could tell, was the foreign country to which I could admit her.

In some ways, I was discovering, Sachiko seemed to know everything about the world, sampling the products and photogenic images of different cultures as easily as in some International Expo. Yet in some ways, she knew nothing. In geography, as in everything, the Japanese seemed to favor a ruthlessly edited version of the world, converting each country into a collection of gift shop pleasantries and postcard images. The classic example was the TV documentaries in which some pretty young hostess led viewers through a Third World hellhole, either screening out the suffering in search of scenic vistas or treating it as a kind of artificial prop that only increased the quaintness and exoticism. Even the Japanese tourists I ran across abroad seemed not really keen to understand or penetrate other cultures, but content just to collect them, and to snap up a few Taj Mahal souvenirs or pictures of the Eiffel Tower to take back home like trophies. The rest of the world, like Japan itself, they saw mostly through rose-colored lenses or through blinkers.

So when I mentioned Bhutan to Sachiko, she knew every last detail of this picturesque land, where the people, wearing their own versions of kimono, resembled some theme-park recreation of the Muromachi period; Japanese TV had shown a famous documentary on the subject. As for Burma, Central Asia, the caravan stops along the romantic Silk Road, now being featured in every Japanese book and screen, she was all but definitive. Yet when I mentioned Nicaragua, she had never heard of it, and eager only for good

340

news, she, like nearly every Japanese I knew, had never heard of the Cold War, was shocked to learn that Washington and Moscow were ideologically opposed, knew nothing at all about China's difficult reforms.

When I took her later that afternoon to an exhibition of anti-apartheid art, partially sponsored by the tireless *gaijin* crusaders of Kyoto, she was stunned and horrified; incredulous to learn of a place where such discrimination was employed (though to foreign eyes, racisim and segregation were scarcely alien to Japan). And as we watched a video of Afrikaners talking about their experiences with the system, Sachiko's eyes filled with tears and she lost all words. On heading out, she asked me if I would take her to *Cry Freedom* and *A World Apart,* and when I told her that Japanese were considered honorary whites in South Africa, she could scarcely contain her indignation: 'Why this system? Not so fair! This system very terrible!'

It amused me to find that I, least politically informed of creatures, was introducing her now to many of the things that Japan so carefully screened out: to inequity, to unexpectedness, even to tipping (though when I tried to explain this habit to her, she looked quite shocked at the notion of institutionalized bribery; 'service', in Japan, meant not an extra charge but, in fact, an extra dish or gift that the customer received *gratis* – and in any case, every gift here left the recipient doubly indebted).

Through the world I inhabited too, Sachiko was ending up in situations she had never known before. Slipping into the Western world, as through some Lewis Carroll looking glass, she had entered a world of fun-house inversions and fairy-tale shocks, in which new conventions loomed up at her as suddenly and scarily as the glowing skeletons in the Haunted House to which I took her once, which left her clinging to my arm in a state of happy terror. One day, she called my guesthouse and was answered by the eccentric young gay from Harvard who had somehow grown fascinated with her. *Moshi-moshi*, she called out, uncertainly; *Moshi-moshi*, he replied, recognizing her voice. 'I love you.' There was, I gathered, a long silence on the other end, and then an uneasy giggle. 'No, really,' he went on. 'I love you. If you weren't already claimed, I'd want you for my own. If you were my girlfriend, I'd never want a boy again.'

Four days after the incident, Sachiko was still shaken by the conversation. Everything she considered sacred had been defamed. To talk to a self-professed gay was itself an unnerving novelty for her. But to get a frank admission from him, and to hear from a relative stranger intimacies of the kind she had never heard in public even from her husband – it clearly left the ground beneath her shaking.

Just as often, though, her innocence seemed almost proof against the world, making the world seem innocent. When I introduced her one day to an English friend, she looked at him with awe as he politely complimented her on the beauties of her town. Then, unable to contain herself any longer, she abruptly said, 'Your country very beautiful country. I many time dream this place. Cinderella, many big castle, fairy princess. When I high school size, I always dream this world. Your world little Emily Brontë world.'

He burst out laughing and went on rhapsodizing about Japanese teahouses and Sōseki's novels.

But Sachiko was not to be sidetracked, or to be diverted in this rare encounter with an emissary from the land of dreams.

'Japanese person much love your country air. British Airways!' She was proud of her new knowledge.

'British Airways?' he repeated, incredulous, thinking

of rock-hard rolls and hockey-stick attendants. 'I usually try to go with JAL.'

'Japanese person not so like this air. Very cold feeling; little distant.'

'But Sachiko,' I butted in, 'isn't that how all Japanese service is? Isn't that, in fact, the glory and aim of Japanese service?'

She looked confused.

'We in the West usually like to go Thai Air,' I went on, 'or Singapore Airlines. Many people think those two are the best in the world.'

'Japanese person not so like Thai Air!'

'Why?'

'Bad Smell!'

'Bad smell?'

'True! Asian air very bad smell! Japanese person like only British Airway. Cathay Pacific too – but very expensive.'

'But, Sachiko, Cathay Pacific is Asian too.'

She stood firm. 'Japanese person like!'

She in turn, of course, was introducing me to many things, not least the shallowness of my own reading of Japan. As I went on blathering about Hiroshige or Buson, I realized that it must have sounded as jejune and uninformed to her as typical Japanese raptures about Chopin did to us. And when I told her, proudly, about my visit to the famous geisha show, she was singularly unimpressed. 'You know Michael Douglas movie?' 'You mean *Fatal Attraction*?' 'Ping-pong! This Miyako Odori, little same feeling!'

I got a similar response, once, when I suggested we visit the love shrine at Kiyomizu and make the ritual walk, eyes closed, along a series of twelve stepping-stones, that was the famous highlight of every tourist's visit. Listening to my suggestion, she could hardly contain her mirth. 'This little teenage place,' she giggled. 'Usually only high school person come here this place.' It was the same response, I realized, I would have received had I invited a mature thirty-one-year-old New Yorker, and mother of two, to a Coney Island photo booth.

Often, too, as I inflicted on her haiku of my own composition, the effect must have been as jarring to her as hearing a prayer rewritten. And once, eager to show off my command of Japanese wisdom, I quoted to her Bashō's famous, plangent cry of wonder, an epic in three words, '*Matsushima ya / Ah, Matsushima ya / Matsushima ya.*' But somehow, in the heat of the moment, I began intoning, '*Matsushita ya / Ah, Matsushita ya . . . ,*' converting the poet's poignant ode to a moonlit island into a call for the Japanese equivalent of Data General. That same day, she told me excitedly, 'My friend give me little foreigner poem. Very beautiful poem. Please you see.' And handed over some verses by Leo Buscaglia.

Four

Green, green, green were the colors of Kyoto in the summer: the dripping green of moss gardens, the thick dark emerald of the pine trees on the temple slopes; the illuminated jade of white-barked bamboo shot through with summer light. Green lichen, green hills, green light. Always the sharpened intensity of solid colors in Japan, so strong they knocked the breath out of one: pink against blue, gold on black, a blaze of reds. And the beauty of a city that measured its year by its blossomings: the coming of plums to Kitano in early winter, the cherries on Mount Hiei in late April, the deepening of moss in the rainy season.

In the early days of summer, with the first suggestion of returning haziness and heat, Kyoto took on a Californian lightness, and the days were motionless and blue. Lazy cumulus days without a trace of wind. Red and blue carp banners drooping from the rooftops, and lazy Bach toccatas in local coffee shops. A Constable world of suspended motion. Then, as the heat came on, a creeping intensity: Sachiko sucking ice cubes in the sultry nights and giving me new wind chimes to keep me cool (as courtiers once had spread silk cloth across the mountains to shield an emperor's eyes from summer glare); shopgirls eating long, fine, pure-white noodles served on ice.

Along the avenue of trees that led to Shimogamo Shrine, weekend painters sat relaxing at their easels above a dry stream, silent on their chairs as they tried

345

to transcribe the intensity of green and blue. Etsuko, meeting me outside the shrine, greeted me with a poem she had just translated:

Ah July,
The rushing stream washed over the stones,
And the stones sparkle.

Then she led me into Kawabata's house, turned this day into a gallery of dreams, lustrous kimono spread out upon their racks like carpets or fine silks, ten-thousand-dollar gowns with fifteen-thousand-dollar *obi*, bearing the faintest tracery of cranes, or phoenixes, across their midnight blue. Farther on, in a room full of windows, we took a traditional meal while a few chattering women tried to set me up in marriage with their daughters.

'I think it is because we are externally so powerless,' she later explained, putting the encounter into perspective, 'that we Japanese women must be powerful in spirit. And so it comes out in these violent and inverse ways, as in the *hannya*.'

'*Hannya*?'

'You must know this?' I didn't. 'It is the current figure in Nō drama and in so many of our stories through the centuries, like *Dōjōji*: the woman who consumes a monk in the fury of her passion. The term, of course, was first created by a monk; it refers to the first word of a very famous sutra. But if you say *hannya* today, most people think instantly of the demon-woman.' She smiled. 'I think it must be a theme men like, it is repeated so often in our literature.'

In the middle of summer, the third great festival of the Kyoto year transformed the city again into a display of scenic backdrops. On the eve of Gion Matsuri, the narrow lanes at the center of town were clogged with thirty-one elaborate, multistory floats, smothered in treasures and portable shrines, wobbly on their giant wooden wheels. Around them, the ancient houses were open to the street now, floodlit, their living rooms on show like a series of illuminated stage sets. House after tiny wooden house set up as in some spectral diorama: paintings, lacquer screens, old men playing cards around low tables. Occasionally, a group of naked-chested boys streaking through the lanes, making a strange cacophony as they passed.

The next day, a ten-year-old boy with scarlet lips and whitened face, crowned with a phoenix, led the clanking wooden floats through the central streets of town, past geisha houses and old inns, towards the shrine that towered above the entertainment district. That afternoon, in the same shrine, I visited a special exhibition honoring the famous, centuries-old sweet-makers of the ancient capital. It was, of course, a private show, but somehow Etsuko, in the midst of arranging her father's funeral, had found an invitation for me, at twenty-four hours notice, and, more than that, had given me a letter of introduction inside a card of Oxford, and, in fact, a picture of the very building in which I had once lived. (I thought with shame of how hard it would be for me, in California, to find a picture of *her* college, or whether I would even try.) Inside a special tent, a kimonoed woman, whose family had sweetened the palates of twenty generations of emperors, took me round the display of sweets, laid out on plates like Harry Winston jewels on a velvet cushion, each of them devoted to this year's theme of 'New Life'. Sweets laid out as teardrop crystals, sweets in watercolor seascapes; sweets alluding to the flower that heralded rebirth, sweets suggesting the imminence of cresting surf. Sweets as shells along the shore, sweets as snakes sloughing off old skins. Sweets that

347

conveyed, with a drop of salt, the heartbreak of new affections. My own guide's display was of Dante and Beatrice, made all of sweets, under the title, in sweet-form, 'Vita Nuova'.

Poems out of evanescence, old myths turned into candied images. And the next day, all these artifacts, the creation of a year, were gone.

One night, Sachiko called me up shortly before midnight, her voice as ever soft and breathless. 'I want meet.'

'Now?'

'I'm so sorry. I want meet.'

'OK. I'll meet you at the market twenty minutes from now.'

A little later, she was walking towards me, smiling in the dark. 'I'm very sorry,' she began, burying her head in my chest. 'I need meet. I cannot patient.'

Together, we walked through the darkened, narrow streets and into Kurodani Temple. The early-summer moon hung above us, ringed with phosphorescence, capturing the eye. Around us, here and there, lanterns pricked the dark. Beside us, in silence, a fire burned. Below, far below, as on a phantom ship, the quiet shimmer of the city's lights.

As I led her through the towering temple gates, Sachiko suddenly stopped and caught her breath. 'My dream,' she whispered. 'I dream this gate. When I little children size, I dream this place.' She looked around in startled wonder. 'I not come here this place before. But I feel come here before.' A chill went through me, and she shivered. 'I little afraid this dream. Dream gate.'

Together, in the shadow of the entranceway, we looked up at the temple, grave against the hooded, dark-blue sky. In the distance, a statue of Jizō; my favorite Buddha; the hills full of graves in the dark. A few dogs skulked across the asphalt. The sudden roar of a lone motorcyclist approaching; then a departing hush. Our features scarcely visible in the sacramental dark.

'I remember,' she began, almost under her breath, 'New Year Day. Very warm night, little same today. I walking in grave, together brother. He say, if we together, very old, we always live together.'

I held her, shivering, against the windless night, and together we looked up at the hazy moon of monks. 'I dream of sea,' she said, 'and many star.' Above us, the moon was balanced on the branches.

Then I felt her hot whisper in my ear, and saw her lying down, her curved eyes flashing in the dark.

The moon, the mild, warm air; the silent, sleeping dogs.

Five

As summer deepened, Buddhism still continued to pursue me much more assiduously than I did it, and the procession of holy men to my guesthouse showed no signs of abating. One day, having narrowly avoided the Jehovah's Witnesses (attractively represented by two young nymphs), I surfaced just in time to get a blessing from another roving evangel, who invited me into the corridor for some *kuriingu* (an alarming sight for a newcomer to the guesthouse, who walked up the stairs, jet-lagged, on only his second day in Japan, to see me and the girl, bowing our heads in the corridor, hands joined in prayer, repeating a mantram together, eyes closed). Soon, in fact, my alertness to the threat was so great that when a man appeared at my room, all politeness, I instantly assured him, 'Thank you very much. But I've been blessed many times in recent weeks. That's enough. Thank you!' and closed the door on the half-terrified face of a TV repairman.

Another day, in Osaka Airport, I was wandering around the customs area, waiting for Sachiko, when a man materialized at my side. He extended a hand and then a business card, and told me how much he enjoyed living in Michigan. I was pleased; this was the first Japanese businessman who had ever come up to introduce himself.

Then, however, my new friend began looking around shiftily. Was I alone? Yes, I said, for the moment. The next thing I knew, he was handing me a four-color brochure advertising a meditation institute that looked disarmingly similar to the one founded by Wayne Newton in the latest James Bond movie. The place was Buddhist, he said, handling the word with all the exotic and elegant associations it held for foreigners, and it had many foreign adherents; his life's work would not be complete until I was among their number.

Just then, up raced Sachiko, out of breath, to rescue me again from a Buddhist career.

In Tokyo, a little later, I was looking for a place to stay. 'Please try the Hokke Club,' a hotelier friend of Sachiko's advised. 'It's in Ueno, and I can organize a special foreigner's discount. It's very unusual.' 'Hokke Club?' I said, wondering whether its associations were with sports or truancy. 'No problem. I'll call up right now. How many nights?' 'How much?' 'Don't worry. Any price OK.'

I wondered what I was getting myself into as I went across town towards a hotel that sounded as suspicious as a members-only escort agency: when I arrived, I quickly got the picture. Through the lobby, like crowds from a Cartier-Bresson portrait of Shanghai in the thirties, filed a sea of strange gray families as far as possible from the polished Japanese norm: squinty little boys, skulking fathers, dowdy mothers. Some of them gathered in disorderly groups around the TV. Others, in summer kimono, filed like sci-fi creatures into an elevator. Others shambled through the lobby with the furtive air of *yakuza* or traveling minstrels, people exiled somehow from the promise of Japan. Like the derelicts downtown, or the snake-eating dwarfs I had seen once in a Kyoto freak-show tent, they seemed to belong to some hardscrabble underside of Japan.

When I presented myself to the desk clerks, they led

351

me up in the elevator, through a long corridor, up an emergency staircase, to a bare little room without a washbasin. Breakfast, they said, was compulsory, and would cost ten dollars. No exceptions were made. I did not sleep soundly that night in the Hokke, or Lotus, Club, at the heart of the Tenrikyo sect of Buddhism, one of the 'new religions' of Japan, so affluent and powerful that it ran a whole city of its own near Nara.

In my own essay in Zen idleness, meanwhile, I was beginning to see how hard it was to leave thought alone. Not unlike Matthew, perhaps, I was realizing that I did not have the discipline to meditate, and because I did not meditate, I did not have the discipline. The analysis itself meant more paralysis; reason proved unable to transcend itself. And everywhere I looked, to my chagrin, I found admonishing injunctions: even in the metropolitan prose of Julian Barnes, worldliest of writers, I came across moments that sounded like pure Zen: 'Stop the loom, the futile chattering loom of human thought. Stare at the lighted window, and just breathe.'

In other ways, though, inevitably, I was also beginning to see that I drew closest to the discipline only when I did not know that I was doing so – in the utter absorption of writing about Sachiko, say, or talking with her sometimes. Happiness came with self-forgetfulness, and it seemed only apt that the Buddhist principle of 'right absorption' was translated often as 'right rapture'. True concentration took one out of time and self, an unacknowledged ecstasy. And if Zen extolled the child as much as any Romantic poet did, that was partly because the child lived fully and intensely in the moment, free of both nostalgia and a sense of future. Only when the mind was not preoccupied could it be fully occupied by something else.

I thought back then to what the abbot of Tōfukuji had said, explaining how even a businessman or journalist had something to gain from a night in a monastery, and a taste of stillness. One had to learn how not to spend time, he had suggested. 'When you're hurrying around too quickly,' he had said, 'there's a part of the world you can't see. If, for example, you're taking a wrong direction in your life, it's only when you stop and look at things clearly that you can revise your direction and take a more proper course. The message of Zen is that in order to find ourselves, we've got to learn to stop.' This whole year, now, seemed a lesson of that sort.

As Sachiko came towards the end of her tour-conductor course and the beginning of her dreams of taking off into the dark, the pressures on her grew more and more intense, till it seemed as if she were wandering through a kind of wind tunnel. Often, when I saw her, she seemed alight with her new prospects, quickened and uplifted by her expanded sense of horizon. Just as often, though, I could see how much her struggle to be free could weigh her down.

One day, as she was excitedly telling me about her plans for travel and self-sufficiency, the phone rang, and she picked it up brightly. As the minutes passed, I saw her face fall. '*Chigau, chigau,*' she kept repeating. 'No. That's wrong! You don't understand!' Finally, after forty-five minutes of discussion, she put the phone down and flopped into her chair, her spirit broken. 'My mother say she want die,' she told me, through her tears. 'I need stop course. I cannot more. I dream bird life, but I cannot. My dream, child dream. I not bird; I human.'

'But, Sachiko, you need a dream if you want to change. If no dream, all your life will be sad.'

'This part I know very well,' she said sadly. 'But I not so strong. I not so have confidence. I see foreigner person, they little giant feeling. Anything do, very easy. But I little scared. My boat very tiny.'

She stopped, and brushed her eyes clean. 'Middle life best, all person say. But I have problem. I cannot stop. Middle life very easy, I know very well. But I want dream, I want more difficult life. This Japanese system: no dream – no problem.'

By now, I could more easily understand why dreams held such a talismanic importance for her. In dreams lay responsibility, in a very literal sense; in dreams lay her only hope for realizing – even transcending – herself. Dreams meant carving out a little imaginative space of one's own – a retreat – in a world as cramped in time as it was in space; yet the Japanese were more keen to have dreams entertain them than the other way round. It often seemed to me, in fact, that all the tinkly amusement-park surfaces and chipper reassurances of the public world here were almost a way of keeping people quiet; or at least of providing them with preshrunk pleasures so that they would not seek out unscheduled dreams of their own – let alone acknowledge any kind of sadness. Thus all the happy communal rites – from Disneyland tours to cherry blossom parties – seemed ways of providing safe, user-friendly forms of organized happiness, satisfaction guaranteed, a little like the bright baubles that a parent might offer a child to prevent him from crying. This was the social contract in Japan: forfeit your individuality and you would receive a life of perfect stability and comfort; give yourself over to Japan and it would never let you down. It was like a kind of emotional welfare system: give up your freedom and you would receive a life so convenient that you'd hardly notice the freedom you'd relinquished.

So when Sachiko went on talking of dreams, I tried to hold my tongue. For her, every dream was something of a triumph, and movies like *Rocky III*, which she had seen four times, were especially liberating tales to one who was struggling to see how an individual could live apart from the system. She had told me recently of a friend of hers, a twenty-year-old girl, whose ardor for a-ha was so intense that she had taken a part-time job and worked around the clock to save up enough money to see every single concert on their forthcoming tour of Japan, following them from Tokyo to Nagasaki to Osaka to Yokohama to Fukuoka and around. Didn't she think it was sad, I said, that this was the closest her friend could get to foreign feeling?

'Not sad! This her dream!'

'But isn't it sad that she must have such a dream? It means her real life is a little empty. She would not need such a dream if she were fully happy. And she would not love a-ha so much if she had a real-life boyfriend.'

This reasoning left Sachiko subdued. It was only later that I realized that to downgrade dreams with her was probably as cruel as to quicken them.

The first time that I ever saw Sachiko really bristle, though, was one day when I told her that I'd just gone to see *The Last Emperor*. She had not seen it and, she said, she never wanted to see it, after what her Japanese friends had told her. 'Why this movie show many Japanese person do terrible thing? Whyyy? All person crazy in war. Japanese, Korean, your country person – all same!'

'But foreigners get upset that the Japanese pretend that the conquest of Manchuria never happened. It's not the movie the Japanese government want to cut; it's the documentary footage of what really went on, the

355

same material that is deliberately left out of all your history books. Japan is too proud to admit its mistakes.'

Sachiko, though, was not appeased, and much as she longed for images of exotic China, and all the mystery and splendor of the Silk Road, she adamantly refused to see this matchless vision of the Forbidden City. 'Why foreigner person not understand Japanese heart?' she went on, somewhat plaintively. 'They say Japan very terrible, many killing whale. But whale very special animal, Japanese person believe. Eating whale little religious ceremony. Other animal not same.'

Now the box was open, there was no putting a lid on it.

'You see this movie, little three lady, devil?' she continued.

'The Witches of Eastwick?'

'Maybe. Jack Nicholson little devil feeling.'

'Right.'

'Jack Nicholson little Japanese man feeling?'

'Japanese??'

'I think foreigner person think Japanese man devil.'

'No, no, Sachiko, that's not true. Maybe sometimes they see him as a little robotlike.' I tried – and failed – to be diplomatic. 'But not devil. You can see in Kyoto how many foreigners want to come to Japan. Besides, in America there are so many Chinese, Koreans, Filipinos, Indians, Vietnamese, and Afghans, no-one has a very clear sense of the Japanese.'

'But my friend say' – this was always the prelude to some Japanese superstition about abroad – 'she go many country Europa, many person not so kind for Japanese.'

'Not so kind to Europeans either, I expect.'

'Really?' But I could tell she didn't believe me.

'Really! Japanese visitors are usually very polite, very gentle, very shy.'

'But I read in magazine, foreigner person think Japanese man little devil.'

She had also, I remembered now, read in a magazine that Howard the Duck was meant to be a foreign caricature of the Japanese abroad, small, well-dressed, polite, and forever put upon by the humans he was so foolishly parodying.

At moments like this, I could see how hard it would always be for her to break away from Japan, and not only because Japan had never taught her to live without it. For something deeper was going on here than the usual conflict between self and society, or, in the Japanese context, between *giri* and *ninjō* (duty and feeling); something deeper, too, than the familiar double standard that allows us to challenge the criticisms from others that we ourselves feel free to make (I can attack my mother, but you cannot). And as fast as Sachiko sought the foreign way, Japan remained as deeply rooted in her as her family did. Watching her waver between a Western and a Japanese destiny, I began to wonder whether the country itself, determined now to turn 'international', as its last divine-born Emperor lingered on his deathbed, would ever be able – or even want – to surrender the beliefs that kept it in a world all its own.

'Japanese need change heart,' she said one day, more able now to see her country's limits.

'But then the whole system, which has become the most successful in the world, must change.'

She nodded slowly. 'Maybe very difficult.'

I could see her extending the analogy towards herself.

'Don't worry, Sachiko,' I said with glib assurance, not even really persuading myself. 'Worry doesn't help; it only clouds or distorts. If you can solve a problem, there's no need to worry; and if you can't, there's nothing gained by worry. Just stay calm, and there's nothing you can't do.'

Sachiko took this in, remaining very silent.

Six

Through all the time I had been living in Japan, the one force of which I had been most conscious was Time. It was not just that I found myself hoarding moments like a miser, taking time as a measure of freedom and painfully aware that hours, once lost, could never be retrieved; it was also that modern Japan, secular Japan, the Japan that was racing into the future as swiftly and smoothly as a Rolls-Royce, seemed strangely captive to Time. In Kyoto, I sometimes felt as if I were living inside a hall of clocks – the digital counters all around counting down the days till the next great exhibition or the minutes till the next train, the little clocks at the bottom of the TV screens ticking off the breakfast hour during morning shows, the dates dutifully printed on many photographs and even on computer screens; everything became a wake-up call or a keepsake, an attempt to hold time back, or rob the passing minutes of a moment. In that sense, I could see that Sachiko's awestruck, breath-held whisper of 'Time stop!' was truly the highest praise that she could give.

It often seemed, in fact, that the greatest of all the forces in Japan was Time, if only because it was the most implacable. Yes, the Japanese could manage Time, better than anyone I knew; yes, they could harmonize themselves with its rhythms and pay homage to it with their rites (a girl becomes a woman on this day, and on this day autumn turns to winter); yes, they could make uncommonly good use of Time.

But still, Time could not be controlled, as Space, or Nature, or even Truth, could be.

That was why, I sometimes felt, the Japanese were such connoisseurs of memory, the faculty that allowed them to package Time and turn the bumpy chaos of successive moments into an elegy as beautiful as art. It was also, perhaps, why they excelled so much at slowness and at speed. Most of all, it began to explain why so much of Japan was set up as a retreat from Time, a way to stay Time, or step out of it. The monastery, where one took off one's watch as soon as one entered, was the purest expression of this; the water-world, where life was inverted with such Bacchanalian precision that women called out 'Good morning!' to one another at midnight, was another.

I got my own most vivid taste of this one day when I missed the last train home from Kobe. I could not find a business or city hotel nearby, and even if I could, I knew that it would be painfully expensive. I could not see a capsule hotel. The only alternative, I knew, and the only place as reasonable as a monastery, would be a love hotel.

Off a side street, just under the gleaming boutiques and ethnic chic of Tor Road, I came upon a collection of these brightly decorated dream chambers, recently renamed 'fashion hotels', and lined up with the implausible, synthetic neatness of buildings along Main Street in Disneyland. I peered into the Rabbit's Ears Hotel and saw an aging couple shuffle off into the futuristic Charon. But the one that appealed to me the most was the Gatsby Hotel. It had an especially sharp, cream-colored stylishness to it, with sports-car stripes down its middle, and its name, I thought, could only be auspicious. As soon as I ventured inside, a robot greeted me with a Japanese cry of 'Welcome', and I was faced with a panel of photographs of rooms, some of them illuminated. I pressed the cheapest one that I could find – it looked like a gentrified, modern one-room apartment, a palace by Japanese standards – and an arrow flashed in the hallway above me. I followed it up a bright flight of European-style stairs, past framed Barney's ads, a message in Greek, an article about Christopher Isherwood, an old London playbill, a glossy profile of Natasha Richardson, and a sign that said, 'Some of the best-dressed beds will be wearing white linen', all of these West Hollywood artifacts set smartly against the white, white walls. Through the bright, noiseless corridor the arrow kept blinking, silently, at the level of the EXIT signs, leading me on and on and on to a room with a flashing number, whose door swung obligingly open before me. I went in, slipping into a pair of wool-lined sandals at the entrance.

As usual in Japan, the photos had not lied: the room was possibly the cleanest and most stylish suite I had ever seen. Everything was color coordinated in elegant, Art Deco hues of black and gold: black Kleenex boxes, black matchbooks on a gold glass table, black beakers with the gold logo 'Gatsby' on them. In the spotlessly clean bathroom, black-and-gold bottles of aftershave, neatly wrapped toothbrushes and combs, black-and-gold-rimmed mirrors; the door on the shower just fuzzy enough to turn movement into the haziest suggestion of movement. In the dining area, a table, a refrigerator, a black kettle for tea. And beside the spacious white bed, on its slightly raised platform, a digital, remote-control switchboard from which one could soften lights, select music, switch on TV or warm the room. One could play video games on TV (explained in a slim black-and-golden book), pen endearments to one's sweetheart (a black-and-golden notebook was provided for such purposes), or enjoy

Rental Wife on the special hotel channel, in which Yumi, a long-legged nineteen-year-old, lent herself out as a friend to the lonely. Reclining on the bed, in a space as chic as some SoHo café, I felt in command of the world.

Or, better yet, exempted from the world, in a space all my own. Time and the self were ritually annulled in this capsule; all noise and distraction were screened out in this soundproof chamber. There were no windows, really, no maids, no noises from the hall; for once in Japan, there was total privacy and freedom. Not a trace of the world outside the designer fantasy.

I had expected – I had feared – in coming to a love hotel, to find something more rococo or stridently theatrical: a room like a space-age rocket, perhaps, or a caveman's den, some other-worldly setting to accommodate the demand for a holiday from self. But just the insulation, the hushed spotlessness, of this elegant space was fantasy enough; entering it, one stepped into another world. The compact apartment in black and gold was not only the smartest place I had ever stayed in, it was also the most relaxing. And the main decoration in the room, I noticed as I settled in, was a beautifully framed poster announcing 'The Still Center of the Turning Worlds (Intensive Seminars in Zen Buddhist meditation with Zen Master Rama)'. After giving a brief synopsis of Zen, the black-and-scarlet poster provided an address from which one could procure a book called *Zen for the Computer Age*. It was, all in all, the perfect prop: for when I woke up the next day, and walked out into summer sun, the robot calling 'Welcome' as the automatic doors slid closed behind me, I felt as cleansed as if I had been staying in a temple.

I got my final taste of how the Japanese secede from

Time when Etsuko invited me, one late summer day, to a traditional teahouse along the Philosopher's Path. Inside a spotless antechamber, we sipped some piquant apple juice, in tiny tumblers, fresh as mountain water. Then we followed a woman in a kimono out into the exquisite garden, one small stone wrapped in black marking the direction. Again we found ourselves inside a waiting room – all polished black tables, and a single paper lantern, plover-shaped.

Within the tearoom itself, every detail sang the shifting of the seasons. The poem in the *tokonoma* alcove spoke of hearts resembling the autumn moon. An incense holder reproduced the circle of the harvest moon. The seven autumn grasses poked, haphazardly elegant, out of a long-necked vase. 'In tea,' said Etsuko softly, 'we can get a taste of eternity – if I may use such a term.' She giggled self-consciously. 'And that is completely separate from our real, quotidian lives. But tea gives us a concentration, and helps us empty ourselves out. By concentrating on the ritual, on all the forms and details, we can clean ourselves out. And then we can return more strongly to our usual lives.'

In the distance, I could hear the faintest implication of a koto. The temple bells were beginning to sound along the eastern hills. A faint chill of autumn could be felt now in the air; the moon was dimly outlined in the blue. I wanted, desperately, to escape time now; autumn, and departure, were quickly drawing near.

Seven

Not long before I left Japan, I got a chance at last to see Sachiko take her first tremulous steps abroad; my work was sending me to Korea and Australia, and I arranged my schedule in order to be able to meet up with her on foreign soil. It was, as I had expected, a pleasure unalloyed to see her setting foot abroad, so electric with elation, and so high that, as she readily admitted, 'My stomach little hurt. Too much excited. Cannot control. Cannot sleep!' Eager to be charmed, ready for delight, she felt herself swept up in such a surge of freedom that, her first day out of Japan, she literally began skipping across her hotel room like a hopscotch-playing schoolgirl.

I felt like skipping, too, at times, so magically did she remake the world with her fresh Miranda eyes. Usually, I could not bear even the mention of discos, but Sachiko was so excited to see these wonder worlds that I took her dancing every night, and saw these gaudy pleasure-domes anew. Once, when I invited her to an expensive French restaurant in Seoul, she was so confused and overwhelmed by the list of delicacies, this smallest and most ladylike of women, that she started ordering one dish from every section of the menu – poultry, meat, and seafood. Later, when I took her to the nightclub area, I could feel her tensing up, as anxious and excited as a girl on her first trip into the big city. That night, back in the hotel, she was so full up, in every sense, that she simply flopped down on her bed and fell asleep in her best clothes.

Often, too, I could see how her buoyancy actually reshaped the world it met. One night, I took her to a country-and-western bar in the red-light district of Seoul, where huge, big-necked GIs straddled bar girls while 'Maggie May' and 'Smooth Operator' rasped across the system. After we took our seats, a harassed, pretty Korean girl sauntered up to take our order. Sachiko, however, was so disarmed by this kind of place, and so intrigued, that she started asking the girl questions, and with such happy sincerity that the girl in turn responded – and soon the two of them were sitting side by side, chatting away in an unlikely English and telling one another, through shining eyes, their hopes for one another's future. Around them, bargirls squealed over darts, and Asian hands fondled Asian thighs; but all the world was lost to Sachiko and her friend as, earnestly, they exchanged their hearts. When finally we got up to leave, many hours later, the hostess extended a warm hand to each of us, eyes bright.

Whenever we went to a restaurant, Sachiko greeted the waitress with a happy *'Kansahamnida!'*, her first Korean word, and if ever she got a reply in Japanese, she let out a breathless sigh of relief and returned to her native tongue with a happy *'Yokatta!'* (I'm so glad). In sushi bars, she looked on in horror as Japanese businessmen, in golf shirts and crisp pants, picked their teeth and stared into the distance, with an air of lazy ownership, while their local girlfriends slurped down noodles. And when, on her last night in Korea, I took her to a performance of classical dance, she came out shaken, close to tears. 'Before, I always thinking Korean person little animal person. Very big voice, very tough, always fighting! Now I'm so sorry! I very embarrassed! I see Korean person have much pride!

365

They make very beautiful dance, very special custom. But I not know. I so sorry!'

In Australia, the first time she had ever seen a non-Asian culture, she felt, not surprisingly, even more transported, as giddy as if she had walked, quite literally, through a screen. 'I feel I little living in TV,' she reported in quiet wonder, displaced by something more than jet lag as we walked Down Under streets. 'This dream world? I sleepy? Maybe soon wake up?' As we sat in a restaurant outside the Opera House, white tablecloths snapping in the lazy sunlight, and the chic young things of Sydney stretching out their golden limbs, she let out a gasp. 'This not Kobe movie? This not Nagasaki park? This true? That lady, little same Olivia Hussey feeling! This man, little Hall and Oates! That man, Robert Redford! This true? My life? Why movie not stop?'

Sachiko in Australia was the spirit of delight incarnate, bending down to interview every child she passed, surprising old ladies by asking if they would pose with her in pictures, cross-questioning teenagers about their dreams. She could hardly walk past a single shop without letting out a cry of pleasure and rushing in to look more closely at their unimaginable discounts, and after visiting the beach one day, she felt so light that she simply took off her shoes and scampered barefoot through the Sydney streets. As our plane took off from Brisbane, she gasped with wonder, and sat by the window throughout the flight, peering out into the clouds. She had never seen a green-eyed child before, never heard buskers playing music in the street, never spent a whole day driving. She had never ordered a cocktail before or ridden a horse, been approached by men on the street or visited a noisy pub. Dressing up each night in her very best clothes, she had left the old Sachiko far behind.

'This true not dream?' she asked more than ever, and I did not know what to say.

I noticed, too, as Sachiko rhapsodized about this new world, how familiar her rapture sounded. Every child here, however runty or unexceptional, seemed a 'doll'; every person impressed her as 'very kind, very warm'. Every new street hit her like some otherworldly dream. She sounded, in fact, like me exalting the lanterned lanes of Gion.

And nothing ever fazed her here except the signs of a Japan that she was seeing as if for the first time. She had never noticed before how the Japanese always wore black and white; she had never noticed before how incongruous they looked in their scuba divers' goggles or 'Wombat' ties (as incongruous, almost, as big-boned blondes in kimono). She had never, in fact, felt so estranged from the group. Brisbane Airport, she pronounced, was very dirty, 'because many many Japanese person here'. In Surfers Paradise, as she watched her countrymen moving in tiny hordes to snap up Gucci bags and Cartier watches, she could hardly conceal her shock. 'Why they all want same-same? Before, I thinking Japanese person coming Australia very special! But this style person very different. Not so special.'

And as we wandered through the latest outpost of the Japanese Empire – a Gold Coast cluttered now with o-bentō stalls and koto-Muzaked malls, where couples in 'Homey Honeymoon' T-shirts walked along side-walks thick with signs crying, 'Irasshaimase!' and koalas advertising prices in yen – Sachiko, in a fit of mischief, tried out the new phrase she had learned in her tour-conductor course.

'I think I want vomit. Please can I have an airsick-ness bag?'

* * *

Later, as the summer drew towards an end, back in Japan, we traveled to the Izu Peninsula, the mountainous resort not far from Tokyo, and soon I found myself sitting at dawn each day in a secluded cedar bath, high above the rushing of a stream, encircled by a ring of tall pines. The mist lifted off the water like a screen behind a stage. At night, in our small room, Sachiko curled a finger behind the shoji screen, making the shadow of an evil-eyed wolf.

After dark, in the distance, we could hear a pagan pounding through the trees, reminiscent of the distant drums in Kawabata's famous 'Izu Dancer' story. Lanterns, red and white, were strung across the hillside, like light bulbs in some high school carnival. A long line of grannies circled slowly around a central tower, to the shrill notes of traditional music, flapping their arms around, slow and ceremonious as dying coquettes, as they summoned spirits back to earth, marking the start of the Night of a Thousand Lanterns. Along the edge of the trees, toddlers in indigo *yukata* scooped goldfish out of tanks, while tourists from the city ascended the tower to deliver heartfelt, deep-voiced renditions of melancholy love songs.

Together, Sachiko and I meandered in and out amidst the trees, along the roaring stream, a gauzy summer moon high above us. The music was carried faint to us, and eerie, through the trees.

'I think,' she said mistily, 'this little Heian Age. Many curtains. Very quiet. Man, woman, not so direct feeling. Japanese person much love poem life.'

Emboldened, I told her how much I found of her in *Genji*: in her devotion to flowers, her fondness for cats, a quickness to sorrow that could almost come to self-pity. So much in her reminded me of the spirited, dreamy, quick-witted women of the Heian period, less conventional, perhaps, than their men (if only because they had less to lose), and pledged, as the author of *Sarashina Nikki* had it, 'to walk across the bridge of dreams'. Sachiko, however, did not seem uplifted by this.

'I not so like *Genji*. Much much baby-making ceremony there.'

'But in the Heian period, it sounds so poetic. Lovers together in kimono, looking at the moon, then leaving at dawn with a morning-after poem.'

'Maybe,' she said. 'Maybe very beautiful letter. But all *Genji* little "sex machine" feeling. *Genji* little same Rod Stewart. This story little singles-bar style. I not so like.' With that, she went into a rapturous tribute to John Denver.

By now, Sachiko and I were bypassing language altogether very often. And though there were parts of me she could not see, and vice versa, they were really, I thought, the parts least worthy of being seen, the verbal and the analytical sides that made up nothing but a captious surface. Not seeing them, in a sense, allowed us to see one another more clearly, just as the bareness of a Japanese room sharpened attention and heightened intensity. The words we could not share left us more room for ourselves.

The Japanese, of course, had long prided themselves on their ability to communicate without words (in part, no doubt, because this served to bind the tribe together and so keep aliens out); in phrases like *ishin-denshin*, they enshrined the Buddhist ideal of speaking through actions more than words. And Sachiko, living her life in subtitles now, and resolving herself into the simplicity of a haiku, was, without trying, teaching me gradually to see a little below the surface and grow more attentive to the small print of the world. Once, when she handed me some chocolates wrapped in a stylish green pouch, I tore open the bag and gobbled them down. Only later did I gather that the present was not, in fact, the candies but the bag. It was the green, she explained, of 'little cartoon eating food' (she burst into a rendition of the 'Popeye' theme song). And the Japanese word for 'spinach', she said, was a homonym for their word for 'secret love'. Thus, ever since the Heian period, giving someone a present wrapped in a bag of spinach-green had been the most eloquent way of giving him one's heart.

Eight

One day, towards the end of summer, wearing a long red dress to offset the blinding green, and carrying a red silk umbrella against the rain, Etsuko invited me to the fable rock garden at Ryōanji, its enigmatic stones a natural koan, and one stone omitted so that each visitor could make the meaning something different. Along one side of the Dragon Peace Temple, a washbasin read simply, 'I learn to be contented.'

As we sat on the platform, in the early drizzle of a hazy afternoon, Etsuko asked if I had been following the news about the Hanshin Tigers. I knew that the summer had not been treating my favorite team well. Japanese champions just two years before, they were now in last place. Their longtime star, Kakefu, or 'Mr Tiger', was said to be contemplating retirement. Taxi drivers squirmed and sucked their teeth whenever I brought up their favorite subject, and Sachiko, in a characteristic burst of impishness, had happily asserted. 'This year Tigers not so strong! They not true Tigers; they Hanshin Cats!'

The drama had come to a climax, though, when the son of their leading star, Randy Bass, had developed a brain tumor. Bass, who had led them to the championship, had compiled the most impressive statistics of any American ever to play in Japan; more important, perhaps, he had adjusted philosophically to the Japanese system, not only slugging fifty home runs in a season but bowing when requested to do so, stoically refusing

371

to complain when rival teams conspired to prevent him from breaking Japanese records, and even inspiring a chant that went, 'God-Buddha-Bass!' Recently, though, he had flown off to San Francisco to be at his eight-year-old son's bedside. The Tigers had grown restive. Complications had developed, bringing the boy even closer to death. The agreed-upon deadline passed, and still Bass had stayed by his boy. Finally, the team had offered an ultimatum: come back or get fired. Bass had remained with his son, putting family before company. That, to the Tigers, had seemed the ultimate heresy. So, in a kind of strategic suicide, they had fired their Most Valuable Player.

To replace him, they had scouted around for another *gaijin* and, somehow or other, had ended up with a famous malingerer whose indiscipline was so legendary that he had already been jettisoned by both the Yankees and the Angels. (The next foreigner they signed slugged thirty-eight home runs but incurred the wrath of all Japan when caught by a photographer making breakfast for his son, while his wife slept in.) Loss followed loss, of games as well as face.

'Did you hear what happened yesterday?' Etsuko asked me in the quiet of the rock garden, face pale.

'No.'

'The general manager of the Tigers jumped to his death from the eighth floor of the New Otani Hotel.'

Meanwhile, in lesser ways, the cross-cultural collisions were continuing all around me. Each night, from my room, I could hear the former president of Harvard's Spee Club stalking up and down the corridors, complaining of the 'epistemological uncertainty' of a land 'where nothing was real', while someone else marveled aloud about how he could earn $250,000 a year here as a translator. A group of thirteen Israelis began camping out in a single room downstairs, part of a circuit of foreigners who lived off the Madonna and Mickey Mouse posters they could sell on the street, making three hundred dollars or more a night. Another newcomer from Santa Barbara appeared, called, as if in some bad movie, 'Beach'.

Matthew, by now, was living in Thailand, and Siobhan had returned to the Haight with a tall, silent, ponytailed Japanese boy, with whom she had no common language. Etsuko was making plans to take off for California herself – as soon as her daughter was out of school – and write a thesis on folklore and Christianity, picking up the intellectual interests she'd had to keep in storage for so long. And Shinji, the *gaijin*-lover from Nagasaki, had managed somehow to make it to the outside world – Australia – which he now proclaimed to find 'very easy, very boring'. One day, I got a package from Sydney, and tore it open to find eleven different tapes, all handmade, and carefully labeled, and based on the stray preferences I had expressed in Nagasaki almost six months before; later, another shipment came, and then another. For all his willed rebellion, I gathered, Shinji was as thoughtful and kind as every other Japanese I had met, and as skilled in the way of obligation: having showered me with presents – David Lindley bootlegs, Amazulu tapes, ancient Buffalo Springfield tapes, and the latest from the Waterboys – he now felt free to ring me up at 6 a.m. and ask for a Burberry coat or information on helicopter licenses, advice for his friend in her college applications or a letter in support of his American visa. And since any favor I did him reduced his emotional credit, as well as the interest he could collect on it, both of us kept trying to outdo the other in kindnesses, in part so as not to have to do them again. It reminded me a little of the 'you first; no, you; no, please, I insist'

373

routines that had so charmed me when first I arrived.

No place, of course, is an idyll to its residents, as no man is a prophet in his own household. And foreigners everywhere are more solicitous about the traditions of their adopted homes than natives are (as converts are more zealous, often, than those born into a faith): Asians in America sometimes seemed as intent on keeping up the 'American Way' as foreigners in Kyoto were on preserving the ancient capital's streetcars and old wooden houses. Yet still, in Japan, the divisions seemed uncommonly intense, if only because Japan lived at the other extreme from the self-analytical and abstract ways of the West, and was anxious to enforce that distance. The Japanese drove on the right and read their magazines from back to front. They put their verbs at the end of sentences and took their baths at night. Sexually, they 'went' where we 'came'; emotionally, they smiled where we wept. Even their baggage carousels moved in the opposite direction. Translated into terms we understood, two plus two made five here.

This it was, I suspected, together with the maintenance of a public face that never cracked, that began to account for the unusual violence of so many foreign responses to Japan – the same people who so admired the formality and reticence of the Japanese aesthetic complaining, often, about the formality and reticence of the Japanese people, and the same ones who so bridled at Japanese claims that Japan could be understood only by the Japanese mocking the way the Japanese spoke English. This it was too, perhaps, that helped to explain why foreigners' responses to Japan seemed so uniform and yet so violently divided – in proportion, perhaps, to the gap between public and private. The tourists who came here for two weeks could not stop marveling, often, at the silence of the place; the longtime residents heard only the clatter of pachinko coins, the blare of right-wing megaphones, the syncopated roar of TV baseball crowds. The people who were sightseers here seemed moved, nearly always, by the courtesy and consideration that they found; the residents saw nothing but hypocrisy. And the visitors went home, very often, wishing that the West could be more like Japan; while the residents stayed here, unable to forgive Japan for not being more like the West.

For my own part, I began to realize that every statement I made about Japan applied just as surely in the opposite direction. I might think it odd that Japanese girls covered their mouths whenever they laughed – until I remembered that we were trained to cover our mouths whenever we yawn. I might wince every time I read dismissive talk of 'foreigners' in Japanese novels – until I thought how we use 'Orientals' in our own. I might be surprised at the formal rites of Japanese courtesy – until I remembered how firmly I had been taught to say 'Thank you', even for gifts I did not like.

The best advice on the subject, though, seemed to come, appropriately enough, from a baseball player, Ben Oglivie, the famously literate right fielder for the Milwaukee Brewers, celebrated for reading Plato and Thoreau on the team bus. Now in his sunset years with the Kintetsu Buffaloes, Oglivie had only one problem here, a friend of mine who knew him said, and that was his philosophical bent; while other imported stars took the money and ran, Oglivie dwelt and dwelt on the challenge of different cultures. And his conclusion seemed infinitely more enlightened than that of many thinkers and social critics. 'It's no good coming over here and criticizing the Japanese game,' he told my

375

friend. 'That's like going into someone's house and criticizing the way he's arranged the furniture. It's his house, and that's the way he likes it. It's not for the guest to start changing things around.' It took a ballplayer, I realized, to teach us elementary civility.

The complexities of cultural cross-breeding came home to me most poignantly, however, when a Japanese friend from California came to visit in Kyoto. In Santa Barbara, Sumi had always struck me as a typically sweet exemplar of her culture: an accomplished listener with a computer memory, an earnest, almost guileless, optimist, and a model of hardworking consideration, holding down eight jobs and taking four courses while still finding time to design her own cards for birthdays, Thanksgivings, and Halloweens. Now, though, after three years away, she found herself as estranged from her homeland as from an America that conformed less and less to cliché. She was shocked, she told me after she arrived, to see, for the first time ever, the sorrow and frustration of this endlessly hustling country. I was shocked to see how she had slipped, without noticing it, from first person to third when talking of the Japanese.

Returning to her small hometown, moreover, Sumi had found herself shunned by all her high school friends, not only because she had made it to the land of which they only dreamed, but also – and especially – because she presented it back to them now as something more complex than a beach poster. They could not forgive her, so it seemed, for importing some reality. She, in turn, having read about Japanese history for the first time abroad, and about Buddhism, could scarcely believe now, or forgive, the distance at which Japan lived from that knowledge, and from the source of its traditions. America, she said, seemed so optimistic, and I, thinking of how I viewed Japan, could only bite my tongue. It was, perhaps, the old half-empty/half-full conundrum; but we are optimists when faced with another culture, and pessimists when faced with our own.

Such confusions were growing more and more common now as more and more Japanese women began going abroad – or joining foreign firms – to gain the possibilities denied to them at home. This, the papers proclaimed, was the *Onna no Jidai*, or Era of Women. And even those who played by the accepted rules seemed far more complex than the smiling pietàs by whom I had been so enchanted when first I had arrived. Through Sachiko now, I was meeting all kinds of women with lives quite as quirky as any in the West – one who did not even know what her husband of ten years did for a living, and another who, in three years of marriage, had never had it consummated; one mild-mannered girl who ran a pyramid-game fraud, and another who patiently waited for the one day a year when she could spend a night together with her married lover. The acupuncturist Keiko, meanwhile, after four months of living with both her husband and her boyfriend, had finally broken down and tried to slash her wrists. Filing for divorce, she had moved back with her parents, who every night received anonymous phone calls from a woman who gave them details of their daughter's infamy.

Only Hideko, the testbook model of a decorous mother and wife, seemed to be keeping up the role of a perfect *ōtome fujin* (or 'automated wife'), and that was because her emotions were so little implicated in the role. Now she was just returned from Australia and could not stop talking about the strip shows she had enjoyed, this prim and tiny lady, every day of her stay. The little girl she led around with her was already a mistress of distances; eyes huge, she hid behind her mother's designer skirts, keeping the world outside at bay.

Just as I was trying to put all these lives into perspective, I chanced to pick up a collection of short stories by Tsushima Yūko, one of the leading women writers in Japan today, and the daughter of the famous novelist Osamu Dazai. And suddenly, racing through her sad and suffocating tales of single mothers dreaming of flight, waiting for the men who invariably walk out on them, I felt I was seeing modern Japan for the first time, the world that all the great male novelists so scrupulously sifted out. Tanizaki and Kawabata loved young women mostly for the use they made of them, pygmalionizing them, treating them as flowers almost, totemizing them as perfect emblems of threatened purity ('It's as if Kinko has no personality of her own, and that's why she seems so extraordinarily feminine', Osamu Dazai himself had written, in the voice of a fictitious schoolgirl). Even contemporary female writers seemed often to embrace the assumptions forced upon them ('A rational woman is as ridiculous', writes Enchi Fumiko, 'as a flower held together with wire'). But here in Tsushima's gray and rainy tales of lonely, wasted women exchanging intimacies in coffee shops and love hotels, I felt I was seeing Japan through the other end of the telescope at last: the concrete blocks behind the cherry blossoms.

Most of her stories were set within the moody, blighted landscape of modern industrial Japan, amidst smog-shrouded, look-alike station cafés or lonely, boarded-up seaside resorts where it was always out of season. Always the main character, like Tsushima herself, was a weary single mother, surrounded by her children, hemmed in by her duties, and hostage to her culture's expectations, and always she was dreaming of escape – to the sea, to an inn, to anywhere other than her clangorous apartment. Women alone in the dark, dreaming of the day when they'd grow wings 'and everyone would finally realize that she hadn't been just some mother'.

The men in her stories were not cads or fiends; just married men in search of pleasure, with other matters on their minds, giving their lovers children, and giving their children presents, so that they would not have to give themselves. They were not so much members of a household as sightseers there. 'A man was the sort who'd give you any number of children and then run off when the mood took him'; a father was 'a mere shadow in a photograph'. The setting of the story, often, was the day after, in an age that did not believe in morning-after poems.

Yet even as she described the transaction as a woman's plight, Tsushima did not, I felt, overlook the reserves of strength that Japanese women kept in private: all her women were living in a transitional age, when the reality of their inherited powerlessness was tempered by the first suggestions of a dawning freedom. In one story, a woman known only, and archetypally, as the 'Mother', absently cleans up around her drab room while waiting for her runaway daughter to return. With half her heart, she fears for her only companion; with the other half, she almost envies the girl for laying claim to a freedom that she herself has always been denied. Again and again in the stories, Tsushima alluded to the overgrowth at the side of a garden, the wilderness just beyond the neat suburban parks. Always, around the immaculate public places, there lurked a few 'dark tangles along the walls'. And it was in these undomesticated spaces, she suggested, that the women were beginning to gather their strength unseen.

Nine

As summer drew towards an end, Sachiko got ready
for her biggest move of all: taking off on a new life of
her own. She had finished her Osaka course by now
and passed the qualifying test, and she was ready to
begin working as an international tour guide. With her
monklike swiftness and one-pointedness, she had
already mapped out a concrete plan of action: how she
would file for divorce, move into a new home with her
children, reassume her maiden name, and set up a
professional life, leading tours around Asia and Japan.
It was hard for me to recall now the Sachiko who, only
a few months before, had hardly stepped outside
Kyoto.

As she closed in on her dreams, the cavils of her
society only mounted and intensified. On a practical
level, her friends were extraordinarily generous: when
her Walkman broke, Keiko promptly gave her another,
and when she started looking around for a home,
Hideko promised her an electric range and a VCR.
Emotionally, though, they seemed determined to box
her into the same narrow compartments to which they
had resigned themselves. The best way to express
yourself was to efface yourself, they kept reminding
her; a woman's strength should come from weakness.
Foreigners were dangerous, and so were dreams; a
woman should fulfill herself within the family. Speaking her mind, they said, was almost worse than telling
lies.

Sometimes, Sachiko seemed exhausted by all this. 'Woman's world very complicated,' she often told me. 'Japanese woman, not so easy heart. Much jealousy there! I want say true. But always say true, soon biggg problem.' More often, though, she sped along unstoppably, her air of confidence intact. 'Aren't you worried, Sachiko?' I asked her once as she prepared to commit herself to an unknown future. 'Worry not so help,' she sang out, mirroring my own words back to me. 'I not want worry. You know this song?' "Que será será".'

As I got ready to leave Japan, Sachiko asked me one day for a copy of a photograph I had taken, a thoroughly unremarkable picture of my own long shadow in the eerie light of late afternoon. The last time I visited her home, I noticed the picture on her piano, set in an indigo frame, and suddenly resonant – a way, I guessed, of keeping at least my outline in her life. And before I left her house that day, she gave me, in return, a golden lacquer box decorated with a cosmos flower – to remind me, she said, of the walks that we had taken when the days were bright with flowers.

Autumn this year promised to hold even more elegiac weight than usual, as all Japan, in a sense, was holding its collective breath, waiting for the Emperor to die and a new imperial era to begin. And for me, as I felt the first chill entering the city and saw a whole new generation of foreigners beginning to appear, the season itself seemed to have grown older, as the city had. By now, I felt, I knew Kyoto's moods so well that I could almost tell the time without looking at my watch: how the light lay silver on the river in the sharpened afternoons, how the temples exhaled mist in early light. Autumn seemed much deeper than spring, as sadness is deeper than brief joy, or memory than hope:

the age-old Japanese assumption. Sometimes, in the dying days of summer, the beauty of Kyoto was almost hard to bear.

Just as I was packing my final bags, though, Sachiko gave me the finest farewell gift of all: a sense of what the discipline of Zen really meant. For as she readied herself for a new kind of life, living at a tangent to the norm and seeing people turn away from her whenever she told them that she was about to leave her marriage, the only friends who came unfailingly to her assistance, encouraging her to extend herself and disinterestedly offering her all the support she needed, were those she had made through the temple. Sometimes, when her confidence was wavering, she called up Mark for inspiration; sometimes, when she needed to be reminded of how even a woman could have a 'strong heart', she turned to Sandy.

Most often, though, when she found herself in need of counsel, she went to see the abbot of Tōfukuji. And he calmly told her that he would give her anything she needed to keep herself and her children in good health. Would two thousand dollars a month be enough? If she wanted more, he said, she only had to ask.

Though Sachiko politely declined the offer – she was determined to do things by herself – the incident gave me a glimpse at last of what all the meditation was about. 'The ultimate purpose of Zen', I remembered the *rōshi* telling me, 'is not in the going away from the world but in the coming back. Zen is not just a matter of gaining enlightenment; it's a matter of acting in a world of love and compassion.'

On the final day of summer, Sachiko took me to Arashiyama to watch the cormorant boats. The night was navy blue and gold when we arrived, a lone torch burning against the dark-blue hills. On the top of the

382

distant mountains sat a round white moon. Along the riverbank, red lanterns shivered in the faint, chill breeze, their echoes wavering red in the reflecting water. A single pagoda, lonely as a plover's cry, jutted up into the heavens. A solitary canoeist pulled himself soundless through the dark.

Far in the distance, car lights glided silent across the Togetsu Bridge; in a teahouse nearby, the upswept coiffure of a geisha flashed briefly in an upstairs window. Occasionally, above the water, a firework shot up into the dark, and then, with a quiet hiss, streamed down in a sad, slow extravagance of gold.

There was a sense of elegy about the river tonight, the smell of spent fireworks, the faintest hint of autumn chill, the happy, clapping songs of summer's final parties.

Cool in her summer kimono, Sachiko led me over the bridge to where the boats knocked against the dock, lanterns along their sides bearing the faint outline of cormorants. Stepping behind her into a boat and steadying myself, I saw the moon shivering in a row of silver lanterns.

Without a sound, our boat set off across the lake, the darkness deepening above the dark-blue hills. The boats, with their crisscrossing lines of lanterns, looked eerie now, and ghostly in the gathering dark, their white globes doubled in the rippling water. From across the water came the dull thud of an oar. The teahouses cast reflections, red and white and blue, across the rippling water.

And so we drifted through the night, approaching, then receding from, the other silent boats. Occasionally, an open cormorant punt came past, torches burning at its prow, scattering sparks across the dark. For a moment, in the torchlight, the aged fishermen's faces were lit up, in a flash of Rembrandt gold, and

383

then, as soon, their wrinkled features and medieval grass-skirt forms vanished again into the dark.

Another boat glided past, ringing with the laughs of company men lined up around a long, low table, served strange delicacies by white-faced geisha. A firework shivered off into the dark, and then came down in a shower of white and gold and pink. The torches singed the water gold. Every now and then, a bird plunged down into the water, emerging with a fish within its beak.

'This place before, I little goodbye ceremony,' said Sachiko, face whitened in the dark. Behind her, the lanterned boats were slow and soundless in the night. 'I not know this. But he say he want only friend.' Her voice trailed off into the dreamy dark. A boat bumped up against us, and the gold reflections blurred and shivered in the water.

Along the bank came the sudden sound of children laughing. A grandfather bent down to light a firework for his toddler, and it veered off into the sky, a shooting, soundless bird, then slowly came back down again. Lovers wandered off into the cicada-buzzing dark. Across the water, the lone canoeist pulled his way in from the shadowed, distant mountains.

'Summer soon finish,' she said softly. 'Soon weather little cold again. Tonight last summer party.' Thoughts turn to autumn, and to separation. In the distance, the sound of ancient folk songs, and of grandmas dancing.

It was only later, after I had left Japan, that I realized that everything had been there that night: the lanterned dark, the moon above the mountains, the dreamlike maiden in kimono. There was the Heian vision I had sought since childhood. And yet, by now, it was so much a part of my life that I had not even seen it till it was gone.